HUNTING *from* HOME

HUNTING
from HOME
A Year Afield in the Blue Ridge Mountains

CHRISTOPHER CAMUTO

W. W. NORTON & COMPANY
New York • London

An early version of "Caught by the Way" was published in *In Praise of Wild Trout,* ed. Nick Lyons (New York: The Lyons Press, 1997).

In a few places in the text, the author has altered names to protect fragile places.

Grateful acknowledgment is made for permission to quote from Robert Bringhurst's "Jacob Singing," *The Calling: Selected Poems 1970–1995.* Used by permission, McClelland & Stewart Ltd., the Canadian publishers.

Manufacturing by The Haddon Craftsmen, Inc.
Book design by Charlotte Staub
Production manager: Julia Druskin

Library of Congress Cataloging-in-Publication Data

Camuto, Christopher.
  Hunting from home : a year afield in the Blue Ridge Mountains /
Christopher Camuto.
     p. cm.
  ISBN 0-393-04915-9 (hardcover)
  1. Hunting—Virginia. 2. Natural history—Virginia. 3. Hunting—Blue
Ridge Mountains. 4. Natural history—Blue Ridge Mountains. I. Title.
  SK137 .C36 2003
  799'.09755—dc21
                                        2002015948

W. W. Norton & Company, Inc., 500 Fifth Avenue, New York, N.Y. 10110
www.wwnorton.com

W. W. Norton & Company Ltd., Castle House, 75/76 Wells Street, London W1T 3QT

1 2 3 4 5 6 7 8 9 0

*For everyone who lives a border life,
for anyone who hunts from home*

What I am I have stolen.
These mountains which were never mine
year after year have remade me.

—Robert Bringhurst,
"Jacob Singing"

Contents

Prologue

Some of us are drawn toward the life of things.

Despite all the unnatural changes in our landscapes and despite all the beautiful, wild life that has been lost from the world, the essential experience of nature is still available to anyone anywhere—that frisson of recognition that catches us unawares—the world and its weather reaching you through all your senses at once, fusing the strange and the familiar in a thrill of connection that leaves you feeling perfectly at home and profoundly homeless.

I am silently walking the river woods road in the predawn dark, heading for a deer blind. Half awake, I sense some sound and motion in the air. An owl's wing brushes my face, leaving an imprint of strong primaries and soft coverts on my mind. This happens too quickly to startle me. The musty wing revives the memory of an odor ancient as pine sap or river-washed sand-

stone, fragrant trace of a time and place far from here, as if the
owl had alighted from some Carboniferous-period conifer and
been dipping toward me in the dark for as long as my being had
been walking toward it. A few hundred yards from my cabin, I
wonder if I will ever find my way home.

I am standing in the old pine planting at dusk, red elm
longbow in my left hand, cedar arrow nocked. Still as a tree, I
watch day and night exchange gifts beneath the dead limbs of
those stout conifers, trying for the thousandth time to see what
light and dark are. As the earth rolls slowly toward nightfall, a
sharp-shinned hawk rustles onto a nearby branch. For an infinite moment we are face-to-face, two hunters occupying the
same space. The universe trembles with the anomaly. When the
hawk sees my eyes move, it stiffens in recognition. If this were
a myth, we would speak and exchange tokens across the gulf
between our natures. Perhaps the hawk would drop an indigo
bunting at my feet and I would offer it the liver of a deer. I try
to hold its amber eye, where day and night swirl strangely, as
long as I can.

I am sitting on a canvas stool one winter afternoon, sketch-
ing trees in the barn woods. I'm trying to capture the subtle
differences in the shapes of oaks and walnuts and hickories, the
characteristic way they aspire to capture light with their well-
formed crowns. A red fox threads its way toward me from the
upper spring. I watch the wary animal coming unawares. I study
its astute otherness in the cold, bare woods, enjoying my terrible
invisibility. When, passing at arm's length, the fox finally senses
me, it calmly turns its head as if taking me into its confidence.
Its perfect face leaves me wondering which one of us had been
watching the other.

An owl, a hawk, a fox. I am left to consider whether these

ordinary encounters near home are the beginning or the end of experiences too large for me to sense completely. But a hunter is, above all things, a pragmatist. A hunter in the broadest sense possible, I'm content to take the part for the whole, to bring home what game falls to my share. This book is, in part, an attempt to understand the wholeness of such fragments, to report on the thread of experiences that seem to lead elsewhere. A musty wing, an amber eye, the perfect face of a fox.

Hunting from home. The home of this book is a two-hundred-acre farm tucked into the rumpled upper end of what used to be called the Valley of Virginia about halfway between the trim-and-tidy college town of Lexington and the rough-and-tumble factory town of Buena Vista. Rockbridge County lies just south of the Shenandoah Valley proper, its woods and fields drained by the east-flowing James River rather than the north-flowing Shenandoah. One of the James's principal tributaries, the Maury River, flows along the western edge of the farm, having sliced through the imposing ridge of Tuscarora sandstone I can see from my back porch. The Blue Ridge Mountains, a few miles off, are visible to the north, east and south. The Allegheny Mountains, from whose slopes the Maury takes its flows, lie farther off to the west. *Allegheny, Blue Ridge, James, Maury, Shenandoah, Tuscarora, Virginia*—this is to be well situated among names that are, for the moment, still attached to a landscape worth looking at. I've taken advantage of that moment and taken Highland Farm as a coign of vantage, a good place from which to observe the life of a barred spiral galaxy, to practice what Henry Thoreau called "the discipline of looking always at what is to be seen."

One purpose of this writing is to re-present this farm in detail as a place to dwell in and on. For the sake of clarity I've had to bluntly name its pastures, woodlots, springs and gates—the front pasture, the river woods, the strong spring, the old clear-cut gate, for example—although when walking about I do not think of these places as named. Narrative requires naming (hence *Allegheny, James, Shenandoah, Virginia . . .*). But I don't want this naming to make it seem as if I am taking hold here in a way I am not, trying to fix what I hope will, in the end, escape me and the hunting I do here. I love language as much as land-scape, but so long as denotation is firmly rooted in the precision of the tangible, I root for the wild connotations of living things to exceed my grasp and lead me on. And although I'm prone to enjoy the common and scientific words for things—particularly the names of birds, trees and stars—I understand that naming and discovering are different processes and that the former should always defer to the latter.

I should admit from the outset that beyond trying to under-stand the poetics of this place I have no title here. A notch above squatter status, I rent a relatively snug four-room log cabin where I live and work. I say "relatively snug" because from May to October, I share my office with a rat snake that seems to enjoy the tangled company of computer and printer cables balled up behind the desk. Not to mention the opportunity of an odd mouse or two. When I am working late at night, it is not unusual to see its finely wrought face float out from behind the monitor, its hunger and curiosity stirred perhaps by the warmth of humming gigabytes and the ultrasonic ping of pixels. The mesmerizing appearance of this snake blurs the line between the tame and the wild, a distinction nearly always in need of reconsideration. I've never yet observed an animal that didn't have a culture of its own. If I am downstairs when *Elaphe obsoleta* begins to make its rounds, its discreet rustling sounds like a fax coming in. By morning, it will have made its way down from my loft office. One day I found all three feet of it wound up in an empty tier of the fruit basket that hangs over my small dinner table. While coffee brewed, I gathered the snake, which coiled tightly around my hands, and set it on the front porch, hoping to instill some sense of the boundary between inside and outside despite the imperfections of the cabin's chinking.

But blurred lines are the rule, not the exception, here. For a writer, there is no difference between living and working: I am writing or backing off from having written or sidling back to it, sentences beginning to emerge from my mind due to some hunger and curiosity of my own. Like many writers drawn to what is left of nature, by necessity I live what Thoreau called a "border life" and have over time learned to use the resources of my disenfranchisement to continue the writing that keeps me disenfranchised. A good system, I've finally come to realize, and the only way to *be* a writer as I understand the practice. I have learned to enjoy the freedom and responsibility and to tolerate the loneliness—what Emerson called the "solitariness"—of life along this border between *seeing* and *saying,* where an acute self-consciousness is left the task of discovering the *other* in whatever guise the other chooses to take—owl, hawk, fox, snake, fax.

Writers, like many critters, prefer what biologists call edge habitat. Looked at closely, edge habitat is a series of exposed centers, good places to forage for the subsistence that supports more foraging. A writer is all edges, hence our edginess, and Highland Farm is all edges, edges with—I'd like to say an infinite number of centers, but this place, like the earth itself, is quite finite. So far as I know, the expansion of the universe has no local benefits, adds nothing to the tax base the Chamber of

Commerce worships like a fetish idol. But consciousness, the great Romantic writers reminded us, has an infinite reach or at least, through the imagination, plays with illusions of infinitude in wholly convincing ways. Since we cannot get out of the way of our own consciousness, we will never know for sure. Best to pay attention to the tangible details of the visible edge of things—all those exposed centers that offer themselves for appreciation—to humbly trace the mind "in the act of finding/ What will suffice," one of Wallace Stevens's gleaming beams of insight into this saving process.

Beyond home lies the horizon I can see from here. Fluid and static at the same time, the oldest mountains on earth are distinguished company, easy on the eye and hard underfoot. Since most of their forested slopes are a great public commons—National Forest land—I roam them at will as a fisherman and hunter and solitary backcountry walker. The chapters that follow oscillate between Highland Farm and its long blue horizon, the structure of this book imitating, as best it can, the relation of one to the other.

Although this is hardly a conventional hunting book, hunting is central to it. That love of nature includes hunting may strike some as perverse. Thoreau theorized that, ideally, men, like cultures, outgrow the desire to hunt. But I grew into hunting, having taken up the pursuit of grouse in my thirties and deer in my forties. I see nothing regressive in it and have come to believe in what I can only call the *radical biophilia* of the hunter, borrowing the term *biophilia* from the sociobiologist Edward O. Wilson. Hunting has weighted my time outdoors and clarified a great deal for me, taught me innumerable practical lessons and taken me in certain dreamlike moments through the transcendental concentration of the hunt to contact with

what I assume is the sacred pulse of being, my own and that of
the game I pursue.

But hunting is mostly practical. In the fall, when I hunt
day after day, I move better through my nonhunting life. I
am leaner, quicker, more attentive, gentler. Most women are
immediately put off by a man who hunts and seem to assume
that hunting is part of some macho-militaristic facade which
overlays an atavistic love of violence. But a few learn that a good
hunter comes back from the hunt chastened and quieted, honed
to a somber, joyous, thoroughly peaceful core. And, of course,
a woman, too, may step into the woods to explore the hunter
in herself, to watch herself watching in the most fundamental
way of all.

I offer no defense of hunting beyond the depiction of my
practice of it here. The arguments on either side fail to settle
the issue. Like many things in life, hunting cannot be justified
on purely rational grounds. Although it is not necessary to hunt
for food—you can hire someone to kill animals for you—I take
the right to hunt to be an extension of the right to eat, no more
or less important or problematic than that, and no more or less
heroic than reading or vegetable gardening or stargazing. I do
not recognize my own hunting in most of what I read on the
subject.

Beyond what I hope is honest observation, nothing remarkable follows. The year or two I planned to spend at Highland
Farm somehow became a decade. Half that time was given to
travel, once to the ends of the earth, which only made this
humble place seem more important. A year or two of taking stock became a kind of continuous stock-taking. Passing
through became staying. Perhaps taking stock is all writers ever
do. Perhaps staying is a way of passing through. These happened

to be years when I was negotiating my way around the regrets that loom large in middle age, those trailless boulder fields and stretches of ankle-turning psychological scree that stand between the first and second half of a man's life. Between the usual worries, I finished becoming a writer—the oldest goal I can remember and one that connected me to my youngest self. I had made myself a writer here at Highland Farm—by which I mean only that I learned to practice the art of carefully joining words and things—and came to understand that, for me, as for most writers, there was no practical difference between failure and success. That grim realization, the pleasure of practicing an art for its own sake, and a love of the life around me, got me through the boulder field and across that scree into country where I might make myself useful. But when I turned to write about the saving details around me—the grain of logs, the shapes of trees, the flight of birds—I found the writing hard, very hard. So although nothing personal follows, in retrospect it all seems personal, terribly personal. In language, intense subjectivity and intense objectivity are mirror images of one another.

Captured here is a year in the middle of my life when I par-ticularly needed to run my fingers along the grain of things, to exercise my senses deeply, to feel my body and mind working together toward a well-weathered well-being. This was a year when I had plenty of good work to do, a year when I could fully enjoy the balance of slender means and slender needs, practicing what my dog and I have come to call the Tao of breaking even, a year when I could at least try to live with the circumspection of the owl, the hawk, the fox. I simply wanted to write straight-grained sentences, frame up square paragraphs and sheathe brightly lit, roomy essays, roofing the whole with the best natural material that came to hand, proceeding from day to day as if I were building a home with words. I wanted to enjoy simple tasks and simple pleasures, to work hard at writing and when not writing to indulge my native laziness and my most important prejudices—a fondness for hand tools, cast-iron cookware, full-sized pickup trucks, mixed-breed dogs, good books of all kinds, trout flies tied from fur and feathers, red elm longbows and flintlock long rifles, antler-polished ironwood walking sticks, brassy hard-bop jazz, the pre-Socratic philosophers, all blues, Chinese landscape painting, the guitar compositions of Fernando Sor and Dionisio Aguado and the wildly complementary insights of astrophysics and mythology. I wanted to spend as much time as possible in the sun and in the rain, waist-deep in rivers and high and dry on ridges, staying intensely still in my watching places and moving briskly along backcountry trails.

At the heart of what follows lies an inescapable convention— an account of a country year. I would apologize for this lack of originality except that an ordinary country year has become as rare and endangered as everything else in nature, and is all the more worth watching now. The natural diversity of an ordinary place remains to be enjoyed and celebrated and studied. However unsophisticated it may seem, I am not ashamed of the preoccupation. The most fundamental and important truths are still to be found in the life around us, in the significant distractions of any odd moment in pasture or woodlot, river bend or forest.

On close inspection, there is nothing conventional in nature. The need for a sustaining relationship to nature is the same as it has been since Heraclitus—a quest for experiences that fuse the literal and the figurative, the phenomenal and the transcendental, the local and the universal, the profane and the sacred. Although the beautiful assumptions of the Romantics have been belied by history—demolished by the machine in the garden that is hard at work destroying the saving landscape of this book—the highest purpose of consciousness and of art is exactly what Wordsworth said it was in the famous preface to the second edition of his *Lyrical Ballads,* "an acknowledgment of the beauty of the universe."

Over the course of several books about the southern Appalachians, I have worked slowly at trying to write a kind of prose that might do justice to a landscape that has captivated me for twenty years—hardly a momentous ambition. My hope is that I might flush a few things of interest for the reader to see, get you out on the ground of my awareness, not to tell you much about myself but to reward your own curiosity, to share the simple pleasures of a place that has been lent, or let, to me.

The traces of writerly self-consciousness embedded in the text that follows are necessary markers of my evolving attitude toward nature and writing, the interplay of words and things as I experience that relation in the field and at my desk. One encounters all sorts of correspondences between the transparency and opacity of nature and the transparency and opacity of language. The underlying poetics of our relationship to nature seems to stand out in stark relief as we watch *nature* disappear from the earth to be replaced by that beleaguered realm know as *the environment,* a phrase that intentionally or unintentionally marginalizes what is essential and, given the treachery of our undemocratic politics, dooms us all eventually to homelessness. In writing, the pursuit of significant form without the benefit of a story to tell pressures language toward displacements that reveal, from time to time, something eventful in the relation of words and things, the possibility of recapturing a hint of those essential relations.

As the critic and philosopher Stanley Cavell has written in *The Senses of Walden,* gracefully adding thoughts to Henry Thoreau's graceful thoughts: "The writer's sentences must at each point come to an edge. He has at all times to know simultaneously the detail of what is happening, and what it means to him that it happens only so. A fact has two surfaces because a fact is not merely an event in the world but the assertion of an event, the wording of the world. You can no more tell beforehand whether a line of wording will cleave you than you can tell whether a line of argument will convince you, or an answer raise your laughter. But when it happens, it will feel like a discovery of the *a priori,* a necessity of language, and of the world, coming to light."

Like an owl flying low through the dark, a hawk frozen on a pine branch, a fox stepping through leaf litter at your side.

I am acutely conscious that, like many other writers, I write for the eye and ear and mind of a reader I will never meet and who very likely does not exist, just as the best version of this book—and of myself—seemed out of reach each morning. In the end, the book I wanted to write dissipated like river mist when the sun rises, leaving this text behind, the trace of years lived between home and horizon.

Despite all the changes, the gravitas of nature is undefiled. It remains to be seen.

Highland Farm
Rockbridge County, Virginia

HUNTING *from* HOME

Solitary in Winter

Alone far in the wilds and mountains I hunt. . . .
—WALT WHITMAN,
"Song of Myself"

I take hunting to be a search for true country, for native contours of place and for wildness.

My dog and I are halfway up an unnamed ridge pursuing ruffed grouse—the finest, most elusive prey we know. From here the Blue Ridge Mountains stretch, if not from sea to shining sea, then at least from horizon to horizon, an earthy rumple of snowbound watersheds that is more than enough ground for us. In ten good winters we could not hunt well all the land we see from here. That blunt fact is equally daunting and reassuring. This is as good a country as we know, both for the hunting and for its own sake.

We're not far from home, thirty miles maybe as the crow flies. In fact, we have receded, like two tiny figures in a Chinese landscape, into the long blue horizon visible from Highland Farm. We like doing that, hunting into the mountains we see

from the pastures where we walk every afternoon and that I can
see from the study where I write in the morning. The Blue Ridge
wouldn't lend itself to the monumental expression of space I
admire in Northern Sung painters, but their Taoist compositions suggest the inner importance of mountains everywhere,
not their altitude in the present moment, but their being across
all time. I might have borrowed the title of Fan K'uan's tenth-
century *Traveling in Streams and Mountains* for the title of this
book. Tenth century or twenty-first, good country underfoot is
what matters for some of us—a sense of self and place. At home,
I watch the blue mountains like a hawk and disappear into their
hard-used forests every chance I get.

No real hawk turns above us as we lunch on this familiar
brow of sun-washed sandstone, although it's not hard to imagine its broad, white wings catching sunlight like a sword. Even
the normally ubiquitous turkey vultures have forsaken the
mountains for the lowlands, where the living is easier. You only
have to get a thousand feet or so up into the Blue Ridge in the
dead of winter to find life thinned out. In mid-January, each
quiet watershed is like an ark—there's one or two of everything
left. But today the sky is empty of anything except the sky.

The outcrop forms the apex of a triangular plateau of
mountain laurel and white pine where, more often than not,
we flush a bird this time of year—a solitary winter grouse we
may or may not bring to hand. Last year, I killed a bird here
and sat on this rough sandstone bench admiring it—a warm
and beautiful thing far finer than anything I could contrive
in words. I felt a humble kinship with it. Still, I was glad to
have succeeded. Nonhunters may not understand this. Anti-
hunters will be appalled. I care deeply for thinking about the
issue but not much for arguing about it. If this most ancient

form of food-gathering became immoral at some point in human history, I need that moment identified and explained. Failing that, I'll hunt and take full responsibility for what I do afield. There's no virtue that I can see in having your food killed by proxy. And the soulless lives of animals grown for food are grim indeed.

I felt no hypocrisy gently smoothing the feathers of that grouse I brought down last year, having overtaken its sudden escape with the muzzle-loading shotgun I sometimes carry afield. I have deep feelings for the animals I pursue, and strong knowledge of them, but I am not sentimental. "One kills," the Spanish philosopher José Ortega y Gasset notes in his *Meditations on Hunting*, "in order to have hunted." That is a difficult sentence for hunter and nonhunter to understand fully, an existentialist formula. Although the hunter should always be "uneasy in the depths of his conscience"—because all death is regrettable—there is nothing worse, Ortega y Gasset implies throughout his thoughtful, passionate book, than hunting in bad faith. So I admired what I had killed and took it for my own, with equal measures of respect and covetousness, making plans as I smoothed its coverts and untwisted two tangled primaries to reuse what its being had left behind for a fine, wild meal and a stash of well-tied trout flies.

That bird flushed without warning, as grouse do, bursting right to left out of the pines as we approached this place last year. Patch had not pointed it, but he had been birdy ever since we reached the laurel slick that leads us here. I readied myself as he wound in tighter coils of interest, very serious and astute, his haphazard tail-wagging steadied to a controlled beat I recognized, his worn old bell clinking to silence. The best of the hunt are these periods of birdiness when the dog takes over and worries the cover. There's a beautiful purposefulness in a hard-working bird dog. Nothing sentimental about that, either. On a good day, I'm a fair shot at best and need all the forewarning Patch's body language can give me. He has turned me into a far better bird hunter than I would have been on my own.

When a dog, with a man in tow, is on the scent of a bird, there is a triangle in the woods. That is where the hunting is done. Hours of walking and miles of mountains suddenly coalesce into a possibility that has a distinct geometry. A straight line drawn between hunter and dog forms the base of the triangle. The squirreling forward of the dog suggests another side. The hunter peers ahead, trying to guess where the birdy apex— which may well be moving—is hidden so that he can anticipate the third side along which he will shoot. If the dog locks up on point, the triangle resolves and the hunter has gained control of the mystery. If the bird fails to freeze on the ground, it will flush on its own, unexpectedly taking the triangle off into three dimensions, four if you count time—the two or three seconds the hunter has to react to a bird fleeing through the curvature of space amid the confusing Doppler of its noisy escape. Most grouse, like most galaxies, are red-shifting away from us.

But last year I got lucky on just such a premature flush, which gave me the kind of crossing shot I triangulate well. The bird crumpled at the first blast, the echo of which replaced that deep bass whir of wings. I followed through, swinging on a bird that wasn't there anymore, ready to reach out farther with the tighter choke of the second barrel. As I gathered myself from the sudden commotion, Patch flounced around the fallen bird, doing the foolish war dance he prefers instead of a clean retrieve.

But today we've nothing for our efforts except the view we get from here, a familiar recessional of ancient uplands that I

take to be a home away from home. The snowbound mountains seem smaller than they do in the fall, when the grizzled
ridges look swollen like the neck and shoulders of deer in rut.
In winter, the Blue Ridge is sharper of contour, the fine structure of each watershed revealed by snow-light scattered evenly
through the ranks of second-growth timber. You can see in the
gentle, uplifted folds how the mountains were made and in
the rough breaks of cliffs and watercourses how they erode,
chunk by chunk and grain by grain. The mountains are brown
in the foreground, blue in the middle distance and a grayish
blue at the uneven horizon, where the distinctive lineaments of
Appalachian orogeny are gathered by foreshortening. The effect
is of a rolling ocean slowly calming.

Although my tattered, tin-cloth vest is empty, we hunted well
to get here. There was good cover from where we parked, along
a state highway, for a half mile or so upslope, a broad thicket of
grape and greenbrier, coralberry and wild rose, and God knows
what else. Amid rotting logs and standing snags, red maple,
yellow birch, cherry and oak compete for sunlight on that
raucous southern exposure. Rhododendron and hemlock have
long established themselves in the shady, rocky places. That
is what we like to see—not the contrived monoculture of a
government-sponsored clear-cut graded with logging roads and
doused with herbicides, but a funky patch of mulish mountain
farmland wildly reasserting itself.

A half foot of wet snow slowed me, if not Patch, to the proper
pace for grouse. My own unpredictable motions were as likely
to flush a bird in those tight quarters as was my companion's
energetic searching. The wind pushed from behind us, which
wasn't good, but I whistled Patch to hunt close. This set him
circling within range of a snap shot from me and got the wind

in his nose enough to put us on to any holding bird. I didn't want him cruising too far ahead, pushing birds up the mountain faster than I could follow. In his younger days, we would have had a battle of the wills over this, but Patch is five now. Though he has plenty of his father's English pointer go in him—which I hope he never loses—his English setter mother's common sense and composure have begun to temper his unruly joy afield. Between the two of us, we hunted that steep, snow-laden thicket well, covering the cover with high hopes and light, if pounding, hearts. We were out in the Blue Ridge hunting, and that always feels good.

That lower edge of this long ridge is as steep as a staircase, but since we hunted here two or three times a year, I knew to pace myself for the first two difficult hours. And I knew that to have a chance on a bird today, I would have to stay both attentive and relaxed, even as the day's fatigue built up in my heart, lungs and legs. You couldn't fill a stadium or sell TV rights to the spectacle of an eastern mountain grouse hunter trudging through the woods muttering to himself and hollering at his dog, but it does take a bulldog kind of athleticism to spend a day this way. The southern Appalachians are a poor man's NordicTrack and, at forty-something, grouse hunting is a free cardiovascular stress test provided courtesy of the U.S. Forest Service. I envy all the gentlemanly, flatland grouse hunting I read about at home—pleasant walks in Wisconsin or Massachusetts skirting aspen cover out of which birds flush with literary clarity. But southern mountain folk learn to deal with life on the vertical, and although I wasn't born here, more than twenty years in these mountains have left me with the stout legs, aching knees and enlarged lungs of a native son. In the Blue Ridge, grouse hunting is more like a cross between one-man rugby and slow-motion fell-running. Much as I love it, I wouldn't want to view the videotape.

Patch is another story. I'd be happy to watch him on film or tape taking the woods on his own terms, coursing the rough terrain—when I let him go—hardly any slower than he runs the pastures at home. When I whistle him to hunt, that flowing energy converts, as the special theory of relativity predicts, into a dense mass of hunterly intensity that I will never cease to admire. In fact, I took up hunting fairly late in life, in my thirties, because I could not get a mesmerizing image of dogs hunting birds out of my mind.

I had been to Russia the autumn that tragic country struggled to emerge from the ruins of the Soviet Union. The bureaucratic chaos of the moment had suddenly opened up previously inaccessible parts of a great and beautiful country. With four American acquaintances and a friend from Moscow, I ventured to the northern Urals to fish for Atlantic salmon in the headwaters of the great Pechora River, mother river of northern European Russia, a giant like the Columbia. Unknown to the dry spirits of Intourist and guided by a handful of hearty Russians from the dismal gulag town of Inta on the Arctic Circle, we floated the bright Kos'yu River from the barren lower slopes of Gora Narodnaya. I've not been in a stranger, more beautiful country.

I am not a salmon fisherman. I was pitifully equipped for the task and fished, if not poorly, then only as well as I fish in the Blue Ridge. Which is to say that I tickled the backs of great blue salmon pools with the thirty-foot casts that catch trout for me on what pass for big rivers here at home. But the serious salmon fishermen did no better. We were a thousand miles from the salty mouth of the Pechora, a great delta that fans out into the

Barents Sea opposite Novaya Zemlya. The salmon runs up into
the Urals were not well understood, even by our guides, who
were content, as I was, to feast on roasted grayling and grouse
every night. After supper, the Russians theorized broadly about
the vagaries of *Salmo salar* in the Pechora, proud to have such a
grand mystery in their country. The salmon would come when
the salmon came. We toasted their absence liberally with bad
vodka and worse champagne. The serious salmon fishermen
were disgruntled, but I thought we were doing fine. The wrong
kind of expectations ruin fishing.

The Kos'yu flows through old-growth taiga, a mossy, fairy-
tale tangle of dark, appealing forest thick with evergreen and
fringed, along the river, with willow and dwarf birch. There are
no woods on earth that fail to interest me, but the Russian taiga
seemed like a forest I knew from another life. While we fished,
the Russians hunted with the passel of dogs that crowded in on
the Soviet M18 chopper that had dropped us off. While I cast,
I listened for the muffled shots of the hunters in the woods, and
I liked seeing the affectionate, well-mannered dogs in camp in
the evening. Catching sleek, iridescent grayling and hoping for
the epic pull of a salmon was fine, but it was the hunters disappearing into that forest with their dogs that centered the scene
for me, then and now. Fly fishing was an American affectation,
something I could do at home. The sporadic, muffled shots
of the grouse hunters in the taiga, who worked the woods as
I now did in the Blue Ridge, seemed like a lost chapter out of
Turgenev, a timeless story backlit with the modest light of a
country understanding of things.

Some days I left off fishing in favor of tagging along with
a keen-eyed Russian, Valery, and his Samoyeds, Touman and
Chara, the latter in training. Circling slowly through the forest

behind the dogs seemed a perfect complement to the stasis of
working a salmon pool. I learned then and there that Ortega y
Gasset was right, that there was no better way of *being in* a country than by hunting it, treading through pathless woods pursuing game. We walked the soft, uneven ground typical of old
growth, crossed glowing meadows fringed by the golden dwarf
birch that gave this turn of season its Russian name—"gold
autumn"—a kind of subarctic Indian summer that attached
itself permanently to my dream life. We skirted bogs where I
would have expected to find woodcock. The dogs looped in the
figure-eight, hunt-search pattern Patch would later teach me on
the pastures and in the woodlots at home. Touman instructed
the younger dog by example about the proper range to keep
from their master and about the ways of approaching spruce
grouse hidden in the alders or hiding in the lee of rotting logs.
Valery instructed me, by example, in the offhand ways of a good
grouse hunter with his dogs—a soft word to Touman now and
then, a sharp call to Chara, an occasional whistle to keep some
shape to the hunt. In a sense I was giving up fishing for hunting during those long afternoons along the Kos'yu; and ever
since, although I love fishing, I fish now only when there is no
hunting to be done.

In the Blue Ridge, as in Russia, lunch is a rich but small refuel-
ing. Today I brought thin slices of deer liver, sautéed this morning in olive oil and garlic, stacked on an onion bagel slathered
with grainy Creole mustard. Civilized wild food—the bounty
of other hunting, a deer I took at home on the last day of the
season. Patch gets some of the liver without the mustard. He
never mooches food but is always pleased by the comradeship
of sharing a meal. While I chomp through an apple and enjoy

clear draughts of cold water, he stares down through the wind-
ruffled pines and paces about in the laurel, disappointed that
we have put up no birds where he is clearly getting faint whiffs
of grouse. But I can tell by how he holds his head that the scent
is not on the breeze—we could easily hunt back down through
the pines—but traced through the nearby understory where
birds have surely been. No tracks betray their recent presence,
but I've no doubt a grouse or two is hidden on the precipitous
slopes downwind of us—impenetrable escape habitat that gives
the game an edge here.

I hitch myself back into the stiff, tin-cloth hunting vest I
fancy and cinch it close in front so that I don't catch my shooting elbow in the shoulder strap. I carry a few backcountry
essentials in the bird bag and a small bottle of water and some
homemade jerky in the left side pocket. The same sharp, bone-
handled little pocketknife I use for dressing deer rides in my
left pants pocket. I keep powder, wads, shot and other accoutrements in a canvas shoulder bag organized, like a fishing vest, to
let me find things by feel. Its weight on my left hip helps balance
the heft of the gunstock in my right hand. Halfway through
a grouse-hunting day I may look disheveled enough to give a
black bear pause for thought, but in my mind's eye I'm as well
put together as a banker.

As soon as I stand up from our fifteen-minute break, Patch
is all hunt, and I have to whistle him back into coherence. I
would not have it any other way. Later, when I'm winded and
leg worn, it's Patch's indefatigable energy as much as the lure
of grouse that will keep me going. Dogs, like children, set an
excellent example, particularly for adventure. And hunting,
first and foremost, is adventure—it wasn't just hunger that
drew mankind from cave mouth and riverbank. As we set off

again up-mountain in the snow, this bird hunting strikes me as
gloriously quixotic. It's as if I have equipped myself very practi-
cally to bag a Phoenix. As yet unfound and unflushed grouse
are, in a sense, mythic—hidden well enough to be as good as
unreal until Patch finds them. We are not hunting *birds*. We are
hunting *a bird,* the next grouse that we flush—a reddish brown
beauty digging through the snow for winterberries ten yards or
half a mile or a mile from here—and we must find that pound
and a half of gallinaceous wildness in this watershed, or the next,
or farther on in these lengthy if not endless blue mountains that
we love—one bird to find between Georgia and Maine.

With a gloved hand I wipe beaded snowmelt from the
well-oiled walnut of the muzzle-loader, a slender straight-
stocked gun with a sighting plane that seems to help my cross-
dominance and a barrel length suited to my forty-something
eyesight. While Patch idles in low, I gently but firmly check the
loads with the ramrod, thumb the hammers to half cock, recap
the gun and then pull the rabbit ears until I hear another click.
For all practical purposes, the flush of a ruffed grouse takes
place in the equivalent of what cosmologists call the Planck
epoch, the first 10^{-43} seconds of cosmic history, during which,
I am told, there was a lot of high-energy hijinks going on in
what astrophysicists call space-time foam, a dense gravitational
gumbo out of which the Big Bang boomed and the universe
in which Patch and I hunt began to form. It may not advance
physics to compare a flushing grouse with the genesis of matter,
but the analogy serves to keep us on our toes here in the Blue
Ridge. When you are hunting grouse, you are preparing for
something like that. If you hunt, as I do, with the nineteenth-
century technology of a muzzle-loading shotgun, then you hunt
at full cock to have any chance at all.

Friends think I exaggerate about grouse until I take them on an early-morning hike into spring or summer grouse cover and have to help them ease their hearts back down their throats after a bird bursts loudly from underfoot, disappearing in the confusion before it can be seen (assuming that something unseen can be said to disappear).

"*That* was a grouse," the explanation always goes.

"You hunt that . . . *noise?*" the bewildered, admiring query always follows.

Suffice it to say that *Bonasa umbellus* gets into the past tense in a hurry, leaving the air behind it laced with a drift of leaf litter fluttering to the ground like rousted space-time foam.

Just above our lunch spot, we pick up a logging road that slabs along the southeast side of the bulging ridge that will overshadow us for the rest of the afternoon. What is still dry powder in the woods has partially melted and refrozen several times on the road and become the worst kind of snow for walking. The breaking of an inch-thick glaze punctuates every step, burning small quanta of much-needed energy. I resign myself to the additional weight of wet snow clinging to the deep treads of my leather mountain boots. Patch prances around my slogging progress, punching through the crust, the eager staccato of his hunting trot ringing into the quiet air around us, his hunting bell clinking lightly with every move.

For a mile, there's not much cover, but Patch works the unpromising second-growth woods on principle. The relative poverty of the understory—the absence of a natural forest-floor diversity of plant life—is the consequence of overlogging, the logging road itself a mixed blessing I would happily live without. Ruffed grouse, like all forest creatures, require a forest. They do what they can with what woods are left. We, too, take the land as we find it. Despite a century of misuse, the underlying ecology of the Blue Ridge still works to restore and reassert itself.

Each time we crest a curving rise, the winter rush of a stream comes to our ears, a vein of silver in the woods gleaming against a dark seam of mossy bedrock. Above all things, I am a student of the theory and practice of watersheds, the commonplace gatherings of land and water which in the southern Appalachians we call hollows. Our hollows do no less than underwrite the natural life of our mountains. Along with many others, I ask no more than that the natural fullness of our hollows be preserved, not for anyone's pleasure or profit but simply because nature deserves to be. In a culture given over to a monomania of moneymaking and the vulgarity of conspicuous consumption, and those peculiar forms of "development" that lead to impoverishment, preserving nature seems too much to hope for. But you will find in those hollows that survive the rarest, wildest things—black bear, bobcats, rattlesnakes and trout; lady slippers, walking ferns, cushion moss and reindeer lichen; and, among much else, life expressing itself as everything from a scarlet tanager to an ancient eastern hemlock four feet thick. You find in each watershed natural processes reasserting themselves—respiration of oxygen and filtering of water—and the subtle play of soil-building and natural erosion that reshape the mountains moment by moment, eon by eon.

The logging road dead-ends at what I call, with stunning lack of imagination, the big cover, which looks less promising in the glare of a sunny, snow-lined day. Since grouse are skittish on bright days, cloud cover would be welcome. The only thing we have now in our favor is a soft breeze cooing out of the northwest to which Patch pays a good deal of attention. The big cover begins at the head of a hollow that broadens out enough to have once supported a mountain farm. It is easiest to visualize this old homestead in winter, when the woods have the clarity of a charcoal drawing and the pathos of its ruins—chimney and hearthstone, logs and window casings, overgrown orchards and sagging hog wire—lie starkly against the rocky, snowbound lay of the land. That one grouse we have hiked and hunted five miles to find is holding in the wild vegetation that has overtaken this old homestead, in the best of times probably a rather poor place but more inviting to my mind's eye than the vanity homes being cantilevered into the mountains in my day, thoughtless gestures of ownership that immediately ruin the stake they claim.

Ruffed grouse thrive at these edges where forests reclaim the land from modest human attempts to till and husband. They feed where the land restores itself and take cover, like bear, in its safest, darkest places. I take each bird we flush to be a sudden reification of an indigenous wildness I love like bedrock and flowing water. Ruffed grouse are not a symbol of anything. They are the thing itself—wild life flying up in the face of human attempts to use nature. But what holds the grouse in this watershed is not the clear-cuts the U.S. Forest Service claims as a form of game management, but a swath of old growth a half mile from here that nurtures the birds through most of the year. Given a choice between a housing development and a ten-year-old clear-cut, you will find the grouse in the recovering clear-cut. But what they really prefer—what they preferred for the millions of years before the Forest Service, with the encouragement of the well-heeled gentlemen of the Ruffed Grouse Society, started managing the hell out of them—is a true forest at their back. For grouse, as well as for those who love the woods, edge habitat without an undisturbed forest behind it is an ecological fraud. But these old mountain home sites are more like natural forest openings than the slash-choked, road-scarred clear-cuts taxpayers have been duped into subsidizing for fifty years.

Before we get too close to that promising old dwelling place tangled in grapevine and greenbrier, I bring Patch to heel. I take ten minutes to fully catch my breath during which, for Patch's benefit, I pretend to tend the gun. This face-saving is pointless. He has been stopping to wait for me to catch up with him ever since we left the truck. When I'm ready, we work our way together through the wooded open slope downwind of an overgrown meadow that has become a deer yard, to judge from the game trails and neat piles of oval scat I always find there. That northwesterly breeze combs through the heart of this good cover right to us.

Just below the meadow I release Patch with his favorite words—"Hunt 'em up"—but whispered, so that he knows I want him working close. With habitat as good as overgrown oldfields and a senescent orchard bordered by coralberry, grape, greenbrier and laurel, it's best to assume game is at hand. Beyond the house site at the meadow, small farm fields regrown in locust, red maple, sumac and yellow birch stretch between the two cold, thin creeks that drain this odd, anvil-flat hollow. At the head of the hollow, ranks of chestnut oak and northern red oak occupy the long ridge to the west and throw sharp shadows on the snow. Hemlock and white oak have settled the rich ground below us, although the heartening diversity of tree species here belies a broad descriptive summary. I'd guess there are a dozen different kinds of trees in any hundred-foot square. Those rocky, twisting creeks are tied together with rusted barbed wire that sags wherever its hand-hewn locust posts have rotted away. What's left of that summer labor now supports tunnels of the dense, wild braid of vegetation where birds and small mammals thrive.

As we approach all this choice cover, I'm birdier than Patch, which is disappointing. I may think, already composing a story in my head, that a grouse will flush from the squat ruins of the chimney or burst from the snow beneath an attractive gathering of laurel, but ruffed grouse don't comply with my picturesque fantasies. If Patch doesn't smell them, the birds are not there, or they are there but he has not yet caught the curling scent plume that will dampen that wagging tail and slow his steps until he locks up on point. Besides, as I say, in winter we are not hunting birds, but *a bird,* a solitary winter grouse on the side of a mountain, something very tiny in a landscape in which we ourselves are small. Watching Patch, hoping his generalized interest will screw itself down to endgame attentiveness, I stop trying to guess where that bird might be because it will not, on principle, be where I expect it. That much I know. Which is to say I know nothing.

Assorted wrens and warblers flush like sparks as Patch works the cover, carving a trough through the snow, a wild Rorschach of his efforts. In the presence of game scent, he pays the song-birds no mind. He may be a mixed breed, but he has inherited good gifts from his parents and is a more robust dog than either of them. He will sleep deeply tonight, but in the field he is tireless. He hunts until I need a break, but he never initiates one on his own. *I hunt, therefore I am,* his driving joy and butt-wagging energy seem to say. And now that he has outgrown his adolescent penchant for chasing rabbits and deer—for miles and hours—he is as good a bird-finding companion as you could want.

I like to think that the two of us look good hunting that

old homesite in winter—Patch studying along the downwind edge of a thicket, me at port arms ready for a wild flush, the snow-eased landscape lying indifferently about us, flat winter light making everything one. We look good hunting, I like to think. It seems fair and balanced—the man, the dog, the grouse that is or isn't there, the invisible but palpable breeze that leads us on. The miles we have walked. The scene is balanced, too, between pleasure and fatigue, between wanting to stop and wanting to go on, between satisfaction with what is and desire for more—for the clinking of the dog's bell to stop suddenly as Patch freezes delicately on point, his right forepaw raised in that dainty gesture of self-restraint by means of which he relinquishes the end of the hunt to me. And then for a bird to flush forever in front of us. You get to thinking like a mountain in the mountains. You get to wanting to be as strong and graceful as the wild land and wild life around you.

Once we get in the thick of things, that cooing breeze swirls about us unpredictably, eddying along the edges of the big timber that surrounds this enclave, and so we work the forty acres in a series of ellipses and epicycles that would have given Ptolemy pause for thought. A high wind with weather in it roars faintly overhead, but we are in the lee of the main ridge and won't have to worry about what is coming from the west until we cross that saddle going back on the logging road. Patch is clearly culling through old scent for something fresh, but we haven't seen bird tracks all day. Deer, fox, plenty of rabbit, and turkey on the logging road, but no short, thick arrow of grouse print—an unmistakable sign—to lead us on. But the birds may be roosting nearby and flying into the cover to feed. Who knows?

Unlike deer, grouse are difficult to observe. Even a dedicated

grouse hunter has very little contact with them throughout the
year. As I have said, they usually introduce themselves by leaving. And books on grouse are an absurd mess of contradictions,
half-truths and folklore. The experts tell us to hunt them where
their food is, which is to tell us everything and nothing. One
study in New York State discovered that ruffed grouse eat a
thousand things (994, to be precise), which is to discover that
they can feed anywhere they like in a healthy forest. They are,
like all wild animals, proof of the health of a forest, a revelation,
when you do find them, of at least a thousand things.

We work the irregular meadow edge thoroughly, expecting
that any moment a bird will flush back into the woods and
start a chase. We are at our best now, dicing the cover up with
our combined attention. Patch effortlessly cuts here and there,
his hunting bell chanting short musical phrases as he stops
and starts, body curved and shoulders hunched in an intense
questioning of all the scents filtering through his consciousness.
I'm conscious that we are up in the mountains with the watershed to ourselves—I haven't heard a shot all day—hunting the
snowbound woods as if it were our job. My legs have recovered
from the burn of the snow-dragging hike. My heart and lungs
feel strong. The gun is light in my hands. I follow Patch, trying
as best I can to anticipate where his interest may lead. But no
grouse flushes from the meadow edge.

Patch slakes his thirst in the snow-cold creek that flows along
the far edge of the oldfield. The brilliant water recharges him.
He bounds downstream through the snow until an overgrown
fence line turns his head. He works it carefully, studying it in
places, circling possibilities, not wanting to miss anything but
not wanting to be misled. He is poised, as a good bird dog
should be, between eagerness and diligence. Once you get on

good cover, your concentration gathers around the immediacy of this intent hunting. The horizon of your attention shrinks to the ground between you and the dog and the cover just beyond him. This hunting is what you hunt for.

The fence line takes us across the slope toward the second stream a half mile away. Before we are halfway through our first pass, a grouse flushes forty yards downwind of us—a gray blur driven by a muffled whir heading downslope. Patch had neither scented nor bumped the bird. Judging from the way he is riveted to the fence line, it must have been running well in front of us, which grouse often do. In fact, I find its pudgy track winding along the fence line a little farther on. A hand signal and my own changed direction get Patch going where the bird now leads us. When he gets down to where the gray blur did its touch-and-go, he looks over his shoulder, seeming to acknowledge that I may have some usefulness on these maneuvers.

Now we need to get down to business. As a puppy, Patch would have chased the bird to oblivion. During his career as a two-year-old flushing pointer, he would have kept bumping it just out of gun range all the way to Pennsylvania. Now he gathers himself like Valery's elder dog and tries to carefully close the distance between himself and the bird, checking to make sure I am still with him, following behind and to one side. Patch is not just a good nose; he has experience in the ways of grouse and remembers every move they have made. We share the same memories of failed and successful hunts. But his awareness of the great birds we have pursued is fine-grained, detailed, subtle and complex. My only knowledge of them is the flush and two or three seconds of escape flight, if I see them at all. We are both more grousy than we used to be, sadder and wiser and a little harder to fool.

But despite Patch's best efforts, the bird gets up out of range
again on its own, farther out than before—another gray blur
tracing the contour of the slope down and away. The confidence of its curving, ground-hugging glide, and the fact that it
is still downwind of us, suggests that this is not our bird today,
but a decoy sent by the gods to exercise our judgment or our
legs. When a grouse, a rich reddish brown bird, is far enough
away to turn gray, it is as good as gone as any deer flashing a fat
white tail at you. Still, we have unlocked our prey from a silent
winter mountainside—effected the metamorphosis we came to
see—and need to follow up. We have two hours of light, and I
know this terrain well. We will suspend judgment and exercise
our legs.

I whistle Patch to circle broadly with me back toward the
first creek we crossed. No point in pressuring a skittish bird
downslope. We follow that creek downstream, hoping to put
at least a quartering breeze between the grouse and ourselves,
which should give Patch a better chance to close in and pin it.
As we hurry along, the snowbound woods look different, full
of our expectation now that we've made game. The landscape
glows and pulses. But except for the thin creek dashing through
a gauntlet of snow and icy rock, nothing moves in the woods
with us. By the look of the open timber, recovering second-
growth oak and hickory, I'd guess that rousted bird is headed
for distant cover.

We slip downstream a mile or so with as little fanfare as possible, but that breeze never turns Patch's head. I call a halt just
above the confluence of the creek we've been following with the
second, larger stream that drains the hollow. We're at the point
of another triangle. Together, the two streams have dug a deep,
oval pool where, hunting here in October, I've watched brook

trout spawn in shafts of golden autumn light. Today, the trout
are tucked away, suspended in the cold, very near the essence
of winter's interior stillness. The empty pool, like the empty
woods, seems full. The trout and the grouse, whose presence we
feel keenly in their absence, are secret sharers of the ongoing life
of this watershed of which we catch only glimpses.

If the bird is above us, we'll find it on the way back up, following the second stream. But I suspect that wary grouse is far
below us in thick cover along the river these tributaries feed,
cover we've hunted hard and well earlier in the season when the
birds were still bunched up and offered easier shooting. As I've
said, we cannot hunt it all at once. For safety's sake, I want to be
back where the logging road dead-ends at the home site before
daylight disintegrates into darkness. In winter, dusk won't hold
a working light for you the way it does in other seasons. The
finest trout you ever catch will rise in the forgiving dusk of late
spring or in the nearly endless, sometimes starlit dusk of summer. But daylight vanishes suddenly, like a grouse or a trout, in
midwinter, and it's dangerous to be picking your way through
these cliff-pocked woods in the dark.

Our futile pursuit had taken us out of the best of the big
cover, but we get back into it working uphill. We have the wind
fully in our favor again—too much wind, really. Gusty blusters
of unfriendly cold hammer at us, and Patch gets giddy with an
overload of information in his nose, impertinent data on every
grouse from here to West Virginia. We pull ourselves together
just below all that good cover. Good cover *looks* good, birds
or no. I stop to get a hooded pullover on, a windproof fleece I
need in this punching cold. I put a fingerless glove on my left
hand but leave my right hand bare. When we get up on those
relatively flat oldfields, my heart and lungs slow down and I feel

enough energy and focus left in me to take a bird.

When we get back to the lower fence line, I cut Patch loose again. He busts through some nasty brier-choked shrub and rotting slash and then gets up in the laurel above me. When the loose, running jangle of his hunting bell shifts to toll the quick feints and tight turns of his making game, that artful decision making—*not here, not here, this way, this way, not here, this way, this way, this way*—I'm all ears. And when the bell tightens down, somehow quick and slow all at once—*this way, this way, this way, here*—I listen hardest to the silence of his taut point. *Here. Ahead. Here. Right here. Right here. Now.*

Halfway through the nanosecond it takes for this final message to spark from dog to man, the grouse gets up, through no fault of Patch's. I'm twenty yards from the point and the flush, but this one I see coming. I shoulder the gun and paint through the bird, letting my hips and shoulders turn my head, which is nestled to the stock. When my lead is right, the bird seems to have stopped moving and I no longer hear the distracting sound of its flight. I'm conscious only of a window of space-time in front of it, which my concentration enlarges, and that there is no light left in the background. This grouse is flying into night, which is waiting in the woods all around us. This day, this hunt, is almost over.

When you hunt well, you shoot well. Deep into the country, the country gets deep into you. A day over rough terrain has steadied me for this moment. Sometimes, as Turgenev wrote, the bird flies smoothly into your shot string. I picked the crumpled grouse up from bloodless snow at the base of a sugar maple, where Patch had come, too tired for the war dance, to look at it. The dog, the bird, the man—the mountainside, the sugar maple, the sudden dark—we are all in this together.

I'm too tired, mentally and physically, to fully appreciate the bird. There will be time for that later. I brush the snow from it and briefly look it over, finding beads of blood on its breast. I spread its wings and tail out for Patch to see and smell. *Bird. Good dog. Bird. Bird.* His grave eyes gleam.

In ten minutes, we are back on the logging road, a good hour from the truck. The glazed snow glows in the dark, curving down the mountain. The woods are familiar and strange, silent inside of the hollow sound of a full-blown westerly that arrived with nightfall, silent against the crunch of my footsteps and the musical rattle of Patch's bell. I listen for owls but hear no owls tonight. In places, I smell deer. The universe expands above us at forty or sixty or seventy kilometers per second per megaparsec, but we are too weary and content to think about larger things. Orion hunts overhead with two dogs in tow, like Valery with Touman and Chara. I trust my Russian friends are well. Patch and I are satisfied with this long day. We've worn ourselves out pretty well on these old mountains and, when we get far enough down the road to encounter our own tracks, we each take advantage of the trail we broke coming up, carefully measuring out the energy we have saved for going home.

On the last day of the season birds were everywhere and nowhere. Patch whirled into a big wind that gusted from all quarters, sweeping scent from each curve and swell of the surrounding mountains, parsing the woods for every last possibility of game. "Here," Aeolus seemed to laugh, "here are all the birds left in this winter. Come and find them."

We hunted through the apple orchard where Patch had flushed the first bird of the year, a dark brown grouse I killed rising into autumn light. I remembered putting fistfuls of small green apples into the game bag along with the warm bird and how the apples were stained with flecks of blood when I unpacked the day's bounty. Now the orchard was snowbound, the trees long shorn of fruit and the light spare and uninviting except where conifers held dark color in the woods. I can't say we worked the cover hard. Patch's birdiness was giddy and unfocused. Satiated by weeks of venison roasts and steaks, I had lost the appetite—and the leanness—that quickened my step in October. We were out to enjoy one last day afield, a cold Saturday in February when only unrepentant bird hunters know there is still some hunting to be done.

We worked downslope, crisscrossing from laurel slick to laurel slick, worrying any shelter wood we could find. I needed feathers for trout flies, if that excused the desire for one more grouse, but I wasn't unaware that we were hunting birds that had almost made it through. We picked up a silver creek that slaked Patch's wild thirst. He stood belly-deep in the icy flow, full of himself, and lapped his fill like a wolf with big business to get back to. The stream led us to the beaver ponds that flood the woods between the three tines that form the North Fork of Buffalo Creek, a shifting wetland that added much character to the watershed. We hunted the high ground *edge, thick with rhododendron, and crossed the biggest dam to get to the overgrown oldfield where I killed my first grouse a decade ago. That bird, which I flushed and missed twice, led me to my first view of these boggy headwaters.*

There were no birds in the sunlit oldfield, which we did hunt hard, or on the slopes above it, where we tired. The big wind kept up, freezing my ambition and fooling the dog. On the way back down through the beaver ponds, we stopped to admire a stand of yellow birch that gleamed fiercely in the winter light.

Second Growth

Well, there I might live, I said; and there I did live. . . .

—HENRY DAVID THOREAU,
Walden

In midwinter, it's the bare bones of the farm I admire, the clarity of land and light around me. What I can only call the *being* of nature seems most revealed during these undistinguished weeks when the ice-streaked rivers open and close and the earth underfoot freezes and thaws by turns, resettling itself with a restlessness you can feel through your boot soles. The life of the farm seems to stall, as if the turning of the year had hit a flat spot, one of those imperfections in the earth's odd shape on which the workings of the solar system slip for a week or so, leaving the brown woods perfectly empty and the pastures perfectly still. During a long walk around the farm, the strong wing beats of a crow flying silently beneath an ashen sky may have to stand for the life of things.

Once grouse season ends on the second Saturday in February, there is no hunting proper left to do until October. More than half a hunter's year is about not hunting, and a good hunter refines himself from late winter to early autumn. Unknown to the warden, Patch and I hunt every day of the year licensed only by our curiosity. The game is harder out of season because on any given day we don't know what we are looking for. We might see the sun rise, a storm brood toward us, daylight fan through a quiet woodlot, or darkness fall on the back pasture, revealing not darkness but the well-lit universe overhead. We might encounter things we see frequently—turkey vultures teetering on thermals, a red-tailed hawk perched in the crown of a dead walnut, a line of deer crossing a rise—or chance on something we have seen once—a flock of evening grosbeaks along South River, a solitary sandpiper at the barn spring, red fox kits playing with abandon on the limestone outcrop below the barn. Such hunting never stops, and it improves us. For better or worse, we are what we have seen and have slowly learned the obvious—that everything is important—that crow, for example, flying against an ashen sky, its silence a kind of call.

Highland Farm occupies an irregular rise of land buckled between two rivers that join in the woods below my cabin. From my writing desk, I feel as though I'm on a headland built to overlook that confluence—two hundred forty acres of pastures and woodlots molded into ridges and sinkholes, pocked with strong springs and the mossy creases of intermittent creeks, traced lightly with forgotten roads and gouged, here and there, with old logging scars. The flow of those rivers, which I can hear after a heavy rain, creates the illusion that the farm is pointed downstream, that here up on this headland we are headed somewhere. That suggestion is deepened because I look out that way while I write, my eyes frequently wandering to the horizon. I like hearing the rivers while I work, each rushing in a different

key toward where they sweep together, turning with the terrain
to find a way through the Blue Ridge Mountains down near
Glasgow where the Maury River joins the James River upstream
from Snowden Dam. The steady, grainy sound of the rivers
helps me concentrate even as it distracts me.

Like the woodlots and pastures in the foreground, the mountains change throughout the year, their flanks turning through
subtle hues like the coats of white-tailed deer. Those changes
mark the true seasons, the seasons between the seasons which
have no names, like the weeks between winter and spring when
the hardwoods flower, tinting the landscape with an impres-
sionistic haze of the palest greens, yellows and reds nature has at
its disposal, or those days between summer and Indian summer
when you notice sourwood leaves turned red and early flocks of
migrating birds moving through the cabin hollow long before
you thought to look for them.

I like the compact, grizzled look of the mountains in winter
when you can see a forest sketched in detail on their rocky
slopes, the diminutive trees drawn with great care. Reduced to
its essence, the horizon looks as if it were gathering the strength
to support another year of growth. Sometimes, when I raise my
eyes from my desk to look at them, the mountains seem to have
just stopped moving.

Every turn of season invites the close inspection of grouse
cover and trout streams and of the haunts of animals and birds
whose wild presence in that forested horizon I like to confirm.
For years I misunderstood this and thought that for all the life in
view here, literally under my nose, there was wilder, rarer life in
the mountains—scarlet tanagers instead of cardinals, cerulean
warblers instead of indigo buntings, black bear instead of deer,
timber rattlers instead of rat snakes, one brazen raven there for

every hundred desultory crows here. Now I think that the idea of wildness, though useful, has always represented the projection of a human need and that the rarity of certain species, though quantifiable, ultimately leads to a false accounting. In nature, nothing is wild or unwild, rare or common. The wildness in nature that would preserve the world, as Thoreau insisted, is underfoot at every step. Nature sets a passionate example at every turn. A field sparrow gleaning fescue seeds in a pasture is as powerful an expression of the will to live as a peregrine falcon stooping out of the sky. The gray squirrels, twitchy with paranoia, that enliven every woodlot are as rare—in essence if not in numbers—as the rumors of stately mountain lions roaming the hills, the careening shape of an oak leaf as precipitous as any cliff where golden eagles roost.

As property, the farm is an oddly shaped patch of land, its zigzagging fence lines reflecting settlements, sales and inheritances that go back centuries, touching many lives unknown to me. I imagine these are recorded in deed books I could study in the county offices if I were inclined to do so. But that would feel like prying. Occasionally, I find something lost or left behind—a plow point, a drawknife blade, an iron wheel or the hand-forged hardware of a singletree—humble artifacts that speak of honest, well-paced work. I've lost things myself—a fine bone-handled knife, a tin of percussion caps, a saw, a wedge, a few good cedar arrows and innumerable drawing pencils dropped by the way. At least one person has gotten lost here.

The main section of the four-room cabin I occupy is fashioned out of stout logs hewn into shape seventy or eighty years ago by a now-nameless fellow who is remembered only for disappearing. He left the one-room version of this dwelling, situated elsewhere on the farm, empty as an old wasp nest

until my landlord wrested the unchinked logs from the copperheads, blacksnakes and field mice that had set up shop in it.
Whatever his faults or eccentricities, the nameless man bucked
and squared those logs well enough—the eclectic mix of chestnut, oak and poplar that surround me now—even if, perhaps
pressured by the turning seasons that still govern life here, he
trimmed in haste. I consider the thin hack marks of his broadax
honest decoration.

Beyond what years of closely watching woodlots, pastures,
weather and night sky entitles me to, I have no title here. I passed
through that need of ownership Thoreau describes so well at the
beginning of the second chapter of *Walden,* and have found, in
my own way, a kind of purchase. I know the land around me
well enough to understand that it rewards exploration at any
time of day in any season. From stars to birds, you may practice
discovery here. And the modest rewards of finding something
familiar, like the belly-smooth earth of a fox den entrance, or
something unfamiliar, like the haunting silhouettes of tundra
swans migrating under a bruised March sky, or something rare,
like the slender tips of walking fern rooting themselves in wet
cushion moss on a limestone ledge, underwrite, for me, a sense
of place that verifies my faith in time.

From my study in the cabin's loft, I look southeast toward
that ruffle of mountains three or four miles away through two
hexagonal windows set like eyes above my writing desk. I work
better on days when the mountains are obscured by clouds and
my native curiosity and incurable physical restlessness are left
unstirred. But even on the clearest days—in early spring and
late autumn when the cold air is as sharp as a lens—I cannot
see beyond the mountains. They are, indeed, as the Greek root
of *horizon* suggests, a boundary.

Now, in midwinter, the intervening pastures are sere and the woods brown, although that brown cast in the middle distance lightens to gray in the foreground, where I am faced with dense ranks of hardwoods interrupted, here and there, by a few persistent evergreens. The crown of a gnarly dogwood reaches into view out the left window, affording me the opportunity to bird-watch while I write.

Out the right window, the last in a row of scrub pines across the farm road leans into view behind my computer monitor. A relatively short-lived species with a binomial far more elegant than its common name, *Pinus virginiana* has a useful, human-scale life of seventy-five years or so. The sun-bent trunk, haggard branches and dense but broken crown of the tree are as fine an image as you will find on this farm of the humble way life aspires to fulfill itself here. It reminds me of the broken pine that leans into Tai Chin's fifteenth-century *Returning Late from a Spring Outing*.

Sitting at this desk, I can see only one habitation in the distance—a house, barn and some outbuildings set on a hill perhaps a half mile away, prosperous or ramshackle I cannot tell at this distance. This relatively unsettled look of the countryside is reassuring, although it is, in part, an illusion created by the perspective of my writing desk. For now the view reflects a sensible balance between the human and the natural, what used to be called the pastoral.

The front porch overlooks the cabin hollow, a thin corridor of walnut and poplar laced with sugar maple, dogwood, cedar, spicebush and smooth black haw, the principal viburnum here and a fine native shrub when it can fan itself out in the open. This modest gathering of trees follows the faint impression of an old farm road, grassed in after thirty years of disuse and a good walking path into the heart of the farm. The intermittent creek that drains the barn spring follows the old road under a tunnel of coralberry, dewberry, honeysuckle and multiflora rose that will be thick with nesting birds in April and May. At the lower end of the hollow, a rabbit warren is hidden in the dense undergrowth, its mouth less obvious than a woodchuck hole but not quite as subtle as the threshold of a fox den. The stump of an old chestnut, eight feet around, lies stranded just beyond it.

Beyond this wisp of a hollow, the foot of the front pasture rises abruptly from right to left toward the creased prominence that holds this two-hundred-acre farm together like the domed crust of a well-stuffed apple pie. Bleached outcrops of rain-polished limestone and soapstone gleam through thin, dry soil that supports the least favorite forage on the farm, judging from how little time the cattle spend there. A sequence of isolated trees leads the eye up the center of that long southern exposure—a Spanish oak, an American holly, a black walnut, tulip poplars, an American elm, a white pine. Everywhere clumps of multiflora rose, bursts of blackberry and dewberry and tough, drought-resistant eastern red cedar conspire to fill the pasture in.

Through most of the year, it's the tree life that invites attention here—what's called "second growth," although second growth is really a perpetual regrowth, nature's dogged assertion of its vegetative prerogatives against a background of human use, benign and abusive. Over a century or two of random use, the land was logged and farmed and left, and then reclaimed from wild regrowth to be logged and farmed and left again. Half cleared in its current form thirty years ago for cattle pasturage, the main attraction here for eye and mind is its woods and woodlots, strong expressions of ancient ideas the earth

had—what we call *oak, maple, birch, beech, cherry, locust, walnut, hickory, cedar, pine* and dozens of other species that frame
the soul of a piece of rural land that casually harbors much
diversity of life. The forty or so head of cattle that keep the
pastures cropped are not of much interest to me, but I suppose
they make Highland Farm a farm.

Across that steeply sloped hill that gives such character to the
foreground, you can see the near edge of the river woods—dense
ranks of cedar, blackjack and post oak which lead into a dark,
quiet realm that reaches to the fence line on the farm's eastern
boundary. South River, which flows north to south below that
boundary, is not in view from the front porch, but the terrain
suggests its presence. When you get down in the river woods,
you can hear it. A broad field of winter wheat I cannot see from
here spreads from the other side of the river to a rise of land
across the way that roughly matches the mass of the rumpled
hill I live on. Beyond that, the Blue Ridge Mountains gather
themselves as, from this perspective, a graceful and important
edge of things.

The open view I have in winter, from the tattered cedar posts
of the front porch to the stars beyond the mountains, is always
worth a look. By late May, when the walnuts along the chestnut-
rail fence finish leafing in, throwing a cool green shade across
the front of the cabin, the farm will have seemed to have risen
up and closed pleasantly around my dwelling—come toward
it with a great variety of life offered at no cost. Except for the
distraction of nesting birds, it is easier to write at the weathered
drawing table on the porch when the mountains are not in view,
and for half the year I can work there late in the morning and
in the early evening.

Out the back door, another pasture rises gently, flowing

west until it falls away to a county road and that confluence
of rivers which seems to lead the farm toward a string of fine
old towns along the James—Glasgow, Lynchburg, Richmond,
Williamsburg, Jamestown. The view west from the back of the
cabin is dominated by a truncated hill of sandstone that has
been sliced through over time by the Maury River, which flows
in a long, deep, silent pool along the base of it. That stark hill
dominates the western horizon, marking time like the gnomon
of a sundial. The setting sun moves north and south of it as
the year oscillates from solstice to solstice. In winter, the gray
layers of sandstone visible through the bare trees are marks of
even deeper time.

A row of stately Spanish oaks leads from my back door uphill
toward the barn, spaced out crown to crown. These large two-
hundred-year-old trees grew along what used to be a fence line
on the ridge above the cabin hollow. Now these oaks shadow a
new fence strung from the cabin gate to the barn gate separat-
ing the pasture that slopes down to the Maury River from the
rest of the farm. These great trees bear a crop of acorns, and
flocks of raiding jays, every other year and were likely planted
by jays or squirrels. Like all oaks, they leaf out late, in early
May, with slender, deeply lobed variations on the theme of oak
leaves. When new, the leaves of *Quercus falcata* are limp, pale
green and paper thin, fresh and silky to the touch. Then they
thicken and darken, their edges curled toward their midribs.
Trees which delicately reflect morning and evening light in late
spring absorb it greedily all summer, rewarding the world with
small oval acorns in September. In late October, they rust a
subtle orange-yellow and hang stubbornly on every branch, rattling harshly in any breeze until they are shorn by winter storms.
I wouldn't know so much about the life of these leaves—hardly

a subject of importance—except that a large double-trunked Spanish oak leans over the cabin just outside the bedroom window. The shortest walk I can take here brings me to this tree.

There is a gap between the second and third of the big trees where a stunted locust sapling must have been waiting in the shadows of a now-missing oak, of which there is not a sign left except that gap. Given a chance by the oak's demise, the locust grew quickly for forty-two years. I know the tree's age exactly because I cut it down the year after it died and counted the rings. After the tally, I couldn't help but note that I was the same age as the locust, although I saw no special irony in the fact that my firewood and I were contemporaries. And my count might have been off by a year or two. My landlord had generously extended me cutting rights to dead wood, and I made an executive decision that what would have made a fine snag for nesting woodpeckers was going to give me six weeks of warmth in what turned out to be my coldest winter here—seventeen degrees below zero on the front porch one amazing morning when the frigid Arctic air was nothing like any air I had ever tried to breathe.

I felled that stout, nearly branchless tree uphill, to shorten the arc of the fall and soften the blow, which was still impressive, the weight of the locust bouncing and shaking the earth until gravity split the difference and brought tree and earth to rest. I was proud of the neat felling. I remember having my doubts as the chain saw poured out a stream of dark yellow sawdust on my work boots. The graceful, weightless look of trees changes as the cutting bar disappears into the bole, so easily undermining that enormous standing mass. The deeper my cut, the heavier and less predictable that locust looked. But my wedge cut was true, deep enough and properly angled, and my back cut, propped

with badly chewed plastic wedges, just right. I left no spike on
the stump, just a faint ridge across the center where the enormous weight of the thing hinged over due west toward the new
fence line with a deep bass *buuummm*.

I was relieved to get the tree down safely and felt a not incon-
siderable, acquisitive joy at its demise. I learned the first chilly
winter I tended the woodstove for my principal heat how long
and hot a quarter of locust would burn. If I ran Fort Knox, I'd
keep golden splits of black locust stacked in the vaults instead of
gold bullion. A single, seasoned chunk with that thick-rinded,
corky bark still clinging to it will last through a good night's
sleep—enough heartwood for a dream cycle. In the morning,
the firebox reignites with a pop when you spin the stove vents
open, those locust coals as good as a pilot light. So I felt pretty
well off that morning looking at the bounty of forty-two locust
years laid out upslope, so convenient for cutting and so near the
cabin. I've cut my share of wood out of steep, tangled places
where there was a lot of backbreaking hauling to be done.

I cut that tree down this time of year, midwinter, and I
remember the pleasure of bucking the log under a cold, gray
February sky. I cut a chopping block off the base and set up shop
right there, stopping to sharpen the saw frequently as I sliced the
tree up into stove-length rounds. I was working long mornings
that winter finishing a book, mornings that stretched into late
afternoons. I remember how pleasurable it was to go out at four
or so, Patch bouncing around me, and have the locust there to
work on for an hour. Concentration on the details of words and
things left me woolly-brained as a woodchuck in February and
ready for manual labor to wake me up to the world beyond my
own thoughts. I liked the routine so much I nursed the task for a
week, splitting that honey-yellow locust—popping it open with

an eight-pound maul—toting it down the hill, and stacking it neat as milled lumber under the big double-trunked Spanish oak next to the cabin. Crazy, maybe, but I'd stop to breathe in deep draughts of that pungent heartwood, as fine in its way as the fresh scent of a deer hide.

I ate dinner late those evenings, a venison chili I favor in winter. Make a Dutch oven's worth and eat it every night for a week, stoking my own fires with good food—half of it from the garden and the other half from the woods. A small bowl dense with stew meat, kidney beans, corn, peppers, garlic and tomatoes with salad and a hunk of French bread will fill you up but not undo how that rhythmic, physical labor leans and quickens body and mind. I write well after evenings when I work like that, as if honest labor opens up an honest part of me. I'll awake in the morning dark to find two or three paragraphs laid out, like that locust, for the taking. Just follow the grain of the thoughts you find in your head, splitting words and phrases true, following the natural bias of language—where the desire and work of countless others is preserved, just as the labor of that nameless fellow is preserved in this cabin. Stack those words and phrases neatly, but not too fastidiously, in sentences and paragraphs that account for your own experience of things. The locust stump is still there, halfway between the cabin and the barn, overgrown and weathered, its outer growth rings slowly loosening, the nature of the thing worried open by time, the years in it letting go even as honeysuckle vines, tough as sisal, bind it to the ground.

The stately row of Spanish oaks suggests a walk toward the barn at the head of the cabin hollow. As you climb the steep back pasture, you raise the horizon of mountains behind you, the perspective changing with every step should you choose to turn and look. Each stride toward the barn raises another mile of mountains to the north and south, revealing the profound power of walking here. The deeper into the farm you go, the farther you can see into the world beyond it. The watersheds of the western slope of the Blue Ridge Mountains come into view en masse, folded and worn, an incorrigible trace of continental collision, that beautiful tectonic restlessness of the surface of the earth that no other planet we yet know of enjoys, healed scar tissue of a living planet.

To the west, the Alleghenies express themselves in variations on the theme of ridge and valley, syncline and anticline, that culminates in West Virginia's rugged montainscape and extends all the way to southern Ohio. That forested backcountry in the offing is escape habitat for eye, mind and heart and its presence seems to embolden life on the farm. We are all—crows and woodchucks, dogs and writers—a bit cockier for it. Long vistas make us strong.

Beyond what I can see from my cabin, walking is how I come to know things here. Walking is, as Thoreau suggested, not only a way to see things. It is a way to sense them fully, to feel them and begin to establish a narrative relation to them. We are what we cross paths with—not what we are hunting on a given day, but what catches us unawares. Walking invites accidental connections, fleeting associations that leave something casually worthwhile in their wake. Nature sets a good example at every turn. Walking is a way of exposing your own consciousness to the larger calculus of the life of things. Life itself could be figured as a walk through time. Walking is a way of thinking grooved to tangible contours of time and place. Topography, as an expression of local noon or deep time, is best understood step by step, slowly through the boot soles and in the large muscles of the leg, then in the lungs and heart, leaving what gets to the mind improved by physical effort. There is nothing here that cannot be encountered in a walk—bloodroot, oak, fox, hawk. And to be freely tutored in understanding *any* other is no small thing.

The rhythm of walking underwrites in fundamental ways the reassuring continuity of even disturbed, fragmented places. There is something in us that would see the world whole and so, perhaps, be made whole. Walking can pull any injured landscape together, just as it can unify one's impression of a busy city street or clarify the shoddy emptiness of a small town fallen on hard times. Outdoors, we tend to walk in blank verse, striding by small degrees with emphasis *toward* something that catches our eye or ear until that curiosity enjambs us against whatever it is we need to see, or hear, or smell, or touch, or taste. Walking in the same place over time creates a sense of timelessness, as if a given moment might open on all moments, a familiar place liberated by a wealth of details that have fused conscious and subconscious experiences.

In retrospect, the season of any walk extends through past and future:

Walking in winter, the rattle of a woodpecker turns your head. Its shallow arcs of flight through spring lead you on to where the deeply incised bark of a persimmon mesmerizes your eye in midsummer like a brilliant painting in a gallery where, for the moment, nothing else interests you. You make a mental note to return after the first hard frost to share the sweet flavor of its tart fruit with migrant birds fleeing the oncoming winter.

A given moment, properly experienced, embodies all time and tense.

A twelve-point buck flushes out of the brush at the head of the deer track woodlot one September afternoon, its bowl-shaped antlers carrying sunlight into the shadows of dry hollow. Blinded by the trophy, you hunt it hard all season. You see it, too far off, when you are bow hunting in October, and too late when you are carrying a rifle in November. You see it all the time when it is not there. You hunt the image of it and the memory of it and, because you are distracted by it, the deer you do encounter escape you at every turn. The big buck that sounded so heavy running with its antlers full of sunlight takes the whole season away with it.

The Spanish oaks lead to the large black walnut that presides over one side of the barn gate. This ancient tree looks as if it grew in shade for its first century, during which it worked hard to gather sunlight. Perhaps it was shadowed by a long-vanished chestnut. Six feet above the ground the walnut divided into three wandering trunks, one of which died back into a rotting scar some time ago. The other two trunks branched roughly east and west, to gather as much spring and summer daylight as they could. When the tree was released from whatever stood between it and the sun, the walnut filled out a crown that is as beautiful in its irregularity as is the perfectly symmetrical oak that complements it on the other side of the barn gate. There is not a straight piece of lumber in this gatekeeper, but the tree bears fruit well for its age. Gray squirrels glean it eagerly in early autumn. The failed north-pointing limb has drawn heart rot into the great tree, its bark melted around this fatal flaw where lichens, moss and insects have already created another world.

Of course, what seem to be deformities in the barn gate walnut are really the traces of its genius, the embodiment of its strategies for survival, its way of growing, pruning a life for itself out of the air. There are no words for its shape, much less for its strange being. The great tree has grown through time, if not beyond language, then at least out toward that edge of verbal possibility where the literal doesn't quite capture the thing itself, a gnarly old being whose rangy, horizontal limbs, nurtured by the sun, roughly embrace the ecliptic. Rarely a day goes by in spring and summer when I do not walk at least this far into the farm just to mark the evening when bats or tree swallows lace the air while frogs trill from the barn spring and the cabin hollow. In the half-light, the walnut glows darkly, a strong presence, like one of the elders of this place, which of course it is. A tangible, transcendental thing, it bears thought as well as walnuts. Sometimes, when I am at my desk, I imagine I have imagined it, or at least exaggerated its striking posture, the strange runes that flow through its melted bark, the impressive density of its being, animated by what a Zen Buddhist would call its *tzu-jan*, the pure energy of its being. But anytime I walk up the rise behind the cabin, it is there, a strong and fine thing in the world well worth acknowledging, well worth dwelling on.

The farm spreads lavishly in all directions from the barn gate. Climb the board fence behind the barn and you can get into the lower end of the barn woods, a sturdy woodlot dominated by oak, hickory and walnut much favored by gray squirrels in all seasons and by wild turkey in autumn when the white oaks drop their acorns. The understory of the barn woods is graced with spicebush, redbud, persimmon, papaw, cherry, basswood, buckthorn, dogwood, mulberry and red maple and is proof of that casual diversity of life here. It harbors the farm's only swamp white oak and a magnificent Fraser magnolia whose large white blooms are one of the culminations of spring. The magnolia will lead you to a gathering of beech trees up near where the farm road curves toward the back gate.

Through the back gate you could follow a faint track to the nameless woodlot or cruise the north pasture. Descend through the hilly north woodlots, a series of shady sinkholes out of which I have cut a good deal of firewood. Swing back along the brambles, an impenetrable tangle of every thorn-bearing thing that grows here. Skirting the brambles will bring you to the double-helix, a pair of deep sinkholes, one of which is full of the curious plant life that lodges itself on wet limestone ledges.

Return through the back gate and follow the farm road along the near side of the double-helix and the brambles. With the bony pasture of walnut hill on your right, the fence line will lead you to the old homesite pasture, the original site of my cabin, where there is still a pile of crude lumber and sheet-metal roofing. The cabin was situated near a spring surrounded with honey locust. A broken old apple tree, overgrown with sand grape and Virginia creeper, still blooms in April in front of where the cabin sat, facing south, I assume, to gather a full measure of daylight. Beyond the cabin is the dense growth of a thirty-year-old clear-cut, where a variety of softwoods and hardwoods strive to outgrow an untended planting of white pines.

Afternoon and evening light in the old homesite pasture beggars description. Blocked by walnut hill, you cannot see the sunset from back there. You only see the subtle, breeze-borne loss of light and night come on. Even when I know the deer are probably elsewhere, I hunt there all the time in the fall just to watch the pregnant stillness of the afternoon, the way the pasture seems to breathe and move, the way mourning doves come whistling in to roost in the white pines, the way deer appear or don't appear, threading their way through the goldenrod in the failing light.

From the homesite pasture you could wander through the

old clear-cut gate and circumnavigate all that thick head-high cover of pine and cedar, moving deer you'll never see from one side to the other. You could skirt the near side of the old clear-cut and bushwhack your way along the ridge that overlooks the river woods, pushing turkey and deer and perhaps flushing a grouse. Or you could drop down into the big timber of the river woods, where I take a deer every year, moving easily through the open understory until you came out into the breaks, where toothy ridges of worn limestone make walking difficult. The limestone outcrops will push you downhill through chestnut oak and walnut among much else toward the lush world around the big spring, a rocky bowl of numbing-cold water filled with tasty cress in summer and overshadowed by the largest tree on the farm, a northern red oak ten feet around.

Climb steeply uphill through the cedars until you get to the far edge of the pasture on which my front porch looks out. You will see the cabin fronting you beyond a screen of young walnuts, and the Spanish oaks, and the crease of the cabin hollow. Keep the front pasture on your left and hike up the near side of the river woods, a steep pull up along good deer cover, where does and their young hole up during the day. Head the river woods at the gas-line corner, where those deer come out to feed in the evening. As you cruise the upper edge of the river woods, watch for the wild turkey that use that edge and for the big bucks that bed down in the small islands of trees scattered around the fringe of walnut hill. That edge will bring you past the deer track, a small woodlot where I bow hunt both the turkey and the deer, to the cul-de-sac which overlooks the lower end of the old homesite pasture and the old clear-cut gate.

Then make your way straight up walnut hill, where you can catch your breath taking in a perspective I still don't quite know what to do with—sixty miles of the Blue Ridge Mountains in view, from near the headwaters of the St. Mary's River to beyond Thunder Ridge. From up there, the idea of Highland Farm seems to go on forever, a pleasant illusion if ever there was one. Descend walnut hill to the west and follow a narrow hollow of poplar and sumac and ash-leaf maple until you find yourself in a small copse of chinquapin oak, where there is a big white oak stump for sitting. From there you will see the barn and the barn spring and the head of the cabin hollow, which you can descend back to my cabin.

The word *journey,* Thoreau reminds us in his famous essay on walking, has its roots in the French for a day's walk. I can spend a day, dawn to dusk, out on the farm in any season, dawdling for different reasons in different places, and feel like I have gone somewhere, been away on a journey and returned even though I never left home.

I write well in winter, when I am inclined to be lavish with wood and spare with words. Short days encourage economy. Cold mornings prompt me to tighten the long, rhythmic prose line toward which my mind is naturally drawn—a walking prose line, as I think of it. That long line is a vestige, I assume, of Romantic longing—learned or inherited—expression of a need for connection and continuity, a desire to search out some relation to the life of things. I'm not unaware it took me a long prose line to write that—and on a winter morning, to boot. But a pale winter dawn backlighting bare hardwoods suggests the benefit of at least striving for unadorned clarity.

On the twenty-seventh of February, the rising sun moves back into the window to the left of my writing desk. I will have to dodge its blinding beams until early May, shifting the keyboard here and there until it is well up. A week or so later, about the time I plant a row of barrel-shaped snow-pea seeds in the first turned section of the garden, the unwelcome starlings that nest behind the chimney every year reappear to start their work. With yellow beaks full of the pink insulation they pluck from behind the chimney, they stare in at me as I write in the morning and sometimes tap a windowpane to test the reality of it. Sometimes I test it, too, tapping back at them.

When a morning's worth of writing is done, there is other work to do—bills to pay, letters and e-mails to answer, calls to make, books to read, magazine columns to write, sometimes a course to teach at a nearby college. The latter is always a pleasure, since the American literature I peddle is one of the great outgrowths of American nature. There is little difference between a walk in the woods and a walk through the strong prose of Emerson and Thoreau, Hawthorne and Melville, Twain and Faulkner, language that is, paradoxically, wild and well planted. And nothing is as distinct as the sight of a kestrel careening through late-afternoon light, or as revealing as the call of a meadowlark in the evening, or as mysterious as starlight piercing through the branches of an oak than the fine, wild lines of Emily Dickinson's keen verse. It's Dickinson, perhaps, who most understood what there is to try to see in nature.

Of course, there are also practical things to do—wood to cut, a balky old truck to puzzle over, a garden to turn, a dog to run. If you are living well, there is always something to fix or build, to plant or prune or harvest. That's all writing is, after all. Tasks are clear in winter. There is a balance and clarity in things, life pruned back to its essence, wrapped tight in buds not quite ready to burst forth again. I like winter best, perhaps, not because it is a season of darkness, or of more dark than light, but because the value of that pale, evanescent winter light is so clear. In the late afternoons that go dark without an evening, those afternoons of slanted light with which Ms. Dickinson was familiar, every uneventful moment seems eventful. The beauty of late winter here is in the way the weather stiffens as the short days lengthen. A snowstorm in early March frequently forestalls expectations of spring with the lingering reality of winter, covering those newly planted snow peas with snow. But when the sun breaks through on a blinding blue day, snowmelt is as good as rain. Spring may be a riot of new life, but if you watch the life of the woods closely, late winter is the true season of birth and renewal, an unsettled time of year when life affirms itself muddily against gusty weather that is harsh and promising by turns. Nature teaches persistence above all things. Everything that grows will grow in its turn.

So on this Ides of March, I ski in shirtsleeves through four inches of new snow back to a grove of ironwood that established itself where the river woods joins the dense growth of the old clear-cut. If you avoid the rock outcrops and chunks of what geologists call "float" scattered about, there is no finer way to traverse the farm than on cross-country skis. You *shush* along quietly, cutting neat, thin tracks across raccoon, rabbit and fox trails, sliding quietly up to cover where you can bird-watch without need of binoculars. Hungry whitethroats and haggard bluebirds ignore me, as do the rufous-sided towhees fussing with leaves in the bare places and the juncos scissoring about the cedars, flashing that sliver of white in their tails that reminds me of the pure white edge of a brook trout's tail. Harsh crow caws and the liquid chortle of blue jays carry well on the cold air that underscores the silence the snow seems to hold in place. I feel buoyant and graceful moving around this way, eliding that familiar rhythm of walking with a kick and glide that makes the trees flicker by and the snowy ground slide away underneath me. The farm feels good, solid but forgiving, when I dig the poles into the soft earth beneath the snow.

This year, the ironwood grove is a marked place. I killed the only deer I got this winter on the last day of the season, a spike buck that came up the ridge from the Logans' bottomland in the middle of a cold, bright afternoon. I had a fine fall getting close to deer and a terrible one spooking them with some slight move that ruined my chances. Each time out I invented a new way of betraying my presence at the last moment. While my self-consciousness got twitchier and twitchier, the season slipped away as those chances snorted in alarm and burst off. December was coming to an end, the freezer was nearly empty and I was dreaming about deer flushing away from me like grouse. Deer may be numerous, but they don't walk in the back door. You take an animal as wary as white-tailed deer for granted, or hunt distracted, as I had hunted, and you will be sitting on a log in the cold on the last day of the season in a state of deeply rueful attention. At that point you are depending on dumb luck, patron saint of hunters having a bad year, to bail you out.

Dumb luck came up the ridge in the form of that spike buck. You don't forget the deer you kill, or where you killed them, or the way late-afternoon sunlight slanted through the ranks of bare trees as if you were sitting in a cathedral with its roof off. You keep sharp images in your head, like well-made black and white photographs, out of respect and because, although killing an animal is a hard thing to be doing, it is the hunter's necessary task. Short of the kill, you are not only an unsuccessful hunter, you are verging on being a hypocrite—you are not doing what you said you were doing when you went out the door.

I know my limits as a rifleman, what shots I can take and make—a short, clear look at a deer that hasn't tensed up with alarm because it has gotten some hint of me in its eyes or ears or nostrils. I was watching the ridge, breeze in my face, listening to the river, when that winter-gray buck crested the rise and then stopped to look back over its shoulder as if someone were moving down below. That gave me a chance to brace up solid, left elbow propped on my knee as a gun rest. I remember waiting for the deer to step between two well-spaced chestnut oaks, a useful frame that helped me narrow my focus. The buck flinched as I took the recoil from the reproduction of a Civil War Enfield carbine I like to hunt with in the close quarters of the farm's woodlots. I knew by the way it flared its rear legs that I had my deer. It tried to make the clear-cut cover but died just short of that, crumpled into these ironwoods.

I had noticed and admired this grove of *Carpinus caroliniana* many times before. Ironwood stands out strong as its name. It's not hard to see the sinewy beauty of a deer's leg in the muscled trunks of smooth ironwood. The graceful understory tree is as distinctive as beech or white birch. Some field guides call it "blue beech," a name with more poetry than science in it. By any name, smooth ironwood is a valuable food source for wildlife—squirrels, rabbits, grouse, deer browse its seeds, buds and twigs. Like many things on the farm here, it is ordinary and extraordinary, as all forms of second growth tend to be. And any hardwood denser than hickory—the benchmark for density in my trusty bible on firewood—is indeed about as close to iron as any wood is going to get. Poetry and science go hand in hand in some names.

After I field-dressed the buck, I remember thinking that I should come back and cut one of the smaller trees for a walk-

ing stick. The thought probably would have occurred to me
anyway, but it happens that the spike buck that filled the freezer
with good wild food for the coming year led me back to that
grove of ironwood in such dramatic fashion that I finally took
stronger notice of them. I wouldn't read anything mystical into
this, and I'm sure the deer would have preferred to run on
unscathed into the cover it never reached. But slow down and
pay attention on the farm and one good thing will lead you
to another. The walking stick, in turn, will lead elsewhere and
will always represent this spot where a late-season hunt and a
deer's life came together, as serious a juncture as I can fashion
between the seasons.

I got off the skis and cut a well-sculpted tree with the same
folding saw I use to build deer blinds and that I take backpacking. The most useful tools pass easily from one seasonal preoccupation to the next. I trimmed the arm-thick beauty, lashed
it to my daypack and skied out the way I had dragged the deer
home that day, a long pull that wore a bare spot on the hide.

Today, instead of turning toward the cabin when I got out on
the front pasture, I cut a trail uphill to enjoy the snow-covered
farm while I had the pleasure of it laid out in front of me. As
I follow the edge of the river woods back toward the old clear-
cut, I pass some of last season's deer blinds. They have already
been disheveled by a few months of wind and weather, woodlot
entropy at work—the blind behind the locust blowdown at
the head of the river woods, from which I saw more turkey
than deer; the four-sided luxury suite I constructed in some
poplars on one slope of dry hollow, where I spooked more deer
than a man has a right to spook; and a comfy if unproductive
perch I set up on the rock overlook at the cul-de-sac above the
metal clear-cut gate. Since I had gotten a deer in the end, all

those hours of waiting in the cold now take on a more pleasant
glow.

Today, there are deer tracks everywhere but no deer in sight.
During a long hunting season, which in Virginia extends from
October to January, whitetails hone their native wariness down
toward invisibility. They will drop their guard, driven by hunger
and the sweet new pasturage, in May and June, when even the
bucks, just growing new velvet-covered antlers, will be on view
at dawn and dusk.

I flush the tail end of a flock of turkey when I ski up to the
old clear-cut entrance. They hustle off with that offbeat, zigzagging canter they have. Turkey trot. A gobbler out on its own
looks like the noble game bird it is. But in a flock, wild turkeys
seem domestic, big barnyard fowl out on the loose. They had
scratched up the snow pretty good, searching for acorns, and left
behind their telltale J-shaped turds. I can hear deer moving in
the thick cover of the old clear-cut when I ski around it. When
they hear me or wind me, they trot through the head-high white
pines and I can hear them rustling against the soft trees and their
hooves clattering, muted, on the snow. When I get up on walnut
hill, I watch two red-tailed hawks patrolling the snowy pastures,
cruising with effortless speed and supreme attentiveness.

Good tasks wait at home on the cusp of winter and spring.
Tonight is the night to give all the guns a final, thorough
recleaning and to pen a final list of repairs that need to be done
and supplies that need to be replaced so that I am prepared
to hunt again in the fall. Good gear deserves tending. All the
leather gun straps and pack harnesses need to be oiled. I check
the bows and, especially, the bowstrings, which get a rewaxing.
I make an inventory of undamaged arrows and a list of fletching
and points needed to get the beat-up cedar shafts back in ser-

vice. Finally, I clean all my hunting boots and clothing, storing everything where they won't get tainted with indoor scents.

The coming season waits in other chores—seeds to order, a bluebird nest box to repair and a wood duck box to build. I'll have to shellac the exposed ends of the ironwood I cut, to keep it from drying out too quickly and checking with splits that will ruin it. For now, it's hung in the downstairs study along with some maple and walnut blanks. That ironwood may well be the finest trophy of the winter, although it's not trophies I'm seeking from the seasons. There is all that tightly wrapped deer meat in the freezer, a salted hide I'll tan with the hair off and maybe get enough buckskin for a hunting shirt. I have three grouse skins and the feathers from one turkey, taken, I'm proud to say, with a slender-wristed if muzzle-heavy flintlock the likes of which fed many a family in these mountains a century and more ago.

Against the stately background of one of Segovia's early recordings, I tie trout flies tainted with gun oil with fingers stained brown by stock finish. The music seems simultaneously urbane and rural. For a novice guitarist, it's an instructive pleasure to listen to the tonality and phrasing of a master, to hear time casually parsed into rhythmic melody by genius. Art is closest to nature in those qualities that can't quite be taught. While Segovia picks through the compositions of Aguado, Sor and Giuliani—as revealingly spare in their way as a Dickinson poem—I pluck soft breast feathers from a salted grouse skin that interests Patch mightily and must remind him of the season just past. He dreams wildly, twitching and yipping, on these nights when the cherry rolltop desk is covered with the fur and feathers of good hunting. I guess he gets up on those ridges, hunts into the wind and finds birds I'll never see, holding them forever in his mind.

As I lean over the fly-tying vise, he darts around from one side of me to the other, shoving my elbow with his wet nose, trying to assert his priority in grouse matters. I wind hair-thin wire on small wet-fly hooks, cover the wire with thread dubbed with dark red fox fur from an animal I found dead on the back of the farm and skinned before it got ripe. The beeswax I use to coat my bowstring serves for the dubbing wax that holds that fine fur to the thread. Bind the mottled grouse feathers to the head of the hook and you have a simple but effective trout fly, old as fishing itself.

Out the back door near midnight, a wild, well-ordered universe is on display, casting starlight on this late-season snow. Orion has moved on, taking the winter triangle with it, and the Great Bear shifts around the pole star. Next day the sun edges back a little farther north along the eastern horizon, blinding me at my desk and arcing higher in the sky, overseeing in the course of the day a minute or two more of what happens here. The mind of winter fades as the snow melts, gathering in runnels down the drive toward South River, which chatters cold and bright. The long, pale rays of the late winter sun grab hold of walnut hill, and the farm rolls over past this ragged, nameless season between winter and spring.

Rotting snow slumped in the shady lee of shelf rock, or settled in chilly sinkholes, competes with pale green lamb's ears unfolding in sunlit places. The wintering coots leave South River. Honeysuckle and woodbine spin sunlight into the tough green vines that thread themselves along fence lines. Winter wrens disappear following the kinglets that took off weeks ago. Cedars set flowers. Flocks of towhees are replaced by flocks of migrating robins. Woodchucks clear burrows. Spicebush blooms. Hawks shadow rabbit warrens. Foxes stir. The pileated woodpeckers that nest in the woods behind Patch's run return from their winter quarters elsewhere in the county, their flashing wings along the dirt drive the surest sign that not even a late-season snowstorm can stop spring. Their freshly chiseled nest holes shine in the woods like new growth.

*M*y journal notes a full moon near the end of February this year. Patch and I had been hacking around the north woodlots, bird-watching, I suppose, and looking for antler drops or wood to cut. The moon was rising large over the Blue Ridge as we walked past the brambles and then cut through the double-helix to the back gate. As we came down the farm road, six does flushed from the head of the poplar hollow, quartering away from us toward the river woods. I stayed Patch and we watched them run gracefully across the snow-dusted pasture.

The farm has a monochrome cast at dusk in winter, and I noted that the ragged winter coats of the deer somehow looked colorful in the low-slanting moonlight, bluish gray against the snow. By the time we got down to the barn gate, the moon had freed itself from the mountains and assumed its normal size. The deer were long gone, but I remember the way they looked—blue moonlit deer running through a black and white world. I remember the sound of their hooves clattering on the hard ground.

Minutes later, coming down the last stretch of road to the cabin, I couldn't help but notice that the evening sky was full of birds, birds flying hard in the moonlight a month ahead of spring. I did not know what they were. Pale-breasted, dark-winged passerines. I think their wings were sharply bent. They looked to me like the platonic forms of birds, perfect somehow beyond the perfection of the birds I knew. Something otherwordly, like blue deer running on frozen ground. They flew with short, rapid wing beats interspersed with those folded glides ornithologists call bounding. It looked as if they didn't trust the cold air to keep them up, that they sensed they were pressing on well in advance of safe weather. But, encouraged

*by the moon, perhaps, they were on the way north in winter because
it was time for that.*

*There is something profoundly stoic in the lives of animals—the
way they are perfectly weathered to their hours. Still, these birds
caught me by surprise at a moment when, with home in view, I
had stopped looking for anything more in the day.*

*I stood there just beyond the barn gate, Patch nosing woodchuck
scent around the hay bales, and watched those long, loose strings of
hurrying birds with sudden, unexpected admiration, mesmerized
by their confident sense of purpose, their wings ruffling like wind-
snapped silk as they arrowed through the cold.*

Caught by the Way

*From ancient times wise people and sages have often lived
near water. When they live near water they catch fish,
catch human beings, and catch the way. . . . Furthermore
there is catching the self, catching catching, being caught
by catching, and being caught by the way.*

—EIHEI DŌGEN,
"Mountains and Waters Sutra"

Trout, like grouse, lead you on.

I think of trout as an affair of landscape—not something
in it, but something *of* it. In early spring I walk the headwater
streams of the Blue Ridge as if it were my job, cruising watersheds just to enjoy the liberating feel of the open slopes before
they leaf in and to feel the rough lay of the land underfoot. Every
dent in the mountainous horizon that I can see from Highland
Farm has a rocky seam at the base of it—a mossy, hemlock-
shaded flow of cold water over bedrock. In Chinese, the term for
landscape, *shan shui,* means literally "mountains and waters."
Roughly speaking, if you rub a forested mountain with cold,
flowing water, you get a trout. This is to take a compressed view
of geology and evolution, but mythic and scientific ways of
thinking about things converge in extraordinary expressions of
being, like trout. Walking encourages thought like that.

From the bald summit of Highland Farm I can see the
prominence of Thunder Ridge thirty miles to the southeast
and just beyond that another high ridge called Apple Orchard
Mountain. Blue Ridge place names frequently juxtapose the
wild and domestic—*thunder* and *apples*, for example—reflecting how settlement tamed the wild life of that rugged mountain
spine. Although early colonial settlers seemed intimidated by
the mountains as a forested unknown, the height of which they
greatly exaggerated, by the early nineteenth century the domes-
ticity of orchards, hog camps and cow pastures had largely displaced the wildness of buffalo, panthers and wolves. Even so,
the old gods occasionally rouse themselves, and the lightning
that strikes Thunder Ridge still stings.

Just below the gentle crest of Apple Orchard Mountain a
spring pumps water from the Blue Ridge underworld into the
light of day—a trickle in dry years, a rousing flow in wet. This
water wells up through weathered basement rock, a long brow
of Precambrian stonework thrust northwestward by a continental collision that preceded not only the apples, hogs and cattle
but the buffalo, panthers and wolves. In fact, dinosaurs were
just getting started when these dark rocks settled in place and
began to weather down to the haunting mountains with which
I am familiar. That springwater pumping out of the mossy rocks
is wild—wild with numbing cold, wild with the darkness inside
of the mountains, wild with the purity of that unseen aquifer.
Turned loose in colorful beds of gravel, purling over mossy
hemlock roots, that water is, finally, wild with the theory and
practice of gravity, the inner workings of which physics still
cannot explain. While Patch and I await the publication of a
unified field theory, that wild water moves, glistening, from
the unseen heart of Apple Orchard Mountain. Close your

eyes, and you can hear it click along until that chilly rattle of water and gravel quickens into a continuous purl of sound that won't stop until this spring-fed trout creek reaches the James River. Watersheds shed water. From that fact everything else derives—on this planet, at least. Rivers are a wild consequence of the way things are.

Trout are part of that wildness. They are important because they ought to be there, a vestige of the natural *given* of the mountains here in the early Holocene, kin to oak and granite, mountain maple and mountain ash, ovenbirds and great horned owls, black racers and Blackburnian warblers, Indian pipe and squawroot, black bear and bobcat and much else. Kin to wolves and buffalo and elk, long gone, and to rumors of mountain lions, all four species sacrificed here to what is called *progress,* curious word that neatly elides the cost of a great illusion. Trout are, like other forms of native, wild life here, shards of deep time. Their presence in Blue Ridge headwaters bespeaks an epic persistence, an oaken, rocky hardiness, beautiful and supple, conjured out of rock and root by that flowing water. Each humble brook trout I bring to hand in spring gleams as a unique expression of the life of this place. When I release it, each fish holds under my gaze, poised between the stasis of the mountains and the rush of waters as if I were plucking one of Thunder's strings with its lithe body. Those flowing waters do *boom* down the mountains in spring. After some stunned moment of readjustment, each trout disappears into the shadows, losing itself among the rattling cobbles. But even unseen, especially unseen, the trout are still perfectly poised between mountains and waters, not simply *in* the landscape but a being *of* it.

Of course, I am referring to wild, native trout, not the unconvincing imitations produced in hatcheries and unceremoniously dumped into rivers for the marginal sport they provide. Wild trout in their native landscape are part of a strong, distinctive expression of the spirit of a place, whether you think of Apache trout in the White Mountains of Arizona, golden trout in the Sierras, or brook trout—*Salvelinus fontinalis*—here in the Blue Ridge. Love of wild trout and love of forested mountains amounts to the same thing. If you don't find native trout where mountains and waters clash, then the surrounding landscape falls apart downstream of its empty headwaters in the same way that the Great Plains fell apart without the bison and eastern North American skies once paled in the absence of peregrine falcons.

When I moved to Highland Farm ten years ago, one of the first things I did was explore the rivers near my new home to see which held populations of wild brook trout. The essence of that quest is always the same: trace running water upstream. As their Latin name suggests, you will find wild trout, if you find them at all, at the source of things, a heavy connotation they bear with grace. Follow the oily blacktop of a state road along the warm-water reaches of bream and bass and pass the tepid pools where hatchery trout mill about, confused by their freedom. Turn off the blacktop onto a gravel road that pops under your tires as it leads you through second-growth forest laced with the foaming water where naturalized rainbows thrive. These beautiful, rose-tinted fish, quick to rush a fly in spring, are fine to catch, but they are not native here. They are not deeply rooted in these mountains like hemlock and bedrock and brook trout.

Leave your vehicle and hike through even-aged second growth until the diversity of a recovering forest starts to close around you. Fish there. Forests are where you find good fishing, as if trees and trout had common needs. Keep fishing upstream until a brook trout grabs your dancing dry fly as it rides high on stiff hackle tips on the syrupy water that curls through a hemlock-darkened pool carved by time and the river out of two-billion-year-old bedrock. Play the fish lightly as it dances a Celtic war dance at the end of your line, tying you to the water and to the mountains in a way nothing else could, catching you. This warrior is likely to be seven or eight inches long, but it is a perfect expression of the singular form of life that tells you that the stream you are standing in is still *alive* and that the forest around it is, indeed, recovering second growth becoming, log by rotting log, older and older growth.

I learned to fish for trout on the freestone streams that drain the slopes of Virginia's Blue Ridge Mountains. The nature of those streams made me the kind of fisherman I am—an excellent bear of a small-stream angler, if I do say so, but next to useless with a fly rod anywhere else. The close quarters of mountain fishing feels right to me, and I believe I could fish well in mountains anywhere.

On that journey to Russia when I fell in love with grouse hunting, the only place I caught fish was in the headwaters, where the Kos'yu wasn't much wider than the mountain streams I love here in the Blue Ridge. That's the river I want to go back to fish. Strange as the surroundings were, I had no trouble reading the rushing water and seeing where the fish should be—not brook trout, but grayling, a sleek, fork-tailed fish as beautiful as its name, *Thymallus thymallus,* distinguished by its saillike, iridescent dorsal fin that glows a rainbow of purple and greenish grays when you first palm it out of the cold water and hold it in the light.

Those troutlike grayling helped me save face, and reminded me of what I knew. I released all of mine before those brilliantly colored dorsal fins faded and, supreme hypocrite, feasted on the common catch at night, nibbling around those airy fish bones like a caveman before the fire with the others. But as soon as we floated downriver out of the shadow of those brooding mountains and got onto the salmon water, I wasn't really fishing anymore. I cast big colorful flies with the expensive gear I had borrowed for the trip and caught what my skepticism deserved. In the mountains, any mountains, I'm a believer. In fact, I'm a mountain fisherman, which implies—now that I look closely at the phrase—that I fish for mountains, hooking trout occasionally as I go.

I love the look and feel of headwater streams and enjoy the physical demands of fishing these steep, rocky, logjammed rivers. I like rivers you can lean on. Their rushing slows me down and forces me to pay close attention to everything in my path. I can read such rivers trout by trout, punch short casts all day through the roar of water in the air, dance dry flies and swim wets through olive pools and white riffles. I feel like I belong on my home waters in the Blue Ridge backcountry where I can fish quietly and unobtrusively, succeeding and failing in full-voiced silence. When I am fishing well, I am at home in the mountains, part of the landscape, not *in* it but *of* it.

Rivers, of course, are mesmerizing, the source of many things to many people. The sculpting of watersheds by rushing water is fundamental to the way the planet earth looks. Given the lay of the land, we count on rivers being there. We expect, deep in our DNA, to find rivers at the foot of ridges. They are one of the signatures of our world. The next thought is *fish: Are there any fish in there?* And since in the mountains the water is chill with altitude, the fish you are wondering about are trout, those cold-loving salmonids with the gravity of bedrock and the beauty of birds. Hiking in the mountains, any mountains, I'm glad to know they are there. And when I get the itch to fish, I love the bearish feel of following a river's way up a mountain, hooking fat trout, feeling the life in them, earning my way over those logjams and through the gauntlets of head-high boulders toward what I am unashamed to call the truth in the land-scape—not sentimental platitudes but the great natural facts of the way things are. Not that I ever get to the truth, but a wild brook trout in hand, gleaming with the earthiness of its watery perfection, is as sure a sign as I need of the nature of nature.

These rocky backcountry streams also led me to a writer's life after I had given up on that. It's fair to say Blue Ridge rivers taught me to write, although it took me years to realize that I was their student. Blue Ridge trout streams were—almost by accident—the setting and subject of my first book, the compo-sition of which taught me that what had been for years in the back of my mind should be in the front of it. That is not an easy change in focus to effect, but the woods and rivers led me on, became a rough-and-ready way. In that volume, I put the dark headwaters into which I had retreated into the foreground and discovered a good deal of unexpected light, not to mention a sense of purpose that had escaped me downriver where I was supposed to be. Strange to say, I suppose, but I have come to understand that when I fish in the mountains, I am casting for a connection between words and things—that revealing, reas-suring tug between trout and *trout*. My love for language and for the woods, for the way words move like rushing water or coalesce in pools, is no doubt, like all passions, forged out of some half-conscious ratio of need and desire. But even in the most practical ways, following these modest Blue Ridge head-waters to their source led to interesting ground.

Blue Ridge trout streams shaped my understanding of the intimate relationship between words and things. If the rhythm of a writer's prose imitates an underlying flow of consciousness—undercurrents broken into the light of day—then the cascading sentences I find in my mind in the morning derive, literally, from the mountains and waters I know well. Writing in the morning is like fishing in the dark. I cast long loops of prose toward what I hope is the rising truth in things—not toward an idea but, as the poet William Carlos Williams suggests, toward the thing itself. What I consider the sacred being of *any* other will do as a rising truth—mayfly, trout, water snake, trillium, kingfisher, hemlock. What doesn't count? What isn't important? The art of writing about nature remains what it has always been—an act of imitation and of subordination and homage to a given we cannot fully explain or ever improve. Everything in nature is "found poetry." Wild trout are part of that.

So after I moved to Highland Farm, I checked each crease in the horizon for those brilliant, wild signs of life that caught me by the way twenty years ago. I found what I wanted—and needed—radiating from that trickling spring on Apple Orchard Mountain: a satisfying rumple of enfolded ridges shedding waters that spawned wild trout and a good deal else. Gray squirrels and fox squirrels, grouse and turkey, deer and black bear, all wound their way through an oak-hickory forest that rang with diverse birdlife in April and May, simmered mysteriously in summer, bled a revealing palette of color in October, and then bared its soul in late November. From cushion moss to canopy, that watershed quietly recovered from decades of abusive logging and intrusive road-building from which it is still not safe. If I didn't find buffalo, elk and wolves and what mountain folk call "painters," I at least encountered vivid memories of panthers in stories I got from the human natives of the place, who gathered ramps and morels and ginseng with the same quiet passion that I cast my flies for trout.

At first, my fellow backcountry wanderers looked on my fly fishing with frank, if friendly, pity. But the frequent appearance of my battered F-150, which sported local tags and local mud, earned me some leeway and, finally, some credibility. Whatever I was, I was no vacationing dude or sleeked-up fly fishing faddist. I carried my trout flies in a Sucrets tin and fished with a honey-yellow fiberglass fly rod I found in a local flea market I watch like a hawk for interesting old tools and tackle and good pieces of cast-off cast-iron cookware. I carried my tackle in one of those canvas musette bags that should never have gone out of fashion. Eventually, two backcountry walkers with whom I crossed paths suggested with a conspiratorial air that if I was fishing for "natives," I should lash a "lizard" to my hook. I didn't doubt that a wriggling salamander would do the trick, especially in those dark plunge pools that might harbor a fourteen-inch squaretail, but I was the one trying to get caught, and the flies I tied in winter and cast in spring were an important part of the offering.

These mountain acquaintances—whose earthy, long-felt relation to the place I could admire but not imitate—came to understand that I was following some way of my own. They eventually accepted the unnecessary complications of my fly fishing as part of some necessary practice, my way of being there, my way of becoming native to the place. Of course, a fourteen-inch brook trout was exactly what I wanted and in my dreams I fished with lizards.

That mountain stream, wild as thunder for half the year and

tame as apple pie the rest, became my new home water. Its watershed has been the foreground as well as the background for many hours. I walk, bird-watch and sketch there, take friends to see the stream and woods, and once or twice a year backpack into it for a night or two just to take in the heartening life of the place in every season—to listen to great horned owls hoot their eerie blues against the jazzy riffing of the stream, to see black bear moving about in the morning and bobcats cruising at dusk.

I fish and hunt with tools that fit the mood of what I am doing—that syrupy glass fly rod for trout, a slender flintlock long rifle for squirrel, that well-balanced twenty-gauge muzzle-loader for grouse, and the stocky 1858 Enfield carbine for backcountry deer. Thoreau speculates that a man outgrows hunting as his interest in nature rarefies, but I seem to have evolved in reverse. I didn't take up hunting until I was in my thirties, and did so, I suppose, as a way of getting further into the woods I had grown to love first as a backcountry walker and then as a fisherman. My hunting derived from my fishing, just as it had up on the Kos'yu, and to pay one practice back with the fruits of the other, in spring I filled that Sucrets tin with the fur and feathers of fall. Grouse lived on in soft hackles and old-fashioned wet flies, deer in high-riding caddis and humpies, rabbits and squirrels in buggy nymphs whose wing cases were fashioned with bits of turkey feather.

In my mind, this continuity mattered. The fisherman and hunter in myself were mirror images of one another, just as a rising trout in April is a mirror image, refracted through the milk-glass prism of time passing, of a flushing grouse in October. But it all came back to the trout, which centered my backward-seeming ambitions, tugging my heart and mind deep into the mountains. Without wild trout, I would have moved on elsewhere, not just for the fishing but for the hunting and walking and everything else as well.

Like the strange rivers that drop from the mountains in Northern Sung paintings, Rainey Creek comes in and out of view from the trail that shadows it. This quality, along with the occasional timber rattler snoozing in the leaf litter, discourages the interest of casual anglers. It is not unusual for headwater streams to secret themselves underground for stretches, testing the persistence of the merely curious. But loyalty to a mountain watercourse is always rewarded. Every stream and creek leads somewhere.

A mile upstream of the last dirt turnaround where you can leave a vehicle, the river forks deceptively. What looks like the weaker, less productive branch at the confluence—a shallow dribble of water over broken slabs of mostly dry shelf rock—was, a mile up the mountain, a far better brook trout stream than the main branch. On one of my first excursions into this watershed an otherwise unproductive day of grouse hunting revealed a prime mile of brook trout water tucked into the mountain above a steep cascade that fended the rainbows off. The only bird I flushed that day broke cover as I leaned over the tail of a leaf-strewn pool of umber autumn water with my twenty-gauge at port arms. Six hours out, I was footsore and tired and for a split second thought, in fatigued surprise, that I had flushed a trout into the woods. I took close note of the spot and followed up the grouse, which I never saw again. On the way back down the mountain, my empty game bag felt like an empty creel.

That spot where my fishing and hunting selves crossed paths became a center, and eventually I took both trout and grouse within a hundred yards of where, shotgun in hand, I first saw brook trout finning over the gravel of a freshly dug redd. In my mind's eye I keep a painting of a long, olive pool that extends from a white gauntlet of mossy bedrock glowing in the yellow light of the hickory trees that lean over it. In the painting you cannot see the trout or hear the drumming of a grouse from a nearby ridge. But you know from the look of the water and the woods that the trout and the grouse are there. I fish and hunt in and around that imaginary painting.

Every September I cruise the hickory stands along the stream for gray squirrels, wild and wary as trout. I keep an eye out for a fox squirrel with the tawny shades of fur I prefer for streamer flies. In late October, Patch and I pursue ruffed grouse through mountain laurel and hemlocks within earshot of that insistent stream. In early November I slip up a little tributary with that slender longbow and a quiver full of those straight-grained cedar arrows. At dawn and dusk I stand in the shadow of a large hemlock near where a deer trail winds through spicebush at a pinch point between two ridges. In December I hunt higher in the watershed with the Enfield for the backcountry bucks that ghost along the ridges.

Although I'm more a hunter than a fisherman now, Rainey Creek remains the meandering baseline for my explorations of its watershed, the singular feature in the landscape from which I literally and figuratively take my bearings. Its branching tributaries, most dry for half the year, lead me to those squirrel haunts and that grouse cover. I can follow them safely in the predawn dark to the ground stands where I wait for deer. The stream keeps me from getting lost. And in spring, when I need to be a fisherman again, the trout are there, the wise *roshi* that caught me by the way and taught me to love wildness.

·   ·   ·

Rainey Creek tumbles through the year against the background of the shifting seasons, a perfect embodiment of the way change and stasis are tuned tightly to one another in nature. In winter, water gray as the winter coats of deer sluices through boulders rimed with ice. The snowbound woods absorb the sound of the creek so that you can hear the true silence of the watershed between the murmur of the stream and the high sound of the wind overhead. The canopy trees creak and lean, making the wind visible. All day you listen to a rough pruning as branches crack and clatter to the ground.

Rather than fish for torpid winter trout as I used to do—casting flies into the frigid water—I cruise the watershed for its own sake, hunting its rugged, quiet contours for whatever might meet eye or ear. As you hike up along Rainey Creek, the other-worldly call of a pileated woodpecker may break that silence from within, reminding you of all the hidden life there. That rattling cry is both an assertion of territoriality and a warning—the otherness of the winter woods in flight. Bear, deer, squirrel, grouse, turkey are all as remote as the trout you cannot see in the gray, ice-rimed water. In winter, the cold dash of Rainey Creek itself stands for the life of things.

I've learned to relish the cold hiatus between the season to hunt and the season to fish, a nameless time of year that seems to invite the practice of other arts. Walking in winter, you can see the underlying idea of the place—mountains and waters. Some days I sling a tripod over my shoulder like a rifle and try to find vantages from which I might capture on film the way the woods look in my mind's eye. But my landscapes don't capture what I remember, the way the winter woods are simultaneously inviting and intimidating. I have taught myself to draw the stark forms of bare trees and bedrock outcrops, although I do not have art enough to bring the inner life of such things out on paper. I'll sketch the ivory-cold sweep of a shed antler lying on oak leaves or the remains of a meal of walnuts on a mossy old stump. But I can't convey the frank pathos of the small tooth marks on the antlers or the intense hunger implied by the scatter of walnut shells.

Hunt the woods themselves—the stolid trees, the silent ridgelines, the hidden wildlife, the cold and empty air—and you will hunt in a circle and head home with an empty game bag. In winter, nature reminds us that it doesn't exist for our benefit. Best to pass through winter warily, feeling your soul winnowed to bare necessity. On the coldest days, the ridges seem to enlarge and the hollows deepen and you can feel nature demanding to be respected for its own sake. The cold neutrality of a winter watershed gives the lie to the Romantic assumption that man and nature are one. Up on Rainey Creek you get the keenest glimpses, the most undeniable intimations, not of Wordsworthian kinship with nature but of its daunting, unanswering indifference.

The world around Rainey Creek is born again in March as sunlit snow melts and the battered woods slowly come to life. Bloodroot pushes up through the leaf litter, opening finely etched petals to sunlight. Hepatica and early violets appear, reminding you that the forest floor is itself a forest. The first canopy to form closes at your feet. Shrubs bloom above the wildflowers, as do the early-flowering trees—serviceberry, poplar, maples. The oaks and other hardwoods wait with open crowns that let the sunlight through to the midstory growth. Birdlife appears out of nowhere—flocks of nervous redstarts in the red maples tell you that there will be good fishing in a week or two.

The hard-charging river of early spring is barely fishable, but the image of inviting green water clashing through a rocky bed revives the itch to stand in a river and cast for trout. Nothing feels finer than to get waist-deep in that strong flow, lost in the roar of rushing water, keen to hook a trout. Early-season fishing is more like hunting, a fish or two enough to confirm that the universe is intact and that its more important laws are in force—for example, that wild trout take soft-hackled wet flies in April. If these emergers don't work, I'll grease fly line and leader and drift weighted nymphs through the hearts of pools, dislodging trout from bedrock one by one. On sunny days, I'll lighten and lengthen my tippet and cast dark dry flies upstream of rising fish, striking at the subtle rumple where the fly disappears. Once the water warms above forty degrees or so, the trout are mine to catch and release at will. I wade upstream through the strong water, feeding last season's birds and squirrels to the trout, fly by fly, feeling the seasons, and the years, pulled taut with each take.

In April, the rushing stream seems to encourage an angler to hurry, but it's best to wade like a bear and fish slowly, getting behind the pace of the fast water in order to do justice to the deliberation I practiced at the fly-tying vise when I wound the stiffest hackle I could afford on the delicate dry flies I now need to float like corks. Once the river starts doling out stoneflies, mayflies and caddis, I can give myself over to the physical pleasure of fishing a mountain stream.

In the end it is stealth that catches trout. And stealth, when fishing or hunting, is style, a graceful way of being in a river or in the woods, a way of being there without being there, a minor form of artistry, like walking. For taking trout, Charles Cotton's three-century-old advice remains the best: "Fish . . . like an

Artist, and peradventure a good Fish may fall to your share."

In spring, the trout are where they should be—sleek rainbow trout in the white water, stout brook trout just below where the current bulges against the still, deep water. You can tell what you've hooked by feel. Even in a small stream, rainbows fight like western fish, making runs to the heads and tails of pools, as if they remembered longer rivers. Brook trout thrash stubbornly in place, as if they were defending their own turf. Mountain trout are hungry, not gullible, and each spring gives the lie to the myth that these trout are not selective. Still, they don't pick and choose with the serene patience of the spring-creek trout I fish for in the valley on summer evenings. My mountain fly box mimics things well enough, and each year I'm pleased to see how well I've matched the life of this rocky, free-spirited water.

The rest of spring is easy and the fishing effortless in a way hunting never is. I work my way upriver as the rushing water settles down, reacquainting myself with each stretch of woods, spending whole days leaning into the stream lost not in thought, but in the repetition of an ancient craft: wade, wait, watch, cast, retrieve. Study the current and puzzle out the lies. Mend line to keep the fly floating naturally. Stop before you fish each pool or riffle, breathing deep to fill your lungs with mountain air. Feel the complicated woods off either shoulder. Observe anything that moves as a sign of the year revealing itself to you. Then turn back to the fishing.

Study the undersides of rocks like a raccoon to see which insects are about to hatch. Watch the surface of the water and the air for winged insects. As you follow the day upstream, enjoy the minor discipline of tying a well-formed blood knot as you fashion longer, finer leaders. Cast crisply, reaching out to the river with each forecast, bowing to it as you strip line as quickly as the river brings the fly back toward you. Watch the fly disappear in that subtle rumple or float to you untouched. Tuck your rod under your arm as you rustle the fly box out of a vest pocket. Choose a fly that suits the moment, the here and now of the river embodied in a yellow stonefly, a dark Hendrickson or light Cahill. Study the water in front of you constantly. Read it like music. Cast and retrieve, bowing. Cover the water, every curl of current, every seam where the difference of a trout might wait, that unique liveliness poised perfectly between mountains and waters. Then wade on, leaning into the river, using its unsettling strength for support, making your way with the strange, stately, otherworldly progress of a mountain trout fisherman.

By mid-May, winter-thinned brook trout have grown fat and strong again. Traces of their autumn spawning colors remain. The pink in the rainbows, spring spawners, darkens toward red like the red of sourwood leaves. The details of the seasons overlap in these unfathomable ways—hints of autumn colors embedded in spring. The seasons overlap in everything—in the waxing and waning colors of trout, in the way the frost-cracked boulders simmer in the heat, in the way the forest canopy flowers like the forest floor. Meanwhile, the river retunes itself to its rocky bed, rising again with every rain but falling over time with the course of the year, a gradient of change that cannot be denied. As the art of the river changes, the trout, wild at heart in every season, shift into the new lies the changing current creates, where they are shadowed by a heronlike fisherman—the tiny figure in the Sung landscape—who casts and, while retrieving, seems to bow toward the river and the fish.

In autumn, when I have a rifle or shotgun tilted over my shoulder, I'm often shunned by hikers and backpackers. I get hard looks and sometimes muttered rebukes flung at my back,

insults I've never drawn while leaning over the meat case in
the supermarket. But for some reason, fishermen are figures of
innocence. Backcountry travelers will always stop, spook the
trout in the pool I am fishing and ask about the fishing. I tell
them pointedly that I am *trout fishing.* They seem to like hearing
that—*trout fishing*—and I can see myself rise a notch in their
estimation from the fool they thought I was. If they linger, I
try to work in, proud as a father, that the stream is full of wild,
native trout—my way of saying that the world is in good shape
here, that they have picked a fine place to hike even if they
aren't fishing. But most sense a specialist's jag coming on and
shuffle off down the trail before a full-blown lecture or, worse,
a sermon starts up. Just as well. They have their own passions—
Blackburnian warblers, lady slippers, mountain laurel, or just a
healthy, instinctive love of the woods and the day itself.

Innocent as I may seem with a fly rod in hand, when I camp
in the backcountry I allow myself a meal of wild trout. I do
this to remind myself that fishing, like hunting, is not a game
and, in my practice of it, not a sport. Catch-and-release fishing
is necessary if wild trout populations are to survive what little
habitat has been left for them. But when you are in the woods,
the practice smacks of bad faith. In hunting, of course, there is
no release. You cannot call shot or bullet or arrow back. When
you find a deer at the end of a blood trail, or pick a grouse up
from the forest floor, you cannot claim to have not done what
you just did. When you hunt, you are committed to doing
something you will not have the opportunity to undo, or to
pretend you can undo. That finality, and perhaps a middle-
aged sense of my own mortality, may well be what led me to
embrace, for better or worse, the harder ways of hunting. In
fact, when people ask me why I hunt, I tell them honestly

that I like to hunt because hunting is so *serious*. The accusing question I sometimes encounter—*How can you kill animals for fun?*—makes no sense to me.

Given the central, perhaps tragic fact embedded in nature that no amount of vegetarianism or political correctness will erase—that life cycles itself through death—I see, and feel, something profoundly honest in pursuing fish and game. But *fun* doesn't cover what I'm up to or after. The bounty in these watersheds, like the bounty on Highland Farm, is real—the wildest fruits of the world's body, if you will. I need to take those fruits and taste them now and then in the form of grouse and trout and deer and turkey. So in the backcountry once or twice a year, if the stream I'm fishing is full of fish, I'll kill two trout for breakfast on the last morning of my encampment and relish the meal as an earthy sacrament.

Perhaps these dark mountains make those of us who love them a bit too somber, or perhaps pensive people like myself are drawn to these things, but I think it's good to remind yourself that you cannot really undo what you've done in life, let the consequences of your actions simply swim away, as if nothing had happened. Slipping a trout back into a river may be a wise practice, but it is not necessarily a virtuous one.

Up on Blue Ridge headwaters, life is as poignant and dear as life is anywhere. Slitting the silken belly of a trout, for an important meal of wild food, is as strange and serious an act as rolling the heavy viscera of a white-tailed deer onto the ground, or pulling the delicate entrails from the body cavity of a grouse still warm with life and flight. With the blood of fish and game on your hands, a very clear idea of the cost of living forms in the back of the mind—and stays there.

Still, it feels good to let most trout go, just as it feels right at times to let a grouse hang in the air until it's too late to pull a trigger, or to let a deer walk unharmed through the lime-green light of the spicebush it is browsing early in deer season when hunting seems too easy and the deep freezer is still half full.

Sometime in late April or early May I'll hike Rainey Creek mouth to source, a ten- or twelve-mile trek I've taken dozens of times in every season. Most watersheds in the Blue Ridge are scaled to thoughtful foot travel. One daylong traverse will give you a good sense of the whole. A day fishing or hunting provides a narrow, albeit intense glimpse of a watershed. Release those narrower ambitions, and walking frees you to be an accidental part of things.

I follow the river for two, three miles through a hemlock-cooled hollow. If I get out at dawn, I'll flush turkeys along the lower end of the river and, if I'm lucky, I'll spook a black bear between the second and third fords. The trail up the river peters out at a backcountry campsite I sometimes use for observing the spring warbler migration, a flurry of visitation that is also a great assertion of wildness. In winter, you can bushwhack straight up the river, but in spring the growing tangle of vegetation, deadfalls from wind storms and the possibility of stumbling into a timber rattler are enough to keep me on the new trail that steeply climbs up the north side of the watershed.

The rock-studded trail switchbacks to a saddle from which you can hike north into the adjacent watershed or turn up-mountain and stay in the Rainey Creek drainage. That up-mountain trail takes you through a rocky crease of mountain laurel and rhododendron in the shadow of which you'll find delicate lady slippers blooming in June. That narrow corridor is spooky with the possibility of bear, which I prefer to see from a distance in open timber, but the real wildness there is wound up in the heartiness of the laurel and rhododendron—sturdy *Ericaceae*—that are able to root in rock and thrive—or persist— where nothing else will. If there is a symbol of the southern Appalachians, it is mountain laurel—not its beautiful bloom, those delicately scalloped pink bowls that gather sunlight with inexpressible finesse, but its ragged, desiccated bark and the gnarly shape of its slow growth, those twisted, intertwined limbs that rattle in the stiff summit winds.

A short, steep pull will bring me to the Appalachian Trail, a welcome presence that gives me solidarity with many another walker who loves the thin country of eastern wildness. A few miles south along the AT, I come to the little wetland from which Rainey Creek takes its flow. I can shove my arm down into the cold bowl of water from which everything in this water-shed derives and feel the stream's pearly gravel in my fist. The numb ache in my arm from contact with the cold flow of being in these old mountains—that's something to seek in spring.

Coming back, a short detour takes me to an outcrop of lichen-encrusted granite that breaks through the woods like the prow of a ship. From that raven's view of rock I can survey the entire watershed I have just walked, see the way I have come and the shape of the wild terrain. I cannot see Rainey Creek, which is hidden at the base of a rocky seam, but I can see the land that makes it possible—a long, greening dent of valley and ridge, finely wrought and finite, through which, by the nature of things, a river must flow. The lay of the land—from that everything else springs and flows. Wildness from wild places. Mountains and waters.

Strange, the way the deer moved in the river, not swimming but pulsing airily as if it were gathering itself, forming underwater before it crashed to the surface and clattered in place on the cobbles of a riffle which was somehow deep and shallow at the same time, the deer then collapsing to sink and float that odd way underwater, softly expanding and contracting with the currents that played with the form of a deer in the river swimming underwater, and then the river was full of deer moving like otters where I was trying to fish, crowding the river like salmon brushing against my legs and then knocking at me, making me think, in the comically slow way you come to conclusions in dreams, that there was something wrong with the river there. . . .

The first time I tanned a deerskin, I had deer dreams for a week, vivid deep-night productions that always involved a river I was trying to fish filling up with the floating forms of deer. I felt no conscious guilt about taking that deer, but the Spanish philosopher José Ortega y Gasset has written that "every good hunter is uneasy in the depths of his conscience." The moral shock of killing an animal should always leave something in its wake. I killed the deer cleanly, with a single shot, and butchered it well, caching all its fine meat in the deep freezer. I scraped and salted the hide and stored it, safe from insects, keeping odd bits for the deer-hair flies I use for trout fishing. Although I frequently dream about animals, I dreamt no deer that winter.

I took the hide out in spring, before the weather went to work on it. I soaked it in water and hardwood ashes from the woodstove and then spent a long day removing the hair and graining it on a maple log, being careful not to split the supple material that formed

*under my slow work. I thought I might make a simple hunting
shirt out of it.*

*When the hide had to be rinsed, I took it down to the riffle in
South River just above where it joins the Maury. I have no running
water outside the cabin and did this merely for convenience. The
deer hide swirled strangely when I rinsed it and as I felt the cool
river water grabbing at my legs and arms and watched the hide
turning beautifully in that way, a chill from I don't know where
went up and down my spine. Suddenly I thought I might be doing
something wrong, and I looked guiltily around to see if anyone was
watching. The river chattered and the chill of self-consciousness
passed. But seeing the deerskin turn about, laved by the currents, I
sensed I had stumbled onto something intimate and sacred in the
way of such things. After that, I started having the dreams.*

*Now, when I tan hides in spring, I take them down to the river
on cedar poles I have carved to the heartwood with the same knife I
use to field-dress and skin the deer I kill, a modest gesture I thought
might be appropriate to what I now assume is a great occasion. I
don't pretend to know or understand more than that. The tanning
doesn't disturb my sleep anymore, but I wouldn't be altogether sorry
to again have the dream about a river full of deer rising and falling
into being with its currents, pushing me out of the way.*

Early Wood

What is there here but weather, what spirit
Have I except it comes from the sun?

> —WALLACE STEVENS,
> "Waving Adieu, Adieu, Adieu"

April, like October, is an affair of light.

The lambent aura that emanates from leafing woodlots is reinforced by the fresh verdure of pasture grasses and the lingering winter gloss of evergreens. Each day is bathed in a blue-green clarity too perfect to last for long. Working early at my desk, I can feel that silken daylight waiting in the cool dark. I work hard before it comes. Then day dawns, accompanied by a studied colloquy of birdcalls, each of which lays claim to a distinct persistence of being. I would call these wrens, chickadees, titmice, sparrows and nuthatches common birds, except that nothing in nature is common now. Of course, nothing ever was. Their sweet calls cloy only if the mind cloys around them. They have their business in the world, and their rights to it, and each morning they stake a serious claim. By the time the earth here has rolled over into first light, raising the sun through the empty arms of a century-old white oak, my concentration is fully broken. Working fitfully, I steal glimpses of a familiar world resolving itself, deeply renewed, in the subtle shades of color that silently establish April's claim to close inspection.

Long before the farm leafs in, the subtle flowering of trees adds depth of field to midstory and canopy. Haw and redbud tint the woods. I never cared much for redbuds, which people gush over every spring, but I probably shouldn't take the tree or the gushing personally. A fine, wild thing in their own right, I suppose, they look cultivated and ornamental—a bit too pretty for my taste. Smooth black haw is more to my liking, given to understatement, which is what the understory is for, and, much like the Spanish oaks and the ubiquitous black walnuts, an important part of the character of this place. Haw stakes a modest claim in every woodlot, fanning its thin branches out on the southeast side of things alongside buckthorn and spicebush, soaking up sunlight that might otherwise go to waste until some sumac or, better, papaw gets going. If you walk around in early April, you will find yourself naturally following its fine white bloom from place to place in the same way you wandered from one bright yellow spicebush to another in March.

Dogwoods bloom after the haw, in early April, along with the black cherry strewn all over the farm, a few ancient apple trees and a scattering of peach, most of those planted by woodchucks that chomp the ripe fruit off the lower branches the night before you plan to pick it. The oaks flower, casting ruddy tints into their empty crowns. You can see this flowering in the mountains, faint but distinct bands of russets and rusts that have a hint of autumn in them. Look closely, of course, and you will see every season in every season. The purple, bell-like flowers of papaw appear as sassafras set their small flower heads. Then the big beech by the barn blooms on its sunny side next to the farm road, and then the sweet cherry near it.

The farm gathers more of what I would call suspended light in early spring, the way it does it autumn, the light that painters and photographers like, a light that doesn't quite settle on things. In spring, that softly bright, revealing light is a critical presence. You miss it when it fades into the humid glare of summer. Unknown to the county tax surveyor, the farm enlarges with each fluorescence and spill of leaf. A single red maple blooming in the foot of the cabin hollow seems to expand the space around it in the same way that the orange rust in the crowns of the Spanish oaks draws the big trees up to full height and volume. The clarity of the midwinter landscape is clarity of structure—you see the unfathomable strength in things. The clarity of April is something else, clarity of process and growth, of aspiration—the energy of a planet stirred to express itself under the simple offices of sunlight and rain.

There is something painterly in this progression, deft brushwork off a subtle palette, and I'm not surprised to see the same artist working every year down on the flood plain below Highland Farm with a canvas set between him and the mountains. Except for the unfathomable beauty of a woman's face, there is no subject as difficult for the artist as the onset of spring, so casually lavish and finely wrought. In any medium, the challenge is to be precise without being precious but not to lose the life of things in mere precision. In the end, words pale, and sentences written six months ago look as lifeless as last year's leaves.

I've never stopped to look at the painter's canvas, but I wish him well. Brilliant and indifferent work hangs in local galleries. I've got my hands full trying to keep up with spring on the

cramped keyboard of a computer that gives me twenty-six letters and a few stray marks with which to limn the life of things.
What's important? The way after blooming dogwood produces
perfectly green paired flames of leaves? That new leaves of black
cherry are sometimes tinged red at the edges as if color had bled
from its flowers? That the buds of beech and oak are as tightly
bound in mid-April as they are in midwinter? That walnut trees
look dead in spring? That last fall's seedpods still cling, shriveled, on black locust? That the blackjack oaks are full of dead
leaves that rattle with strange life in the wind? That the incredible speed of crows in full flight is inexplicable given the casual
adagio of their wing beats? That the gray winter coats of deer
turn red in spring? That everything in the woods knows when
it is going to rain hours before the wind picks up and thick gray
banks of clouds appear in the northwest, sending me out to drag
tarps over the woodpiles?

Life comes on in spring. Simple enough.

If it's proof of anything, spring is proof that, given half a
chance, life on earth still works. In the country, we can take the
lavish, spendthrift outpouring for granted, but I'm pleased to
find that the leafing in and flowering of trees is of keen interest
everywhere and at all times. Nature is perhaps more striking
where it is not so picturesque and peaceful as it is here. From
deep inside the shadows of history, Anne Frank recorded the
onset of spring with joy. For March 16, 1944: "The weather is
gorgeous, indescribably beautiful." A month later, on April 18,
she is as ardent an observer as Thoreau: "Our chestnut tree is
in leaf, and here and there you can already see a few small blossoms." On the thirteenth of May, she notes the waxing power
of sunlight and that the tree she watches through shuttered windows is in full bloom, "covered with leaves and . . . even more

beautiful than last year." Thoreau, too, looked out a prison window with his sight unchanged. If Anne Frank is willing to risk her fear of rats and burglars—and worse—to sneak glimpses of the narrow band of night sky visible above 263 Prinsengracht, we have no license to take anything for granted here.

If the flowering and leafing of trees enlarges the farm in April, birds bring that space to life. There is considerable tussling for mates and nesting territory around the greening hedgerows. This seems a waste of energy, since the same arrangements are hashed out each year. Whitethroats are so busy in the blooming haw in early April, I thought for years that they nested here. But at some point—all in a night, it seems—they disappear. Field sparrows and, later, chipping sparrows secret themselves in the haw and multiflora abandoned by the whitethroats. Chickadees slip into locust snags and sometimes into the gourds I hung to keep the swallows out of the bluebird boxes. Mockingbirds build flat, disheveled stick nests in the crotch of a peach tree overhung with honeysuckle.

The rufous-sided towhees that remain are as visible and vocal as mockingbirds will be in June. Sparrows and finches glean the pasture grasses rustling last year's seed heads. Titmice appear constantly out of the same thin air into which Carolina chickadees disappear, sleek with folded wings. After March, robins are not much in view, but paired cardinals flush out of every hedgerow and call constantly in the cabin hollow. Bluebirds stake out nest boxes after the usual skirmishing. Goldfinches appear in breeding plumage. Nuthatches inspect tree trunks up and down. Carolina wrens, striking in every aspect, sing strongly in the morning before dawn, capturing the essence of the word better than anything I know. Their response to daylight sets a good example.

A full complement of woodpeckers—hairy, downy, red-bellied—raid the feeders, cracking sunflower seeds open against the cedar porch posts and sometimes stashing them in the grooves. Once or twice a season I may see a redheaded woodpecker taking advantage of the free seed, but there are degrees of condescension in the woodpecker clan. Of course, the imperious pileated woodpeckers keep their distance, but you can hear the big birds working almost all the time carving out two or three nest cavities for the one they need. They get in the more heavily shaded woodlots and work from eight to four like contractors on a job. I've seen titmice nesting in the discarded venues, and I assume other birds do likewise. Flickers are about in healthy numbers, but they also disdain the feeder. You see them on any walk swooping from tree to tree in that falling flight of theirs.

Since the word *spring,* as noun and verb, has roots in ancient words that convey a sense of inherent liveliness and a tendency to quick movement and, going back to Sanskrit, the very idea of striving—of striving to be—no class of animals embodies the seasonal idea of spring as well as birds. I read nothing symbolic or allegorical in their being or behavior. The fact of their presence is enough. In their persistent liveliness, especially in April and May, birds seem to be the finest product of evolution, simultaneously fabulous and practical, impossible to ignore in a setting like this where they are so constant a distraction, they are always at the center of what there is to see. Without them, we would not know how hospitable a place the earth is. For my own needs, the resources of Highland Farm are quite crude—from firewood to venison, I take a rough and selfish harvest here every year. When I see a wren with a beak full of weed stems, I understand how much finer the uses of nature might be construed.

Returning birds confirm a world beyond the horizon and give the life of Highland Farm a stake in other places, from the Gulf Coast to the mountainous interior of South America. I watch for them as intently as one of Columbus's sailors. Delicate blue-gray gnatcatchers appear in mid-April and immediately begin building nests. A week later, sleek and twitchy tree swallows start harassing the bluebirds for their boxes. Brown thrashers move into the cabin hollow, flash their glossy presence and disappear. Veeries call in the evening, putting the wrens and the meadowlarks to shame. Rough-winged swallows, northern waterthrushes and black and white warblers appear down by the river about the time the bass and sunfish are getting on their redds. Indigo buntings and orioles flush from woodlots when I set about cutting up the winter's deadfalls. Red-eyed, solitary and warbling vireos take up posts in the greening woodlots, distributing themselves along the calculus of their needs and preferences. By the time ruby-throated hummingbirds zip into view, and pewees materialize on fence lines and flycatchers in the greening poplars, you know spring has come full course. The presence and insistent pressure of ordinary birdlife around you tells you life itself is humming and that there are natural enclaves in Mexico and Costa Rica and Venezuela and Brazil that are as fine as Highland Farm.

Nothing limns the complex seasonality of this planet like birds. Once you learn to notice them, the year seems to be *about* birds—the woods and pastures seem to be built for birds, they use the farm so well. Judging from my journals, most moments of attentiveness are focused by birds. For many people, I think, birdlife schools *noticing* in the way that music schools *listening*. One April, the back pasture was full of tree swallows, or rather the air over the back pasture was full of tree swallows in the evenings. For a week or two, their extraordinary flight seemed a reification of something in the season I could not name, a passion in things, an energy, a design. Of course, all bird flight reflects that skyward skill and earthward swoop that only the consciousness of birds feels directly. This is not to anthropomorphize. Their sensations connect them to life as surely as our own. I imagine that the consciousness of animals is more like music—some seamless, nonverbal sensuality that glows in their brains and central nervous systems and, I don't doubt, affords them considerable pleasure.

The flight of every swallow is simultaneously characteristic of the species and unique to the moment. I remember one bird that performed from twilight into dusk, undercutting that soft, clear April air as I sat on the porch repairing a mossy old bluebird nest box. There must have been other birds about, as there always are—chickadees bounding, whitethroats careening, mockingbirds flashing, crows rowing hard with strong pulls of their broad wings. But, for whatever reason, it is that swallow I see now most clearly, slicing the silken light and then rising to stall, hawking an insect I couldn't see with a quick twist, its deft wings shuddering a bit before it swooped and rose again, twisting so that I could see the way its jet-black back and wings contrasted with its throat and breast, each so perfectly white the bird looked wet, as if it had just been made. Birds are like fish in that way; familiar but otherworldly, they always look new. The next evening the air was empty, and the back pasture had become the place where a swallow had limned the air into something you could very nearly see.

If the species that return to breed here confirm the normal course of things, strays and migrants enliven life with the uniqueness of their presence and give us title to more remote regions, the sweeping polarity of a larger life than, most years, we live here. This year I got up from my desk one April morning a half hour early—stuck or bored or satisfied with my work—and ambled down the fence line along the drive. While the usual birds scattered and Patch protested from the run where I set him after breakfast, a sliver of something flitting around the empty branches of a walnut caught my eye. What I first assumed was a pine warbler, elusive but common here, resolved into a female golden-wing when I got the binoculars on it. I did not know what it was at the time, but I noted every possible diagnostic detail—beak shape, wing bars—jotting down a note or two at each brief stop it made on a branch to peck the bark for insects. It helped mightily that the bird was almost but not quite a pine warbler, that it was both distinctly similar but distinctly different. I've never seen another here and assume the species is either locally rare or that the bird was out of range. But for all I know, there is a farm fifty—or ten—miles away where golden-wings are common as mice. The closer you watch birds, the less reliable you find the distribution maps in field guides. And whenever I stop to glean the fascinating pages of *Auk,* I notice that those distribution maps are often being revised by experts who have not yet finished studying the intimate details of how birds use the hemispheres across which their modest lives are lived.

The benefit of being an amateur is that you are always crossing paths with something you don't know. The pleasure of learning is always at hand. I liked seeing the golden-wing, knowing at first only that I didn't know it—that is the finest moment in any encounter. And then I liked coming to know what it was—in name—and then realizing, again, that there was much more to learn about what I had seen, that I should be on the lookout for golden-wing warblers.

Chance bird encounters put an edge on walks—two wood-cocks flushing from the base of that red maple at the foot of the cabin hollow, kestrels courting over the back pasture, a grouse drumming from the old clear-cut, a sharp-shinned hawk snatching a songbird in the barn woods, a wild turkey raising its head in alarm in the deer track woodlot, a scarlet tanager strayed down from the mountains to visit the barn spring, a meadowlark on the phone line at sunset or an unidentified skein of birdsong defying the middle of a starlit night. Wander up the farm road at noon in April and you may encounter a flock of yellow-throated warblers sparking around the canopy of the oaks with a flock of yellow-rumps, née Myrtle warblers, mixed in. Some of the former may stay right here to breed, finding some nearby bottomland to their liking, but none of the latter will think of nesting short of the north woods. A few can be envied for a summer in Newfoundland or along the southern shores of Hudson's Bay.

While birds put on a show, other life emerges. The mourning cloaks of March have given way to the fritillaries, whites, sulfurs, and small dark blues which nectar on the blooms of April. The solemn, long-lived box turtles perform some strange local migration. Rabbits breed like, well, rabbits, a talent which brings out the best and worst in red-tailed hawks. Woodchucks mate with more circumspection than rabbits. Foxes increase secretly. The adults bring live mice and voles back to the den mouth below the barn and teach their kits to crouch and pounce.

Weather in April hems and haws, a predictable unpredict-ability which is good for the life of things. Fronts come and go as if some big work is being done overhead, days of strong weather briskly moved in and out—sun and rain, stillness and bluster. No weather stays long. Something interesting is always on the horizon. The variety of nature, the very forms of things, is of course honed by this hemming and hawing in the weather. There is as much winnowing in spring as in autumn. The vagaries of early spring weather determine how fat and plentiful the berries of summer will be and how well littered the ground will be with acorns, walnuts and hickory nuts. That's an easy planting I don't have to tend. The garden I can handle and, week by week, I turn the heavy soil, let it dry in the cool sun and till it fine with the steel fingers of the cultivator, string stakes and dibble seeds in place, planting enough vegetables to complement last fall's venison as it comes to table.

On the best days in April, I keep the windows open and a fire going and let the woodstove warm the cool, fresh air that blows through, rustling the morning's work, turning the pages of books left open, fingering new words to read and write. The wood floors are littered with the detritus of fly tying and wood carving and the caked mud that calves from my heavily lugged boots. Nothing that can't be swept clean right out the door.

The growth of trees during spring leaves behind a pale band of early wood. In April and May, this outer layer of sapwood is a spongy mass of thin-walled cells only loosely bound to the older sapwood and cambium between which it is sandwiched. Cut a green locust in June and you can pry the sheath of pliant new xylem out with a penknife. This milky pulp is the living tissue of the tree, as fresh with life as leaves. As spring turns to summer, growth slows, leaving behind a darker band of thick-walled cells known as late wood.

In a warm, wet spring this Dionysian growth quickly adds bulk and reach to trees—volume and height and breadth. Stirred by sun and rain, early wood aspires to greatness. During the long days of summer, the Apollonian late wood adds strength—that graceful, flexible strength peculiar to trees on which architecture has schooled itself for millennia. It is no accident that the columns of Greek temples and Gothic cathedrals are flared like the boles of beech and magnolia or fluted like ash and elm and hickory. Autumn, of course, brings the process to an end, and this year's growth, early and late, settles into place alongside all the other years, where it dies and begins to become what we call simply wood. Winter seals the lamination, leaving an annular ring that is both a record of the local weather and a shadow of the earth's orbit around the sun.

Perhaps the years here are revealed in their purest form in the wood I cut in winter and spring. I count the time in every tree I fell, an act of curiosity and respect, like carefully observing the plumage of a grouse or the pelage of a deer I have killed. My journals are pocked with numbers—rings, diameter, circumference, height—and other odd notations on the startling growth spurt of some boom year or of decades so compressed that I need a 10x eyepiece to perceive the years.

Of course, each year's weather is embodied in those rings. Dendrochronologists retrieve history from them. Find a stump that takes you back to the Jamestown settlement, and you may see the razor-thin bands of drought into which Virginia's first colonists unwittingly sailed. You can see warm, wet springs in broad rings of early wood and a dry summer tightly wound in a pencil line of late wood. A prolonged winter or a dry spring will curb the early growth in the most eager of trees. A summer visited by frequent thunderstorms will leave a heartening band of late wood. You can see the steady growth encouraged by a southern exposure and the way shade suppresses the years. You will see in every wavy departure from the idea of a circle the

way life reaches into the light. You can see where a tree has been
released to grow at its true pace by the death of some towering
neighbor. You can see the hidden wounds of lightning and dis-
ease festered in rotted hollows and you can see the rich, broad
bands of good years.

Species seem to vary widely in their habits, the late-leafing
hardwoods wisely preferring the slow summer growth that
leaves them strong in the long run. Given decent weather
to work with, the oaks and hickories, as well as black locust
and walnut, wrap broad dark rings around thin pale ones.
Understory hardwoods like dogwood, ironwood and hornbeam pack vascular sapwood even tighter around heartwood
fine-grained as sandstone. Most softwoods leaf out early and
grow like weeds in spring. The poplars outstrip their roots in
twenty or thirty years, toppling over in storms that overpower
the collective surface area of their broad leaves, as if they had
too much sail for their keels. Everything in nature answers to
the way it grows.

Mesmerizing as they are in the abstract, I don't pay tree rings
much mind while I'm working. Cutting wood is the hardest
physical labor I do. I might bring my walking curiosity with me
to the woodlot where a windblown oak lies waiting, but a half
hour with the chain saw and the double-bitted limbing ax leaves
me as disinterested in the nuances of nature as any jobber in the
woods. This is especially true when I cut in warm weather, when
the work of undoing what a tree is will punish you sorely. I may
go out with good intentions, bringing my banged-up hunting
binoculars and a notepad, but on a hot day I doubt I'd stop to
glass an ivorybill or, for that matter, a pterodactyl, should one
flush nearby. But when I get the load home, I stop to cut what
botanists call "cookies" out of the lower sections of the trees I've

bucked. I stack them like books in a corner of the downstairs study to read at my leisure.

The biggest, most interesting stumps on the farm are not mine.

Five years ago the farm was logged. For several weeks one winter I listened to the muffled buzz of the chain saws in the distance and the shrieks of the crankiest old skidder I have ever seen, some engine left over from the siege of Troy. When the loggers were cutting their way up through the barn woods and the poplar hollow, I could hear the big trees crack and thump, just as I had cracked and thumped that locust to the ground pretty as you please. I could feel the farm lightening—the big woods thinning, the birds and squirrels clearing out, and I knew it was a loss.

I've made my stand against logging on public lands, more often than not just another subsidy of big business in that con game corporate conservatives call "the free market." (Free for big business, I guess, but not for the taxpayer or the lover of the woods.) Such subsidized resource extraction is welfare for billion-dollar corporations like Weyerhaeuser and Georgia Pacific which have done much harm, at great profit, to the ecology of the southern Appalachians. We have gotten the pesky poor off welfare, but the rich seem to be malingering. In any event, forests need to be left alone in order to be forests. There is no getting around that. For hundreds of millions of years, the ecology of forests has depended on the recycling of nutrients, especially all the beautiful biomass of dead wood. A single rotting log in a forest supports more biodiversity than a suburban neighborhood doused with Chemlawn products. "Harvesting" a forest for timber, as is the current jargon, turns it into a tree farm, a monoculture. The implied metaphor reveals how an agricultural mentality has extended itself deep into the woods.

Woodlots, as the name implies, are another matter, especially woodlots on private property. I am myself the beneficiary of some generously extended woodcutting rights. Even so, after an ancient knuckle-boom log loader arrived on Highland Farm a few years back, it was hard to ignore the implications of the logging trucks rumbling out every few hours under my nose. I could hear them bouncing down the back pasture and then breaking for the rippling gauntlet of the cattle guard before they downshifted for the sharp turn beneath my study windows and the steep dive down the drive. The cabin shook and diesel fumes filled the air as early wood and late wood were carried off for days. That wasn't just biomass going by. I'd guess it was a third of the canopy in places, a third of the shade and light and look of things—the heart of many places I knew well, exposed and changed. And overall maybe at least a quarter of the hard mast production—all those acorns, walnuts and hickory nuts that covered the ground in fall—and more than a little habitat for everything from insects to squirrels. I rarely stood up to look down at the passing loads and saw mostly big white oak boles when I did. My shoulders and neck tensed when the empty trucks rumbled back, their big iron cradles clattering.

The loggers were a local family operation, native to this county for as long as the oldest trees they cut. The men weren't a stereotype of southern Appalachia. They were where the stereotype came from—laconic, hardworking when they got going, tough as nails and good at what they did. A mossy, hard-barked bunch, they looked like they had grown in the woods themselves. Local outfits are still willing to high-grade, or select-cut, relatively small affairs like Highland Farm, splitting the wholesale value of the timber at the mill. High-grade indeed—they did their work well. I've never seen a logging job like it. When I finally got up the courage to have a look around, my eye and mind sorely missed the standing mass of all the lost trees. The farm seemed too bright and open, even for February, and I knew that many fragile microclimates would be changed by the loss of canopy, and that by midsummer the understory plant and tree species were in for a shock. I worried about a few things, like those walking fern in the double-helix woodlot, which need deep shade to survive a southern summer.

The barn woods, the poplar hollow, the double-helix were so thinned and changed it took me until midspring to be able to enjoy a walk in those places. The north woodlots were much changed also, no longer so dark and deep. Not as wild as they once were. But when I recovered from the visual shock and got into the suddenly younger-looking woods, I was amazed. I've seen clear-cuts on National Forest land that would make an unsentimental person weep for the stupid waste of it. But these men downed trees as if they were working indoors and had been sternly told not to scratch the furniture. They had dropped the largest specimens with little damage to what was left standing.

The first place I checked was that beautiful grove of beech near the head of the barn woods. They took some of the biggest red and white oaks out of there, but there wasn't a mark on the smooth-barked *Fagus*. There was slash, of course, and a few busted limbs in the understory here and there, but they had felled trees with a precision I found instructive, dropping massive trunks into narrow openings, leaving what was left to take advantage of the new flood of sunlight. *Release,* foresters call it, a technical phrase with considerable poetry in it.

In the spirit of making lemonade out of lemons, I toured the new stumps that spring and learned what history I could from them. Each stump told its story as laconically as the Sioux calendar history in which each year gets remembered by a single event. Those big white oak stumps, convenient seats now for bird-watching and deer hunting, embody the living history of this place better than I ever could in words. I know now that *Quercus alba* thirty inches thick here represents about a century of growth, at least the way they grew last century along the southeastern edge of the barn woods. Northern red oaks can bide their time, wrapping eighty years in a foot-thick trunk. Cedars, too, grow slow, especially when they grow up together, shading each other out, an arrangement that encourages uniformity and makes for strong trees in the long run, their trunks composed mostly of heartwood. Along with black locust, those cedars make strong, rot-resistant fence posts.

The telltale beauty of wood grain is the beauty of time itself. Read against the backdrop of deep time, growth rings take us back to the Devonian, when the idea of wood arose and began to ramify in coniferous and, later, deciduous strategies of survival. More recent years come to hand in the hickory-handled ax and maul and wedge-driving sledge I carry afield, in my ironwood walking stick, in the curly maple of my flintlock and the oiled walnut of other gunstocks, in the red elm of my longbow, in the white ash of canoe paddles, in the spruce top of my guitar and in the well-worn cherry rolltop on which I write these words. Some nights, the dark timbers and pale chinking of my home look like bands of early wood and late wood, the inviting interior of the cabin a kind of airy heartwood where I live and write and think about such things while Patch dreams under the desk or impatiently nudges my elbow as if we might take off hunting into the cool spring night.

·   ·   ·

At the end of the first week of May, the rising sun moves out of my office window. By then I'm working on the front porch in the morning and can turn to see it break the horizon over a low notch in the mountains. Minutes and hours are arbitrary conventions. In May, you can see time, and feel it viscerally, as movement through space, a turning not of clock hands but of a planet whose fragile life is predicated on many motions, at the heart of which is a tilted, wobbling ellipse. In spring, you don't need to tell time. It declares itself.

I write slowly on May mornings, searching out the sense of certain rhythms that come to mind like a breeze that pulls on my attention, trying as best I can to get inside of the way life works around me. When I am concentrating well, trying to wed the liveliness of words to the life in things, I can keenly feel each moment flutter, *something* about the life of things reified at the edge of my peripheral vision. Life hums in the weathered floorboards of the porch, twists in long strips of tattered cedar bark hanging off the porch posts, sits in the sun like a sparrow on a chestnut rail, emerges from the cabin hollow like reddish deer grazing placidly into a lime-green pasture. But held up against the world itself, writing seems inadequate. Nothing around me needs words, or uses words. Birds move, in and out of sight, responding keenly to the demands of their existence, deftly eluding any sentence I could fashion to capture the significance of their largely secret lives. Sunlight catches the pale green undersides of the swords of new walnut leaves and the glossy, freshly minted leaves of the big double-trunked Spanish oak reflect a rich light around the cabin that seems to increase depth of field.

Some threshold is passed in early May at this latitude, some ratio of temperature and photoperiod which cuts loose everything that lives here. The farm passes through that subtle season of trees flowering and then gives itself over to growth in earnest. The oaks and walnuts finally leafing out is a sure sign that the long beginning of spring is over and that another nameless season within the seasons has passed. Morning birdsong settles down, the bold jazz of mating replaced by the ceaseless bustle of nesting, a largely silent industriousness interrupted by occasional declarations from strong-throated wrens and bluebirds or sonarlike chips and pings from sparrows. Contact calls, communication beyond what human consciousness can understand. Even here at the edge of the twenty-first century, the simple beauty and vitality of spring declares itself openly, as it has every year for all those centuries and more, inviting, not a sentimental response, but a refined respect for everything that aspires to succeed in the stirring sunlight.

The barn spring is a hundred yards from here up the cabin hollow. Casual midmorning walks in May there and back unveil enough life to stock a continent. Some days I walk out and never get beyond the cabin hollow. If I move slowly, or wait patiently, the local diversity of life comes to me. The birdlife is always instructive and heartening. The silent lives of trees seem to augur well. Common animals move through as I do, parting the way through weeds and wildflowers. My growing list of plant and animal species for Highland Farm is impressive, a raucous mix of natives and exotics that have worked out coexistence here. And this is not a nature sanctuary, just an old rural place partly in use and partly gone to seed. It strikes me every day that nature is most productive where it is left alone.

One of the great books of my college years was Martin Buber's *I and Thou*, a meditation, written in the difficult tradition of Hasidic mysticism and German philosophy, on the reciprocal respect for being—any being—that underwrites true morality. Knowing the names of things is one way to walk up to the near edge of that respect, that Thou-ness. Very little of the book has anything explicitly to do with nature, but Buber writes, with chilling insight, that our relation with nature "vibrates in the dark and remains below language. The creatures stir across from us, but they are unable to come to us, and the You we say to them sticks to the threshold of language."

The names of birds, animals, plants, trees, stars are doorways into an instructive otherness. The rich diversity of life I casually encounter walking up the cabin hollow shows me, at every step, expressions of forms of life that have nothing to do with me. Nature doesn't, as Wordsworth, Whitman, Emerson and the Romantics assumed, mirror the presumed goodness of our own nature back at us or, to my mind, give proof of some divinity. My guess is that things are what they seem to be in and of themselves and that if the presence of nature is a test, it is a test to see if we will respect the found world for its own sake. Which is not to say we see all of what is. Heaven, Thoreau suggested, was underfoot, not overhead. That sounds right to me. There is enough beauty, order and beguiling wildness in the mere presence of things to satisfy my earth-loving soul. The world is sacred because it is, not because it is a sign of something else.

Every day here is a gentle argument to respect what is for its own sake. And though I hunt and fish and cut wood and wear my own selfish trails into this place, respect most often means leaving things alone. Spring is the time for that, a season when hunting is reduced to its essence as *noticing*. Naming follows not as a way of taking possession, but as a way of opening the possibility of a relation. Each species name, each word we have assigned whimsically or scientifically to some form of life, marks a Thou, a commitment made in language to recognize the being of some other, something not ourselves—it doesn't matter what. This puts a brake on the notion that the world was put here, by accident or design, primarily for our *use*. Spend enough time in the sunlight that stirs the life of things in May and you will come to feel, I think, that the world was put here, by accident or design, as a place for us *to be*.

But the life of things doesn't resolve into a list of names. Birds enliven walks as the keenest expression of particular moments afield—mockingbirds squawk, clattering noisily through the densest foliage, from which they throw catbird imitations and other confusing mimicry into the air; a glossy brown veery disappears into a tangle of honeysuckle and haw, flashing sunlight off its broadly fanned tail; blackbirds burst from a pasture in a ballet of flock-flight; cedar waxwings gust into a black cherry still in bloom; pine warblers enliven midstory trees, raiding the ground in quick forays; a lone warbling vireo sings in the rain from somewhere out of sight; an indigo bunting clings to a weed stalk and sings passionately in plain view. Walk with respect and you'll find a morning's pathos in a freshly chiseled hole, beading with sap, some woodpecker has carved into a pine tree.

Nature's liveliest stimulus to enhanced consciousness, birds lead awareness on to the edge of what we can know about nature—a flock of stately crows quickly flies in and out of view, not barking that cartoonish *caw* but calling to one another as softly as swans, a voice you have never heard them use before, a voice that makes you wonder where they have been and where they are going; a gobbler walks down whitetail ridge, all blue and black in the shadows, a study in impenetrable self-possession; a kestrel slices the air over a pasture into something finer, whetting its wings with abandon. The range of being here is humbling.

Details of form persist as brilliant abstractions—the gleaming, flatly arched eye stripe of a wren and the fine checking in its tail; the subtle spectrum of iridescence on a blue jay's back, the inky streaking on a thrasher's white breast and the orange in a kestrel's tail.

Hunting in autumn, the first thing is to scout for sign— grouse cover, turkey scratch, buck rub. In May, everything is a sign. That walk around I took in midwinter through bare woods has changed in every sense. The bloom is off the haw and redbud. Dogwood is past its showy prime. Sumacs start leafing in, while the poplars fill with flowers, each a light-gathering work of art. Black cherry remains in flower as persimmon leafs in. Bunches of green keys hang in the box elders. The pungent scent of skunk cuts the cloying perfume of the paulownia, awful aftertaste of their hideous bloom in the air to join the more subtle scents of black cherry and locust. The uninspired bloom of multiflora rose throws a dingy white into the hedgerows. Sweet scent of black locust fills the air. Poplars set their extraordinary flowers—deeply sculpted, perfectly white cups of light that rival the bloom of the farm's one magnolia. Shellbark hickory leafs in, while the bitternut hickory flowers alongside the honeysuckle and sand grape. The pale, limp leaves of beech stir in the wind. The American holly in the front pasture has bouquets of small white four-petaled flowers sprouting from its twigs and protected by spiral shields of stout, spined leaves. Even so, it is full of insects—wasps and bees and orange checkerspots. Pipevine swallowtails decorate the honeysuckle, zebra swallowtails festoon the papaw.

A subtle array of wildflowers blooms underfoot in the woodlots and in the pastures, a casual extravagance that seems to mirror the diversity of birdlife according to some calculus I can't fathom. I recognize the obvious—mayapple and violets, fire pinks and fleabane, rue anemone and tickseed sunflower. You could spend the season crawling around on your hands and knees caught between seeing and knowing—periwinkle, larkspur, mustard, geranium, waterleaf, lyre-leaved sage, wild cucumber and wild strawberry, garlic mustard, gill on the ground. Squawroot and bloodroot persist in the river woods. The sand grape that vines the sunny side of woodlots flowers in small green clusters. The stiff-branched coralberry sets off-white clusters of trumpet-shaped bloom. There are crops of herbs, medicinals and fungi I should be harvesting, as well as lichens, spleenworts and ferns I should identify for the sake of knowing what they are.

By mid-May, young of the year are underfoot and in the air. The fox den below the barn is busy with kits, the entrance strewn with crow feathers. I find fawns no bigger than rabbits curled up in clumps of milkweed. All eyes and ears, for a day or two they are at the mercy of everything. Sometimes I wonder how anything survives its first days. Week-old fawns skitter away with the sparrows when I march into a woodlot with the axes and saws. Their tilting bounds are odd. At a month old, they will run like deer. The females are nervous in the spring, but the bucks and bachelors are eager to put on weight beneath their sleek, reddish brown coats. They are as unwary as they will be all year. I can't deny that their velvety racks, branching out into the sunlight like vegetation, stir trophy-hunting ambitions in the back of my hunting mind.

Of course, there is as much predation as birth in spring. Patch and I may be at bay, but hunting never stops. Hawks hawk. Swallows swallow. Foxes outfox. Rat snakes gorge themselves on bird eggs and nestlings. Birds raid the cocooned victims of spiders' nests and, when that cupboard is bare, bring the well-fed spiders themselves back, pinched hard in those dainty beaks, to feed their young. The spiders that remain at large, set nets in their good hunting places as carefully as fishermen. Everything hunts. The beauty of spring is underwritten by the frank striving of all forms of life to live. The bluebird is as much a red slayer as the copperhead. I read no grim lesson in this, only the way life works, thriving in diverse ways, competing in time for space to grow and express whatever its genetics have gathered from its long past.

The Maury River is quick with fish in May, sleek smallmouth bass that crash crank baits and wobbly flatheads and turn on streamers quartered to them as if they were defending territory, which of course they are. There is something strong and hawk-like in bass, a pouncing fight in them that is different than the elegant fight in trout. The river itself is strong in May, which is how the fish get strong. You feel strong yourself, bracing up against the green and white flow of the Maury while you cast to these eager fish.

I could hunt turkeys, but I have a deep freezer full of venison and no appetite or need for more meat. Had I grown up in the South, I might take the cocksure strutting toms more personally, the way grouse engage me in late October, and hunt turkeys for the sport of it. I've lucked across birds in fall when out for deer, but in the world of turkey hunting that doesn't count. The skills are surely admirable—the backcountry scouting, the calling and especially the ability to remain invisible to the keenest eye in the American woods. And there is the great fact that turkeys are, in many respects, the apotheosis of southern Appalachian hardwood forests, in their way a finer, keener thing than bear or timber rattlers or ravens. But turkey hunting, like writing, is a dawn affair, and it's all I can do, in April and May, to stay working at my desk when some strange birdcall starts up.

This year I kept my cedar call box near the writing table on the porch—a concession to good manners. For a week I answered a bird gobbling in the lower river woods by giving the box a tentative shake or two. Usually that would silence the bird, like putting down a rising trout with a bad cast. But one foggy morning I drew a turkey closer and closer and thought I nearly had it out to the edge of the front pasture where I might glass it when the mist burned off. All this gobbling got a second bird going in the poplar hollow, at which point I was caught like the one lame musician in a good jam session. My calling couldn't keep up with the conversation. The far bird shut down quick—it may well have been a poacher come across the barn woods fence line. And then the near bird lost confidence in whatever I was saying. I never saw it.

By late May I'm harvesting snow peas from the garden, the bounty of those barrel-shaped Sugar Anns I planted in mid-March. Lightly steamed and heavily peppered, they gleam an unreal emerald and perfectly complement the thin slices of rare venison tenderloin with which they get served. Those are the best meals, the food that comes from the woods and the garden. Spring chores pile up quickly, afternoons and evenings are rich with easy tasks.

Nature teaches that the obvious is worth a second look, and in the end I don't mind admitting that little beyond the obvious catches my eye and ear in spring—a cool red dawn, beautiful confusion of birdsong, the wind gusting unaccountably, turkey gabbling in the river woods, rain on the sheet-metal roof, the sound of the big river below sorting stones like a shaman, geese honking in and out of view overhead, the back pasture shrouded in night mist, the moon sailing through clouds, the wild stars beyond it swinging planets in wild orbits where atoms and molecules wait for the opportunity to express themselves in ways we can't yet imagine.

Overhead, nothing is obvious. The night sky, as always, is as wild as the woods. The stars shift as the birdlife shifts, and I'm not surprised to read that some species of birds have star charts in their brains and navigate by stellar cues. At night, when I walk into the back pasture, the universe is angled differently than it was in winter, another useful consequence of the imperfect journeying of the earth through space. Castor and Pollux greet me out the back door in early May. The Great Bear hunts, upside down, over the crown of the cabin oak, Polaris and Cassiopeia hidden behind it. Arcturus and Spica become my locator stars, useful guides in the dark. The Milky Way shifts out of sight, but the River flows into view. Galaxies, nebulae and other deep-space Messier objects bloom overhead.

I didn't recognize the stilt-legged bird probing the margins of the small pond that the barn spring fills. Salt-and-pepper head, neck and breast; grayish brown wings flecked with white; seashell-white underneath. Long, stout bill like a woodcock leading to a large black eye lined with a thin, bright white eye ring that seemed a bit tufted. A shorebird, surely, which suddenly conferred the status of "shoreline" on the muddy flat more famous, locally, for raccoon tracks and the delicate claw marks and tail drag of the painted turtle that lives there. Some kind of sandpiper, I guessed, a solitary one at that.

The barn spring pond routinely gives up a lot of life, as water holes tend to do. Approach it carefully in wet years and you can lose a heartbeat to a mallard or even a wood duck bursting off the water. Green heron use the pond, and once or twice I've found a great blue heron gracing the shady enclave with its stately presence. Every year, a pair of brown thrashers nests there among the mockingbirds and sparrows. And I've seen other migrants flirting with the place, this year two white-crowned sparrows that I thought might stay to breed. In any season, the resident birdlife peaks in the briery cover around the spring and in the surrounding walnuts and poplars. It's the first place I take birding friends and my most frequent destination when work limits me to short walks.

I watched the visitor for an hour in good light and then, mesmerized by the simple fact of its presence, watched it as best I could as the light failed and the pond darkened. Whatever it was, I knew it would not be there the next day. I wanted to know what it was in name, but for the time I watched it the solitary sandpiper at the barn spring was unnamed, or so I thought. In Martin Buber's sense, it was just below the threshold of language and all the more *luminous to me for that. You can't plan those moments when a casual walk on an ordinary day coalesces into a perfect opportunity to watch something emerge from the unknown and invite a few moments of pure relation between equals, subject and subject.*

Its distinctive checking made the bird seem unusually well drawn, weighty and clear, even though it was, in a conventional sense, well camouflaged. At first I didn't know it was there. Then, once I saw the bird, I couldn't stop seeing it. The stilt-bird walked around the algae-strewn puddles in small, attentive circles, tipping its body frequently and picking at the water with just the tip of its bill, not probing up and down like a drill, but reaching out with it at an angle to pick at something I could not see. Its bill rippled the water, which was blue in the late-afternoon light.

*It was, I figured out at home, exactly what its form and the occasion had named it—*Tringa solitaria*—the solitary sandpiper, not a rare bird in the world, but a rare bird at the barn spring on Highland Farm, where it chanced to set down two-thirds of the way on its journey from the Argentine pampas to the Canadian subarctic.*

Bend of a River

Everything flows.

—HERACLITUS

June, fishing the old Poor Farm water hard.

For the nonangler, the phrase "fishing hard" is an oxymoron, but fishermen know what I mean. One of my favorite fishing writers, Sir Edward Grey, refers to the "wildness and hard work of fishing." That's it exactly. What we call Poor Farm is a stretch of what is left of the Jefferson River, the best big trout river near home. That *big* modifies both trout and river. Although no westerner would be impressed with it, the Jefferson is a broader, deeper watercourse than the tumbling mountain streams I love to lean my shoulder against in early spring. And it holds at least the promise of far larger trout than I can catch in my favorite brook trout streams. So, a big trout river.

A twenty-inch fish is, in my mind, the standard unit of measure for a large trout. When I built the rod I do most of my large-stream fly fishing with—a nine-foot, three-weight graphite—I wound a few wraps of scarlet thread twenty inches up the blank so I could confirm the long, fat fact of such fish before I let them go. I think at the time I vaguely intended to make a national inventory of such trout. Wood smoke, I guess, particulates in the lungs reducing oxygen to the brain. Winter dementia. After ten years, the wet noses of a few fish have come within an inch of that mark but none have touched it. So, in Sir Edward Grey's manner of speaking, I still have hard work to do and much wildness to suffer. It seems that scarlet wrap sits right on the border between "a man's reach should exceed his grasp" and "a man has got to know his limitations."

Tucked into the Allegheny highlands about an hour and a half to the west, the Jefferson is beyond my local horizon but hardly an exotic destination. Years when I have the itch, I'll make thirty or forty visits to the river. I'm like that, returning to the same place until I feel I've gotten to the heart of it, which, of course, I never do. You can't get to the bottom of the fine places on this earth. I no more finish my business with my favorite stretch of the Jefferson than I finish with a woodlot at home.

In March, I'll fish from midmorning to late afternoon, probing the strong water with nymphs and emergers between the spare early-season hatches of mayflies. In April, I'll fish half days, early or late. In the morning sometimes there are brief spinner falls when the big trout that have been night feeding rise softly in the thick rings of rises before going off to sulk through the daylight hours. Just past midmorning, the mayfly du jour will appear on the water and you will suddenly see where all the willing trout in the river are. Fishing, like hunting, is hard for long hours and then suddenly it seems unfairly easy. There are some good fish among these midday feeders, but the rises are all the same and you have to guess where the strong fourteen-

and sixteen-inch trout are. It's best just to cast to the fish within reach and work your way along, trusting the river to dole out rewards in some instructive, amusing or mysterious order.

More often than not I'll work from five A.M. to noon and not get to the river until two. On days when I write well, this after-noon fishing is a tremendous pleasure. Two or three good pages on my desk at home—strong, knee-deep riffle of a book or an essay flowing well and maybe a fragment of a poem—make a fine difference and keep me from feeling guilty about my free-dom. There may be a few caddis or small stoneflies coming off the river, but early afternoon is for patiently nymphing until you find where in the water column the fish are feeding. There is a good deal of huffing and puffing about "fly fishing tactics" in books and magazines, but I don't sense anything paramilitary about this fishing. You search out the fish with common sense and drift a fly to them, nicely as you can. Politeness—more often called presentation—is the key. Strike the right notes clearly. If the trout are taking, they will take, and you will maybe hook and land them and then let them go. Not much more to it than that. If not, you fish along, enjoying the river for the river's sake, wading strong and casting well, happy as a bear, maybe learning something or, better, losing awareness of the need to learn anything for a little while. You are not in a war. Fishing is no more about tactics than it is about equipment. It is about being in the river. Dig the river, if you will pardon some archaic language, and you will catch all the trout you need to catch.

May, of course, is the Fat Tuesday of the trout fishing year, patron month of the mayflies for which fly fishing was named. In May I'll make the drive in the dark, tires hissing past silent farmhouses and sleeping towns, and fish from first light. Those days are quietly wild, and I feel as healthily detached from

things as I do when I am deer hunting. I rarely stop casting or
even get out of the river and at the end of the day feel more like
a bear than a man. I'm the shaggy river keeper. I sometimes take
elaborate notes I rarely ever look at again. I don't need to write
down what I need to remember. I remember it.

*The way the river sounds loud in the dark, full and empty at
the same time. The loneliness of crossing the first ford under the
fading stars. Birdsong at dawn and then the river quieter in the
sudden light. That deep, dark sluice of water below the second ford
where I lost a good fish years ago. The overgrown trail through
the wetlands backed up from a network of beaver ponds. Heart-
scuttling flush of ducks. A water snake sliding off a beaver dam.
Frog spawn. Green heron cronk. Bream zipping circles in the back-
water. The way walking warms you on a cool morning. Then the
river again in view, thrumming in the riffles, silent in long pools,
twisting through the fractured bedrock that gives it character. Trout
sipping spinners before the light has got on the water, dark rumples
in the flats that widen your eyes. The tug of the good fish, the way
they bore down into the river and spoil you for the day. The way
the river shuts down when the sun gets on the water. Trying to find
and feel fish you can't see with a long leader and a tiny nymph.
Small trout rising to the late-morning hatch. Covering ground back
upstream through the water all day, thigh muscles humming to the
river thrum, head foggy with concentration. Getting tired of fishing
at midday. Then seeing a rise while bird-watching and suddenly
being eager to fish again. Probing difficult places with odd flies that
might turn a difficult trout. Lazily swinging wet flies downstream
in the hopes of getting lucky. Bearing down in midafternoon when
shadows start to grow from the west bank, making slices of the river
look like morning again. Casting deftly into these promising slicks
with buoyant caddis and stoneflies or with ants you can barely see,*

hoping a big brown trout might be inspecting the flow along the bank. Facing the best water of the day in early evening, tired but still keen to fish, waiting for a hatch or a spinner fall. Ignoring the small fish that start up as soon as the bugs are on the water. Waiting. Watching. Hoping the light will hold. Guessing where to be. Then that heartening and heartbreaking half hour when the river blooms with the rises of the day's best fish just as the light fails. Too many good fish, suddenly, the way you imagined it on the drive to the river. Eyeing the best rises within reach. Deciding where to cast as you enjoy the strong feel of the river rushing around you, through you, taking a part of you off with it.

Strange, what rivers do to consciousness. Lord knows what the fish are thinking.

Now it's June, and the fishing is getting tough again. The river is still flowing well, but it's thinning out, paring itself down to the bare essence of a trout stream. You can't hunker down and hide in the river anymore. You loom over it, and the fish can see you coming. Feel you, too, when you stumble on the rubble of the riverbed, cussing yourself as you visualize all the trout in front of you for a hundred yards darting for cover. All the easy lies have disappeared, those windows of slick water where you popped bushy dry flies in April. A hard-running, thigh-deep riffle through which you swung wet flies is now shin-deep frog water. The boisterous white water that hid your approach to the chutes and deeps at the heads of pools has subsided. The structure of a river, from a trout's point of view, is a matter of flow. As a river thins into summer, its currents become transparent, invisible. You can see everything and nothing. The river bottom is clear but, as Heraclitus pointed out, the river bottom is not the river. The river has changed and the fish have moved. In April and most of May, you can present a dry fly to the river,

prospecting for nymphing trout easily distracted by its appealing silhouette. But in June the gullible fish are gone or wiser.
Fat Tuesday is way downstream. The party's over.

Sulfurs save trout fishermen in early June. Not the large yellow
mayfly, *Ephemerella invaria,* but the little beauty, *Ephemerella
dorothea,* delicate as its name. Fly fishing, of course, is an affair
of flies. And although caddis and stonefly imitations bail out
many a fishing day, the essence of fly fishing is and has always
been the art of catching trout with imitations of adult mayfly
duns. It might be fair to say that the day you start distinguish-
ing, without much thinking about it, between *invaria* and *dorothea,* is the day you become a fly fisherman. Once you've sailed
across that line, you are pretty far gone and as keyed in to things
as a birder who can parse a field sparrow and a chipping sparrow
at a glance, or a tree lover who knows a mockernut hickory from
a shellbark before the fruit is on the trees.

What fills your sails is the fact of the hatch, the subtle way
dorotheas appear on the water in the evening, as if blown there
by the breeze. You notice one sailing by and then another. Then
a handful together on a yard of stream. The first flies seem
to take a while to get off the water. They trace for you those
nuances of current you couldn't see all day long no matter how
hard you stared at the river. The silent music of their emergence
builds quickly to a sustained, understated climax—five or ten or
maybe twenty minutes of sulfurs coming off the water upstream
and down with the kind of regularity the eye and mind of a
fisherman can keep up with. "Pale evening duns," these insects
are commonly—and poetically—called. The pinky-wide yellow beauties are the platonic form of the mayfly, their diapha-
nous yellow wings as pale as the pale evenings into which they
disappear. Unless, of course, a plump trout should slurp that

diaphanousness down before *dorothea* takes flight. That unpo-
etic slurp is at the center of those riseforms that set up some
fine, if difficult, fishing.

Every June I backpack into the best water on the Jefferson
to catch the sulfur hatch. As backpacking goes, this is an easy
gig, a mile or so of level trail to a flat rise I like on a big bend
of the river. I can make several trips and even shoulder a small
cooler downriver to camp if I want some luxuries—venison,
fresh fruit and vegetables, eggs, bacon, fresh bread. Not exactly
a wilderness experience. More like extended car camping than
backpacking, I suppose, but I've eaten my share of ramen
noodles and dehydrated food. I trust my truck despite the van-
dals who seem to prefer the gleaming, late-model SUVs and
spic-and-span Honda Civics that have become fashionable at
the trailhead. There is something to be said for Old Ironsides'
missing hardware and body rust. My fourteen-year-old F-150
is a truck you could easily love but not quickly sell. I'll sleep
on the river for two nights, fishing for the better part of three
days and be pretty woolly-brained by the time I leave, more on
account of the river than the fish. This will be the last good trout
fishing until late September. I fish hard and well, if I do say so,
because it's the time of year for that.

I make camp on a bend of the river. Something in the back
of the human mind draws us to river bends. A sense of security
and comfort and company. There is something eerie about the
featureless middle of the woods—as if we were on an equal footing with animals there, too much in the thick of things without
being equipped for that. Given our relatively poor senses, an
equal footing puts us at a distinct disadvantage—something I
feel keenly when I am hunting. In the middle of the woods, you
don't know where to look, even when you are not looking for

anything. Life is hidden in the open, every bird and branch a purloined letter that eludes your attention because there is too much to see. You don't know where to rest your gaze, and that is unsettling. The depths of a true forest are as directionless as deep space. Steps in any direction don't seem to make a difference. When I get in what's left of old growth, I feel that way, a feeling I enjoy only in small doses.

A river is as good as a topo map and a compass. When you are on a river, there are only four directions in the woods: upstream, downstream and over one ridge or the other to an adjacent watershed, where another meandering stream waits, purling over rocks toward some near or distant rendezvous with another river. If you fashioned yourself a short-masted dugout with outriggers and threw in a little ocean travel with the help of the stars, you could find your way around the world that way. Of course, that's exactly how human beings did find their way around the world.

This is big talk for a guy camped a mile or so downstream of his truck, but the woods, thank God, are still the woods, and they work on your mind the way the woods have always worked on the human mind. In many respects, a night or two sleeping out on the Jefferson is no different than the nights I slept alongside the Kos'yu in Russia. Same planet digging into my shoulder blades. Same universe outside the tent flaps. Same gravity drawing the river along. I'm confident that, if pressed to do it, I could make my way from this bluff of hemlocks on the Jefferson to that first camp on the upper Kos'yu tucked into the alders and dwarf birch and pine with the uninviting lower slopes of Gora Narodnaya brooding all around us. Of course, that camp was on a riverbed, too, and I wouldn't doubt that men and women have been poking fires at both places for ten thousand years, if not longer. And fishing, hard and well, whenever it was the time of year for that.

You could do worse than wake up on any river bend in early June. Here on the Jefferson, daybreak is pleasantly uneventful. I don't need an alarm clock to get up around five A.M. at home, but for some reason I sleep late in the woods. More like a healthy critter, I guess, than a man pressing himself to accomplish something. In the woods, time accounts for itself. Go with the drift of things along a river and you can get pretty close to the pure practice of being alive.

Wealth comes to you effortlessly in the morning on a riverbed. Birdsong. Fawn bleat. Turkey gabble or grouse drumming. Otters sleek with disappearance. Waterfowl skimming by—mallards flying low, Canada geese high, the occasional pair of wood ducks a colorful, eye-level blur. Great blue herons a study in studiousness. Green herons cranky as the pileated woodpeckers that give your presence away to the thrushes at the water's edge and the warblers in the canopy.

Variations on the theme of morning light play from the pale sky into the canopy and down the trunks of stout oaks and hickories into an understory of rhododendron and mountain laurel. I used to try to photograph this play of light, but as photographers know, you take pictures *with* light, not *of* it. Unless you are willing and able to recover in a darkroom or on a computer screen what you think you remember of what you saw, your images will be lacking the soul of a scene best *taken,* if that is the word, by your consciousness of the experience. Light not only makes life possible, it makes it interesting, whether it's scattered in the crown of a white oak or gathered in the unspeakably delicate bowl of a laurel flower. The *Kalmia* is in bloom in early June and along some stretches of the river so unapproachably beautiful as to be almost a visual nuisance. Of course, if you want to fish well, you've got to ignore all this, but it's pretty nice to have that luxurious bloom to ignore along with a fugue of birdsong for background noise.

Being on a river for a few days brings out the best in most anglers. There is more than enough time to try every clever stratagem you planned to try, but that's the least of it. There is time for things to happen that you don't expect, gifts and challenges that make the day, that make you a better fisherman regardless of whether you succeed or fail. If you are a human being as well as a fisherman, not all of this is about fishing. You take your character afield with you, and fishing well or poorly has an edge to it. Mostly I try to enjoy casting along that beguiling, watery seam between what I know and what I don't know about the river in front of me. That's where the trout are, egging you on like grouse or deer hidden in the woods, like the voluble birds and silent stars you can't identify. Rising to rises, or to the absence of rises, is the way the game of fly fishing is played.

Feeling flush with fishing possibilities that first morning, I may just watch the brief, early-morning spinner fall sitting on the gravel bar eating the kind of heart-stopping breakfast I deny myself at home—pancakes, eggs, bacon, endless cups of burned coffee. I don't stop to wonder how a liquid can get burned, but wood fires burn coffee every time and the tang of it is as much a part of the outdoors as the sweet scent of broken birch twigs or the funky odor of wood smoke wafting through the air.

The river sweeps left to right from where I'm sitting, bending away from me, digging a deep run against the far bank. That steep bank prevents anyone from fishing the opposite side, and that dark run carved into the bedrock by centrifugal force is the kind of promising water I dream about at home. Drink too much burned coffee and you'll think you see the broad back of a significant trout hanging six inches below the surface. Take another sip and you'll see it shift a bit to left or right, rising a bit with each feint, the trout's gape winking slightly, and then drop back into its original position. Small trout are rising here and there, slapping at flies with an energy-wasting enthusiasm that betrays their unhoned instincts. Such antics don't interrupt a good breakfast. But that big trout taking an insect emerging through the water column argues for setting down the coffee cup and crawling carefully off the gravel bar.

A really good caster could approach this fish from downstream, throwing a long, curving reach cast such that the fly line stayed out of the trout's view and the fly led the tippet into the feeding lane with that critical moment of drag-free float you need to close the deal. But that's a tall order. Especially since you only have one shot at it. Knowing my limitations, I sneak off upstream through camp with a humbler plan in mind. I come back down the river, keeping low, eventually crawling again to a kneeling position well out of the trout's field of vision. I've got a tiny pheasant-tail nymph—the most delicate suggestion of an insect in my fly box—tied to the end of a three-foot-long gossamer tippet and another nine feet of transparent leader. Fly fishing for big, selective fish is about almost not quite being attached to the fly you present. That tippet is an interesting compromise of strength for secrecy. I keep my casting motion low over the river to my right, the fish being downstream left. I make one short cast to get the measure of the distance. I can no longer see the fish, but I marked his spot carefully against the bank.

The idea is to swing the fly in front of the holding trout with just enough slack in the tippet to fool the fish but not so much I can't quickly set the hook. This is far from ideal, since a fly swinging through the current is not at all like an emerger rising through the water column. But the compromise in tactics is the cost of the limits of my casting. Fair enough. If I haven't stimulated any other suspicions in the feeding fish, it may tolerate that one anomaly and suck the bug down. My first cast to the spot brings the take I imagined, a tap that becomes a tug. But my attempt to set the hook is blunted by the slack I threw into the leader to get a realistic float. When I pump the rod a second time, I feel the fish, momentarily. Through the arching graphite I can just begin to sense the weight and fight in it, an unmistakable fire in its stiffening resistance. And then nothing. Or worse than nothing. The absence of the presence of a fish, not a deconstructionist conundrum but a big trout touched and lost. Somehow I could feel the weight of the thing in the slack, the trace of what lawyers call "negative history," facts no longer relevant to the case. *Damn!*

I'll spend the rest of the day making up for that miss and, by the time of my evening fire, be more grateful to have touched the wildness of a trout like that than disappointed I didn't bring the fish to hand. Success afield is sweeter for the missed connections—the outraged trout that frees itself, the grouse that flushes perfectly screened, the deer that winds you and walks the other way—assuming you have enough success to assuage these disappearances. What matters is the fire in the river and the fire on the ridges and in the woods, the fire of your being there in the river, on the ridges, in the woods. Although I would have preferred to have seen that fine trout, clear and real—felt the riverine heft of it—and started the day with a classy, one-cast triumph, I'll be content, poking the fire in the evening, to leave it hang there six inches below the surface of my consciousness, shifting a bit in the current, gape winking slightly.

The short-term effect of the miss, of course, is much muttering and some profanity.

Since I'm up, I fish on. Casting encourages casting. The off-beat rhythm of fly casting is the metronome of the fly fishing day, the pronounced pause on the back cast contrapuntal to the incessant melody of rushing water. Eager as you may be to fly-fish, you won't be able to cast until you learn to pick your line up briskly and then pause, rod high, while the line straightens out behind you. Although that pause is merely part of the physics of fly casting—you are waiting on one of Newton's laws—the requirement to wait, poised but momentarily doing nothing, is the fulcrum of the cast. Fail to wait and your fly line will meet itself coming and going, snapping or wind-knotting in protest. Wait too long and it will collapse behind you, deflated by a loss of Newtonian zing. You can cheat the length of the pause with a deft haul or two that increases line speed and decreases the wait, but that pause will be there like a musical rest without which the music, fore and aft, doesn't quite work. The entire fishing day is built around those pauses. The fact of it—the right arm gathered shoulder to fist just behind the right ear while you eye the slice of water where you want to see the fly appear—is as close to the essence of fly fishing as anything else you do all day.

I hook up with two of those smaller trout, rainbows, that were fooling around behind the fish I lost. Nice to play them for a few moments off the twitchy rod tip, but multiply their respective tussling together and you don't get anything close to the tippet-stretching fun the big fish would have provided for the morning's entertainment. But all trout count.

You take what wildness from a river you bring to it—that's

the measure of the day and of yourself. That's what you will
remember, reshuffled by your subconscious, at odd moments.
That's what you will dream years from now along some stretch
of strange, familiar water and on nights when you are far from
any river. The wildness is there in many forms without you, but
you must practice discovery to find it. Casting trout flies is part
of that—the hard work of fishing frees the watery back of the
mind the way the concentration of hunting sharpens awareness
of the woods.

If I hike downstream through the blooming mountain laurel a
half dozen river bends, I'll have enough good fishing to bring
me back to camp in time for the evening hatch and spinner
fall. River bends make rivers, playing out useful local wrinkles
in the space-time continuum, a poor man's wormhole, if you
will. They are the hardest places to fish, because their underlying
structure is so jumbled, but river bends spill into pools set up
as clearly with trout lies as billiard tables are with pockets, or
fan out into forgiving riffles where some methodical searching
will get you into trout. There is no finer local horizon to have
all day than a bend of a river downstream of you and another
up ahead. For those of us who love rivers, there is a comfortable
feel to the gestalt of that scene. No matter how precipitous the
ridges or cliffs are on either side of you, being between river
bends seems safe and secure in a way that does not forestall the
exciting possibilities in the river itself. Even a limestone stream
wound through a dead-flat pasture shapes the space around it
into something homey and centered.

I break the woods on my way downriver, which is to say my
walking through scatters things, including a grouse and her
new brood. A bit of gabbling and peeping suddenly becomes

a confusing scatter in the leaf litter along the river side of the trail. It's odd, the way your consciousness gathers sensations in the morning, slowly decoding whatever is happening around you. When I stop, the hen appears, spreading and slapping her wings, hopping on the bare, dusty ground ten feet in front of me, puffed up a bit and, in its way, impressive as a bear. Then she crosses the trail and slowly struggles up the opposite slope, wing-dragging a bit, although not as theatrically as I have seen some grouse do that. By the time she is twenty yards away, the lively, mottled chicks are as silent and hidden as quail-sized chunks of dead wood.

I scatter other birds walking downriver, but my mind is on the fishing. The woods are lavish in the morning, spendthrift with detail. When you are on your way to fish, it's fine to ignore all that flutter and scurry, take the brightening woods for granted. Part of fishing seriously is taking all that in passing. Down in the Smokies, I've walked by black bear with hardly a glance when I was headed off to fish a good pool I knew. Of course, a bear preoccupied with something important will hardly glance at me, and I take no offense at that. To nonanglers, the itch to fish is unfathomable and the focus of fishermen, I'm told, a little bizarre. But, walking alongside a river in the morning with a fishing vest stuffed with a day's provisions on my back and a fly rod in hand, I'm happy in a way that is both simple and complex. Five centuries of fishing books have tried to explain this. I just know that my stride feels different when I'm off to fish, purposeful and truant at the same time.

I eye the river as I walk. The water slides opaquely along the shaded far bank, making the river there seem deeper than it is. The dark flow rumples silkily around rocks and piles thickly into logjams, burbling in the throaty way of heavy water. I know there are good trout in the humming riffles and beneath the gunmetal slicks of pocket water upstream and downstream of the big rocks. There are deep, complicated runs where the river makes sweeping turns against sheer cliffs of monumental bedrock and long pools that hide the flow of the river in perfect stillness. Sunlight turns the near half of the river transparent, making it seem shallow from the height of the trail. I can see small fish lying over gravelly depressions in riffles and begin to guess where the better trout are. Big trout, like big deer, don't stand around waiting to be admired. They spend their entire lives, every ounce of energy and wit of consciousness, shying away from every false move around them. You fish and hunt against the intensity of that desire to never be seen. Where the river is transparent, I can see where such fish might be but not the fish themselves. You have to fish for that.

Once I'm knee-deep in the river, time becomes the day itself, the way I believe time seems to animals. Between the moment I tie the first fly on and the moment when I unjoint the rod, I don't feel the minutes and hours. There's the rushing water keeping me braced all day, as if the hours had some extra force in them, and the slight pressure of sunlight on my shoulders. On a river, you feel time deeply, that thrum of mountains and waters. The river takes care of time the way the woodlots at home tend my hours.

I start in a good riffle where I know I can catch fish. I tie on a small whitetail caddis—a tuft of Highland Farm—and cover the water in front of me, sidling a few steps across the river after every few casts. Small rainbows take in the bright water, but the dark water seems empty. Nymphs find trout there, larger rainbows and stubborn, fourteen-inch brown trout that have a serious feel to them when they get in the current. The finest moment in playing modest-sized fish is when they make that turn downriver. Surprised by the set of the hook, most trout will bore upstream for a few moments. The resistance of the rod triggers the downstream run that brings the contest to life. A decent fish on a downstream run feels like the river itself—what Heraclitus couldn't quite get a handle on. If there are essences in nature, trout are the essence of cold flowing water, and the thrilling fight of a good trout downstream of you is as close as anyone gets to arm-wrestling the river gods.

After I've caught a half dozen trout, my fishing metabolism settles down. You are not fishing until you start catching. Although my gaze rarely strays from the water for more than a moment or two, I'm willing to eye the scurrying of a water-thrush along the muddy near-side bank or glance at the dancing flight of a pair of swallowtails. Everything you see in the woods sharpens your eye and mind. When you are standing in a river, all that quickness around you, the keen energy of living things, seems to emanate from the river itself, as if sunlight and rushing water were the source of everything in the watershed.

On a long day on the water there are many forms of fishing to be done. The flow and structure of the river dictates how long and fine a tippet I knot onto my leader. Every blood knot has a thought behind it, a stratagem as clever as the coils of the knot itself. A true fisherman ties knots well, briskly like a sailor but without any apparent hurry. To the novice angler, the blood knot is a fumbly chore, an impossible arpeggio performed in midair with monofilament. Watch a seasoned angler and you'll see her studying the river as her fingers spin the neat barrels of the knot until she nips one tag end in her teeth to pull it taut. Like the pause in the back cast, the time it takes to fashion a trim blood knot creates time, moments good fishermen use to advantage. The bulging rise you spy with the knot in your teeth may be the fish of the day.

I work a lot of water with that small, dark caddis cast on a long tippet that lays it on the slowly moving slicks as if my fake bug were part of God's Plan. Sometimes a puff of wind will catch it just before it alights, creating the illusion that my caddis might fly away. Once it gets into the flow, the fly is hard to see, and I have to guess its progress toward me and strike at anything that looks like a take in the line of its drift. There is far more guesswork in fishing than hunting, which is more a matter of narrowing down the odds until you are sure of what you see. Fishing is a school of trial and error. Deer walk in the world with you, and although grouse disappear through the air, they start out, fair and square, on the forest floor. Fish are hidden and, more often than not, have to be divined, teased or enticed into joining in a fray with the angler.

Give yourself over to it and a river leads you to the fish. After I work a long riffle and the head of the pool that creates it, I clamber up the jumble of a river bend where trout wait in impossible places, deep pockets where it's tough to work a fly. I cut the leader back and tie on a weighted streamer, plunking the big fly into the white water that swirls it down into the deep green slots. But the runs are short and the fly rarely ever gets deep enough for the choice fish tucked out of sight on the river bottom. Still, you've got to work the water.

Every long pool is an invitation to start life over—fishing is more than a tad forgiving, which is maybe why a lot of us keep fishing. I'll build the leader back to something long and fine and work the deeper bank along the rear of a pool, especially if a fallen sycamore or spill of boulders breaks the flow up into what might be feeding lanes. What makes you a fisherman over time

is being interested in the same things as fish. Being in a river gets
you thinking like a fish. That's the real release. Of course, those
toothy sycamores eat more of my flies than the sullen brown
trout that lurk around them guarded by a picket of branches.
But the trout are there. I'll set up across and upstream from
where I imagine a big, frothy take will swirl around the fly and,
casting long, drift a small nymph in as near as I dare until I hook
up solid with *Platanus occidentalis* and ruin the lie.

A fly fisherman's interest in a pool increases inversely to
the square of his distance from the prime lies at the head of
it. Different anglers have different ways of sidling up to good
water. In June on the Jefferson I like to stay in the shadows along
the west bank as long as I can. If the spot looks choice, I'll stand
and watch for a while, being careful not to shuffle around or
flick flies away from my face. I'll resist the itch for a snack. This
standing in the shadows watching the head of a pool during the
last good week of the early season is perhaps the finest fishing
of the year.

For me, today, on this stretch of the Jefferson, I like that the
river is organized around trout, which seem—when you are
knee-deep in the fishing, wet to the butt—to be a direct consequence of rushing water and bedrock, more an effect of friction
than a product of evolution. The heft of a fourteen-inch trout is,
by my measure, about halfway between the density of rock and
water—solid and energetic, strong and wild, dead-sure tangible
but fine as something dipped in myth. That is why every trout
a fisherman brings to hand seems as strange as it is familiar and
why the most jaded angler gazes at each wild fish with unstinting admiration. That's why after you release a trout, you put on
a fresh fly, walk ten steps upriver and start false-casting out line,
thinking ahead into the river.

In the middle of the day you are more likely to see trout nymphing near the bottom of the river than rising to the surface. Watch for a while and you will see their bellies flashing with the twist of each take. Here and there an adult mayfly will drift along, barely denting the meniscus, executing nature's idea of a drag-free float—an intimidating thing to see. Living flies twist and quiver and turn, flashing small shards of reflected light about, throwing tiny shadows around themselves. My well-tied imitations look good in hand, but they do not dance with life. Even so, you can watch real mayflies sailing along unmolested for thirty yards upstream and down, of no interest to the trout chowing down on the stream bottom.

That tongue of water at the head of a good pool, a perfect half oval of possibilities, is the *mise-en-scène* of trout fishing, although I don't think the how-to books use that term. But it's a stage set for good angling nonetheless, and it's where the heart of a good day on a good river shows itself. A broad wall of whitewater slants down a slab of tilted bedrock, pillows for five yards behind a long, river-wide ledge and then spills over the ledge, breaking up in rocky rubble before fanning out downstream toward me.

That green water behind the ledge will be tough to fish well, but the long fringe of white water is prime for a big rainbow, if there is a big rainbow around. The fan of white water turning every shade of green as it loses velocity offers a lot of possibilities, as if the current gave up an opportunity with each quantum of force it lost. I can't resist starting with a small dry fly, a little Adams that might be a lot of things that are on the water—gnats and little black stoneflies and some small mayfly—a little *baetis,* I would guess.

While wading slowly toward the downstream edge of the

oval, I work out line by false-casting behind me in order to keep the motion beyond sight of where I think the fish are. Then I start shooting casts, covering the near water first, as all fishermen do, enjoying the way the fly line loops forward with authority, unfurling the leader pretty as you please. Then a fly I tied one ordinary evening at home floats along one of those enticing seams of current bringing a good fish to the surface at every wild juncture in its drift back toward me. Or so it seems.

If I take my time and play the fish downstream, I can catch a half dozen trout from the fan of green water. That's a good part of the day—those fish coming up to close the connection make the fishing seem like fishing, putting a little strain in my grip on the cork. On the Jefferson, that will be four decent rainbows and two smaller brown trout. That's not to brag. That's what fly fisherman do with the heads of pools, at least on the rivers they know well. I'll make maybe sixty casts for those fish, enjoying each cast equally. Today I find four fish in that green water, two rainbows on the dry fly, and a brown and a rainbow on a pheasant-tail.

The recent rain has made more heavy water than I thought I would encounter and renders my admirably efficient fly box inadequate. Wading within close casting range of that whitewater, I'd love to tie a buoyant humpy or some other early-season fly, but they were purged for the year three weeks ago. An elk-hair caddis will have to do, but it doesn't. Not quite, anyway. A green oval slick in the middle of the whitewater is the choice spot in this twenty-five-yard stretch of river. And sure enough, my caddis turns a good trout there, a big rainbow come up for a look. Once.

Turning big trout once is the royal road to insanity. Quick as it is, the flush of a grouse happens in real time in the real world.

Even when you can't see it, you can hear and feel the wing whir, and besides, the dog is there to confirm that, at least in this particular, you are not crazy. Walk carelessly up on a big deer and you may curse your stupidity for missing sign, but you won't doubt your senses as it crashes off into your dream life. But that log of a rainbow that just arced up under my caddis fly, that beauty came out of another realm and, when it disappeared, left me standing knee-deep in a river spiked with equal measures of doubt and desire. Better to pretend you never saw it.

Maybe a bigger dry fly would have made matters worse, but I thought I might tease the rainbow out of there like a salmon, although, come to think of it, I've never caught a salmon. I told myself not to do it, but I stupidly flogged the water with the caddis, childishly hoping to re-create an event that I knew was already downstream of me. My antics weren't going to move the trout, but big fish neurons were firing off in my brain like someone had dropped a cigar in a fireworks factory.

Grouse and deer don't ever come back, but big trout don't have as much choice. That spot in the river was not going anywhere. I finally reeled in and waded to the bank for lunch. Fishermen tend to eat lunch either where they have had a triumph or where they have left unfinished business. Hunger has nothing to do with it. If they look a little ticked off as they munch away, they are not yet finished with the water at their side.

To a trout fisherman, trout define rivers. They mark those places where the idea of a river deepens and widens and something coalesces which suddenly gives the angler access to recesses and attributes of riverness that would otherwise be beyond reach and remain unknown. Which is not to say that the river is not wide or deep enough in its own right. Only that we cannot bring the river itself to hand. As my ancient friend

Heraclitus noted, it slips through our fingers every time. We can drink from the river, of course, but we cannot feast directly on it, lick its sweet bones clean as a whistle.

Trout have come to embody the wildness of rivers, the fire in them, and Heraclitus, you will remember, was a philosopher of fire not of water, his catchy comment about not stepping in the same river twice the least of what he said and the most misunderstood. This idea about trout is a conceit, of course, but if you have ever brought a feisty, wild trout to hand, you will agree the conceit works pretty damn well in practice. You could just as easily admire the stately schools of black-nose dace or, for that matter, organize your worship around the virtues of the loggerheaded chub. Or you might go full-bore transcendental like *roshi* Dōgen himself and satisfy yourself with a handful of pearly, water-worn gravel as the thing you seek in rivers. But I'm no more seeking purity in fishing than in hunting, where the death of an animal forces me to fess up to who and what I am. When I spend a day on a river, I want to get tight to a trout as often as possible, feel the river in each wild fish before I let it go.

I assume the river is well rested when a great blue heron flaps upstream, although that big silhouette may well make the fish skittish all over again. When you see birds behaving with unconcern about your presence, you are seeing nature as undisturbed as you will see it. I don't augur their bones, but birds are a sign that things are well. I bet there are ten thousand people whose minds are distinctly chilled by the phrase "silent spring" for every one who has read Rachel Carson's great book. The genius of the phrase will do—that timely if still unheeded suggestion of the profound emptiness of a world without birdlife.

I start over from downstream, nymphing carefully into the heavy water, pretending I am not headed for that one spot where I turned the big rainbow. Then I stand in the rocky rubble to the left of the heart of things and swing a soft hackle through at every angle I can devise, repeating the operation with a dun streamer and then a flashy one. I feel that telltale knock and set the hook a hundred times in my mind's eye, but the river just sweeps my flies through.

I finally give up that well-worn spot in the river and move on through the afternoon. I catch one nice native brook trout just below where a cool trib tumbles into the river, something that's happened before in the same place. First time it happened, I explored up along the tiny watercourse, hoping to find a pool or two worth fishing. I've spent a lot of time over the years following the traces of these little streams toward their source. It's a habit of mountain fishermen—poking around on the odd chance that there is something hidden in the landscape. Of course, there always is—a grove of old-growth poplar, a bobcat den, a timber rattler that may never before have coiled up for a human being. It's rarely trout I find, but the streambed affords me a safe place to walk and shows me the way back.

By late afternoon, I've fished my way back to camp pleasantly worn down to my best fishing self—sharp-eyed, surefooted, long to look and slow to cast. I drag the sleeping pad out to the gravel bar and rest for a half hour, my thoughts even and easy as the flow of the river, cool as the beer I sip. The evening breeze ruffling downstream eventually turns into a rattling kingfisher, which gets me to my feet. *Last call.* I head upstream to some syrupy water I've already scouted, where I wait for those *dorotheas* to pop to the surface and float toward me as buoyant as mountain laurel flowers. Pale evening duns. As good an idea as anything in nature.

I'll fish the rises in that easy, early-evening light, watch the water get complicated with a spinner fall and a hatch of what I guess are midges. In the end, I'll tie the smallest no-hackle sulfurs I've got to a tippet I can't see on the water. I like the way fly fishing extends, at the end of a long day, toward the finest refinement of wanting to touch something wild in the river, some strong, head-shaking consequence of flowing water. Izaak Walton and all the others who have written about fishing through the centuries are dead right: love of fishing makes sense.

I'd rather camp with company, but few people I know are on my feckless schedule. And Patch has to be left home because it is neither responsible nor legal to have a bird dog charging around after grouse out of season. And, out of spite, I think, he doesn't mind me when I'm fishing. Absent conversation, the murmuring of a fire against the *shush*ing of flowing water will do. A few nights in the woods every season puts me in touch with the frank continuity rivers offer. Backcountry nights serve as a useful counterpoint to the sense of home I have cultivated on Highland Farm. On the banks of the Jefferson, I can roast small new potatoes and grill a venison sirloin steak while I munch on mulberries, poke the fire while supper cooks and, listening to the river, imagine I have gotten somewhere.

Get settled into an evening in what's left of the backcountry along what's left of a river and the truth is you will suddenly see no wildness in the woods. Perhaps the wildness of animals is the measure of their fear of us, something in civilization and not in nature. Perhaps nature, in its essence, is the way Charles Darwin found it on the Galapagos—frighteningly tame and vulnerable.

Perhaps the wildness of our most haunting landscapes is just the strange otherness of the universe seen up close—the intimidating horizonlessness of a desert, the dark closure of a forest, the sudden steep airiness of a canyon. Out in nature, we are surrounded by what astrophysicists call event horizons—the edges of energy taking a sharp turn—a spill of water over rock, the dark forms of ducks hustling upstream, stars winking beyond a skyline of trees.

I'd be a better fisherman if I fished new water more often. In front of a fire I always think about Russia and the Kos'yu, the farthest place I've been. I can picture the wild upper river well—the whitewater, the shallow riffles full of grayling and those dark, moody mountains. I remember bringing my first grayling to hand right off the bar where the helicopter left us, the brilliant dorsal of the fish improbable as a wildflower. Perhaps Valery and his brethren are fishing now, for fun and food, enjoying a subarctic spring laced at night with green sheets of borealis dancing high in the northern horizon like they danced the last night we were on the river.

The night after we returned to Inta, I had dinner with Valery and his wife, Katerina. The apartment blocks in Inta have that awful Soviet look-—housing out of Kafka's worst nightmare. But in Russia, behind each gray metal door you find a world of warmth, food and friendship like the apartments in Brooklyn I remember from my childhood, from which emanated a constant clatter and chatter and the odors of fabulous cooking.

Russian homes are packed with books and music and photographs. There is a good deal to trust in that. Old and honored keepsakes glow from the shelves. After the rough life on the river, this homey hospitality was most welcome, and although Valery and Katerina, both teachers, spoke little English and I

spoke very little Russian, we managed the kind of honest conversation that goes with good eating and drinking. Valery let
me admire a beautifully mounted capercaillie, a turkey-sized
grouse of the Russian north, he had taken one year up along the
Kos'yu. But he was most eager to show me his books—Dreiser,
Hemingway, Jack London, as well as a full set of what I know
from the frontispieces was Dickens alongside his half yard of
Tolstoy and beautifully bound volumes of Pushkin set out on
their own between heavy, well-oiled bookends. After dinner,
Katerina sang Komi folk songs, while Valery accompanied her
on a guitar with a well-worn sounding board, and after that we
drank and joked incomprehensibly while Billie Holiday sang
through the crackles of an old record.

So what was wild on that long excursion from home? Or
what wasn't wild? The rainbow dorsal of a grayling? The brooding Urals? The quicksilver river? Green sheets of borealis? That
wonderful home behind the awful gray door? My Russian
friends' love of life? A familiar opening line of Dickens set in
Cyrillic type? Or the sweet sounds of Billie Holiday's tragic
gaiety wafting, sad and triumphant, through the stifling air of
an old gulag town? Event horizons all.

The ancient Greek philosopher was right. *Everything flows.*
Everything matters.

Good rivers, like good lives, are unfinished business. Even
this stretch of the Jefferson, which I've worn out with my presence the way I've worn trails into the woodlots of Highland
Farm, is full of unfinished business. There's a big trout upstream
and downstream of camp and all the riffs and runs which, in
retrospect, I'd fish a little differently than I fished them today.
There are all the people I would bring to the river, if I could, to
show them what I see—or don't see—there.

Carl Jung reminds us that from ancient times a river has been known as a " 'valley spirit,' the water dragon of Tao, whose nature resembles water." Water not only finds a way—hence those river bends and riffles and pools—it is the life-giving way on earth, Tao of everything we know, a fiery thing at heart. The comfort of being on a river is the comfort of being in an ancient place, a place where you somehow left a part of yourself—not last trout season, but a thousand or ten thousand years ago. In Jung's deep-flowing thought, the thrill and comfort of being on a river is also vestige of an ancient itch, an encounter with an archetype of human experience that transcends our individual lives, a transpersonal experience Heraclitus, a good river man himself, was thinking about twenty-five hundred years ago. Rivers have been showing human beings the way for hundreds of thousands of years and our hominid cousins for a million or two. Birds and animals have understood the importance of rivers for much longer than that. It would be quite surprising if rivers didn't run deep in us, turn our heads at every turn, bring us back.

When the news fools chatter on television about the human genome, they miss the point. I don't need to hear they have unlocked the secrets of fingers and toes so that some biotech firm can clone more movie stars or athletes. I want to hear that they have found imprints of the Tigris and Euphrates in our genes, some trace evidence that we all fished with vine nets in the mist of Victoria Falls, speared lions in the tall grass growing in the warm mouth of Ngorongoro. I want to hear they have found the blackened stones of fire rings, heaps of *débitage* from tool-making and all the old masks we wore as we evolved into the strangely beautiful and strangely destructive creature we have become. The river bend my fire lights doesn't appeal to the mind because it is picturesque; river bends appeal to us because they kept our Stone Age ancestors from going stark-raving mad with a sense of homelessness in an unspeakably vast universe.

A river is also a place where a part of yourself dwells that you can't take with you. Stay long enough on a river and you will slip into its mesmerizing otherness like an otter so fluid it barely parts the water through which it swims. The otter, the kingfisher, the water snake. They are all you. In some respects a better part of yourself than you will ever fully know. The caddis and stoneflies are you. Hatching mayflies, genius of the river, are your bright thoughts. The trout you catch or don't catch is you, its wildness yours. That's why the release is such a relief, such a gain. That's why fishing is so easy and hunting so hard.

Night on the river, poking the fire, you wait for something to happen—owl hoot, deer come through the rhododendron, river sound shift unaccountably from its minor key to its relative major, flutter of a nightjar, maybe. Or nothing happens. Night happens. Time flowing in the dark.

*Y*oung-of-the-year cliff swallows skid in the air as they practice flight over the Maury River on an ordinary evening in early July. I'm river-walking upstream, wet-wading the warm, soft-flowing water of a southern summer river so that I can fish my way back during the last half hour of daylight. Fishing home, I guess you'd call it.

A river walk in summer is as much about birds as fish. A cedar waxwing skitters low over the water and comes to rest in a syca-more, from which it surveys its options. Odd to see one alone. By the time I've jotted down its presence, the bird is gone. Something calls "getaway, getaway, getaway" in a bright, liquid voice I don't recognize. A downy woodpecker climbs an elm. An eastern pewee appears in the dappled light of a box elder, tail-bobbing and peck-ing at a branch. The thin, sweet calls of other pewees add depth of field to the evening air. I note an unfamiliar warbler: "small, thin yellow body, dark eye-stripe, gray/brown wings with wing bars, long thin beak; clatters pleasantly." A blue-winged warbler by name, I figure out later at the desk, a little out of range according to the field guide. Black and white warblers stay busy high in the canopy, squeaking in the leaves. A kingfisher patrols past me, beak cocked to fish in its own fashion. Red-eyed vireos call from the dense foliage. Cardinals, finches and goldfinches break in and out of that green cover, in and out of the blue evening summer light. If it's not the songbirds it's the waterfowl, mallards with flotillas of young, geese low overhead or otters moving sleekly through pools or disappearing with a disjointed waddle up a muddy bank.

The summer river is a sensuous essence, its sluggish currents charged a bit by the thunderstorms that pepper its large watershed with freshets of warm rain. The deep pools on the river remain stolid and reflective of the deep stillness of summer, but those *afternoon downpours show up in thin bands of whitewater that dance downstream of rocky bends where the landscape pinches the riverbed and the river comes to life. Big bass can't be teased back to springtime feistiness by that enlivened flow, but their lesser brethren will hang downstream of those rocky funnels. Quartering streamers through the whitewater into the broad, dampening ripples is one of summer's easiest chores.*

Sometimes the bigger bass get active just near dark, ghosting around trailing enticing wakes. Hook a good one and you'll think you can hold the day in place through the arcing fly rod. But while you are playing the last fish of the day, time slips downriver. You can't see the bass, the sullen tug of which feels like a piece of the river you have snagged, a moment caught insisting to be released. The mystery gets off, or you release its mulish presence back to the dark water. Stand up, knees aching, and just upstream of you, deer materialize out of the woods and start crossing the river as if you weren't there.

Karst

foxes down foxholes sigh

    —JOHN BERRYMAN

Light is the way time travels.

Science tells me, and I believe it, that starlight is ancient. A universe far younger than its years greets our eyes at night. Deep space reveals deep time. Of course, time and space themselves converge, shifting guises at the event horizons of black holes, in the spiral arms of galaxies or along the silken edges of nebulae that dance like the borealis. Goosed by the speed of light squared, matter and energy improvise. It's all worth watching.

The Great Bear prowls in the north, over the barn. Dark-eyed Cassiopeia tilts above the cabin, her hair tangled in the Spanish oak, Andromeda a distinct smudge. On a hazeless night I can twist the galaxy next door into view with the same binoculars that help me parse sparrows in the hedgerows. I can't see the planets that astronomers have found there, but then I can't always see the sparrows, either. Or I can turn the seven Pleiades into an astonishing field of light, a heartening woodlot of blue giants and other species of stars, amazing against light-years of darkness that surround it and separate us.

This year the moon is near Venus and Saturn early in the morning in mid-July, near Aldebaran, the orange eye of Taurus. Just before dawn, Jupiter and Mercury rise over the Blue Ridge, which puts more than half the planets of our solar system in view from the back pasture, if I count the one I'm standing on, which I always do. At night, Mars is close, in the southern sky above Thunder Ridge where Patch and I hunt grouse.

If I had time, I would start a new mythology based on these conjunctions, but it's probably best not to take the larger motions of the universe too personally. Moonlight on my truck reveals only that it's time to sand the rust. Besides, there are enough mythologies, and they tend to be used poorly. I like things the way they are—tangibly mysterious, the known and unknown set out in the open side by side, bright matter and dark. Seems a fair challenge to the mind and heart. And I like the way deep time is revealed every night for free, and the way we are somehow far older than the ancient stars we see. Summer nights, I keep an eye on things not because I am in the market to buy, but because, as Wordsworth insisted, the universe is beautiful, starlight from any eon right as yesterday's rain.

The Chinese poet Li Po, a little tipsy, perhaps, embraced the Milky Way as a great river. That seems like a good idea. Patch is with me, coursing around in the dark, chasing whatever it is he chases when he runs full tilt after something I cannot see, some wild, mythological mixture of rabbit, woodchuck and kestrel that teases his nose and beckons in his mind's eye.

In summer, I cut Patch loose to run only in the relative cool of night. He would hunt grouse in hundred-degree heat if you let him, and die doing it. So I have to control his carousing in July and August, letting him burn off energy under the stars when he won't get heatstroke doing it. Even then, after ten minutes his panting gets louder than the distinct pounding of his galloping paws.

Bats scissor the air at night, adding their wing-twitching practice to the idea of flight. They remind me that the farm is hollow, the ground underneath vaulted with the darkness of limestone caverns. Deep time is stored underfoot as well as overhead. The geology of this hilly valley is known as karst, limestone of marine origin pocked with sinkholes and small dolines and other abrupt topographical interruptions caused by underground erosion, which makes Highland Farm a visually interesting place. You can't see the earth changing shape here, but the fact that the earth has a life of its own lies all around you in limestone outcrops ribbed with smooth, finger-wide grooves of *rillenkarren* and in exposures of smooth-skinned soapstone and the scattering of quartz and sandstone float lying about. Some of my best hunting places are miniature blind valleys where game trails are funneled together by tricks of fracture and differential erosion. I can see the worn path of many deer quartering a slope around rocky impasses in the woods, good places to wait, hidden in spicebush and buckthorn, with a longbow in hand.

I assume the years before I moved to Highland Farm were unusually wet. For the first year or two I lived here, I could hear a stream cascading beneath the back pasture after a hard rain—a dark, wild river flowing under the barn gate laving the twisting roots of the Spanish oak and the old walnut. I didn't understand the sound of it at first, but Patch heard it, too. We both cocked our ears one muddy afternoon until I recognized the muffled rush under us as just another stream in a world blessed with them. Since then summers have gotten hotter and drier, and I have not heard that dark cascade in years. But there is a world of rivers, or at least riverbeds, underneath us.

The art of summer is as subtle as the art of midwinter. The spring landscape invites you in bloom by bloom, bird by bird, spoiling you with constant arrival. The autumn woods release your eyes and mind from the beauty of the year leaf by leaf, educating you with a thousand departures. But the quiet fullness of summer days mirrors the quiet emptiness of winter when nothing seems to move through the woods except time itself.

Day dawns uneventfully in July, which is good for writing. Language flows better in the predawn dark. Even when you are only trying to do rough justice to the world you see every day, it helps to have the negative space of the predawn hours to work in, an hour or two when words have to glow on their own—or fail to glow—with the simple truth of things. The integrity of sentences seems important in the morning. Sounds odd, perhaps, but the first few moments in the life of a good sentence are critical and can't bear much distraction—or much competition from the reality to which they would do justice. For most of the day, the original mystery of language, from which writers secretly draw momentum, is not obvious. In the early morning, with the border between your conscious and subconscious still blurred by sleep, the relations of words and things are fluid, and it's possible that a writer may see something new between *oak* and oak, *hawk* and hawk, *dawn* and dawn. Best to try to catch hold of the underlying poetic of language before daybreak, with a metronome of crickets still keeping time at the edge of night, softly pulsing en masse until a wren announces, with one brief call, that the world you would imitate with words is back in business.

As it happened this year, I had nesting wrens at my shoulder all through June, a second clutch of Carolinas brewing in the canvas musette bag hung on a nail next to the warped, well-weathered drawing board on the front porch. The first clutch, laid in late April, went down the sleek belly of a rat snake, judging from the empty, only slightly disheveled nest I looked into one morning in late May. Snakes don't pull birds' nests apart. After they chase the adult off, they dine at their leisure. I've yanked a few blacksnakes out of bluebird boxes, just because I didn't want to watch them do their rude work, but generally I try not to play favorites among animals. Reptilian hunger is as sound as any other.

Nevertheless, I was glad to see the Carolinas try again in June. Their strong song announces perhaps a third of the dawns here in a given year. That's quite a service. Paul Ehrlich's invaluable *The Birder's Handbook* notes that the male has upward of forty songs. Sounds more like four hundred, but the point is they are vocal beyond our understanding of their need to be heard. Their superfluous singing sets a good example. Why should any art cease evolving? And who can say what is superfluous in art and nature? Scientists discover "useful" organisms and elements in hot-spring basins, rain forest canopies and ocean trenches nearly every month. Perhaps it's all useful, or perhaps our use of the word *useful* needs to be expanded. Perhaps the whole wild universe is one bare necessity—if we took the needs of everything into account. In any case, making more wrens seems to me to be a good idea.

On June 2, the same day I noted that deer antlers encased in gray velvet were starting to fork, four wren eggs appeared in a nest that had been rewoven and relined. A fifth materialized the next morning, and then the adults started sitting. I flicked on the porch light and peered into the nest each morning while coffee brewed. I'd find either five bluish, mottled eggs—turned differently each day, I finally noticed—or the dark form of a wren hidden in the shadows at the bottom of the musette bag. When a bird was on the nest, the bag looked empty at first, except for that strong eye stripe around which other features eventually resolved, most notably that profoundly wide eye—dark as anything in nature—and that stout, curved beak which, small as it was, still looked formidable and dangerous to my naked eye hovering six inches away from it. The fine character of birds is sometimes lost in their beauty. But I've seen no black bear or twelve-point buck with a stronger being than those wrens.

The adults spent more and more time on the nest as the month went on, until their presence was nearly continuous. Every hour or so the sitting bird would flit out of the bag. It, or its mate, would return and settle on the nest in five or ten minutes. I'd check the eggs each time, peering into the bag with a small flashlight. I got used to that routine and was pleasantly surprised each morning that the rat snake hadn't returned to clear out this thriving enterprise. I assumed it, or some other, would, but when I moved out to the front porch to continue work each morning around ten A.M., I found the nest unmolested.

The chicks began hatching out on the afternoon of the sixteenth, the first new wren preceding the others by many hours It took that extraordinarily vulnerable form we are all familiar with—and that especially amazes the eyes of children when they see the sight for the first time—a limp, pink inch or so of body with ungainly head and large eyespots, the barest suggestion of limbs, what looked like little more than a fleshy blood vessel for a neck and a small orange triangular beak. That first hatchling lay limp on the other eggs, heaving with the effort to be, shipwrecked in a universe that, among many other things, had left a small place for the theory and practice of wrens. After four hours, the first chick, still alone, had a faint tuft of down on its head and a bit on its rear. It was growing.

This was not what nature shows on television call the "miracle of birth"; this was the simple, complex fact of it—being taking root as a Carolina wren in the bottom of a moldy musette bag on my front porch with no background music other than the sound of a summer breeze tossing leaves in the nearby trees and the haggling of mockingbirds and cardinals in the multiflora.

The facts about the wrens sprouting at my side as summer began this year were easy enough to chronicle, although I imagine science has noted this with more precision than I did. By nine P.M. there was still just that one chick on the beachhead of the world, out under the stars, if you will, leaving me to speculate on the meaning of a scene that extended from that pulsing bit of pink wren to the faint smudge of Andromeda overhead three light-years away.

Two more new wrens were hatched out the next morning and the fourth was emerging, breaking through the tough, thin shell of its first world, when I looked into the nest with the day's first cup of coffee in hand. By midday, the fifth egg, which had been moved to the center of the nest, was still intact. By three P.M. on the eighteenth, the last wren hatched out—forty-eight hours from first to last. The five of them did not look like they were a match for the world during those first hours—not much more than thinly cauled heartbeats.

The hatchlings mostly slept and grew. Of course, growth at that stage of life is more like metamorphosis, changes that—if I remember my high school biology correctly—recapitulate millions of years of evolutionary guesswork about the best way to be a wren. There is only so much you can do inside an inch-long egg. The wing limbs, which were so inconsequential at hatching, quickly extend, acquiring a dark, scaly stripe from which the short quills of future feathers eventually grow. Those threads of neck thicken as the body fills out and sprouts tufts of down everywhere. Still the head is on its own for a while, too large to be moved by undeveloped muscles. All energy and effort seemed to go to the simple but critical act of opening those small beaks wide. The large eyespots responded to the flashlight beam, but I think perhaps to the warmth of it rather than the light.

Throughout the day, one adult remained on the nest while the other brought food, bits of insects at first—legs and wings and torsos—and then whole spiders, inchworms and small caterpillars. This chow took effect quickly and the chicks were soon all plump guts and eyes, stirred to hunger by hunger itself and, despite their vulnerability—still small enough to pass through the unhinged jaws of a rat snake—a force for much carnage among the insect population. They competed silently for the food that came, shifting their orange mouths about on bare stems of necks that grew stronger with the wavering effort to get noticed and fed.

By the nineteenth, feeding was nearly constant and nature's wisdom in stocking the world with a lot of insects became apparent. When I was at the drawing table working, the adults would come in to the nest with some wariness—stopping first on the chestnut rail fence and then on the cedar porch rail—but the job had to be done, and they soon accepted the neutrality of my interest in what they were doing.

By the solstice, a very thin peeping started up in the nest, faint even from only a foot or two away. Eyes were still closed—

no need for these taxed bodies to waste energy on seeing—but ear holes had appeared. Wing development proceeded and the expense of the specialization of flight was clear. You could see the painstaking work demanded by the idea of a bird's wing, those quills closing ranks and then evolving into finely vaned feathers.

The day the chicks started vocalizing I found a rat snake hatchling under the porch, seven inches of quarter-inch-thick basket weave terminating in a wedge-shaped head too large for its body. Its appearance suggested that adult rat snakes were pre-occupied with their own birthing and nursing responsibilities while the wrens were trying to succeed with this second clutch. Since science now thinks it likely that birds evolved from rep-tiles, this spacing between two now-disparate families augured well for the survival of both. The small snake was as strange and otherworldly lying in the palm of my hand, as were the young wrens calling weakly from the nest. Instinctively sensing perhaps that at this early stage in its life it was more bird food than a predator of birds, the small snake did not much care for being held up to the light of day. I set it back in the shadows where I found it.

These new summer beings grew and disappeared while I wrote. One of the wrens died and was dropped from the nest, possibly the late-hatching bird. Those preliminary beaks, use-ful only for opening wide, grew into the familiar curved beak of mature wrens, perfect tools for insect plucking. Eyes opened on the twenty-fourth, and the chicks focused on whatever came into view. Calls became stronger, a firmer reed starting to trill within the plaintive piping. The idea of feathers continued to emerge, gray quills appearing where only gray down had been, from the head down the spine. The wings, full of airy design, developed into something strong and light enough to support the idea of flight. The adults brought food constantly, not only spiders but the caches of food the spiders had wrapped and stored for their own young. There was now no longer any room in the nest for an adult. They brought food and left, of use to their warm, growing young only out in the larger world, where they hunted with remarkable efficiency and success.

On the twenty-fifth, the nest looked roughed-up and two of the wrens were missing, perhaps another toll taken by snakes on their evolutionary descendants. The two fledglings that had survived most of a month were now standing in the nest looking as defensive and threatening as incomplete birds could look. They fed all day, trying hard to quickly finish the work of growing. That evening, they were nearly all the way there—plump and well feathered, although they still had bare patches on their backs. Their tails were too stubby to be useful in flying, but their legs looked strong enough to taxi them around. They were mostly dun-colored, with hints of chestnut in their wings and on their heads and the faintest suggestion of the bold eye stripe of the Carolina wren—one of the finest brush strokes in nature. They had grave gray faces and dark, liquid eyes full of confidence in what they were. But, even at rest, they still breathed hard with the effort to be.

I hung Patch's hunting bell on the musette bag to warn me of another raid, but they made it through the night without any intervention. I watched them leave on June 27, one by one, near midday. I should have guessed that you get fledglings to leave a nest by cutting off their food supply. Instead of coming to the nest with the usual take-out, the adults called from the fence rail, using that liquid *churtle* and a high-pitched squeaking that sounded like an imitation of the principal call of the young birds. The cheeping of the fledglings in the nest was answered with encouraging responses from the thick cover of honeysuckle and multiflora beyond the fence.

It took the better part of an hour of intense coaxing for the birds to leave the nest. One or the other fledgling would climb to the top of the canvas bag, look out, call, flap its stubby wings and retreat. One of the adults would fly to the edge of the bag and call down into it, then fly off to that tangle of honeysuckle and repeat the call. Occasionally one of the adults would give in and bring a small morsel, conceding to the fledglings' need to eat while they got their courage up.

Eventually, each fledgling climbed to the top of the bag and fluttered to the ground beyond the porch, not a flight so much as a glide to a crash—"controlled flight into ground," I think pilots call it. When a fledging landed, one of the adults flew to its side, fed it something and then escorted the young bird, flying short hops to encourage wing use, into the cover, which was now safer than the nest. The twenty-foot journey took about five minutes, the young bird hopping and wing-beating ineffectually all the way.

Two wrens out of the ten eggs laid in two clutches, one of many ratios of survival being played out in early summer, and a good lesson in the expense and adventure of being born. When the birds were gone, I pulled the nest out of the musette bag to see how it was made. The materials list was impressive—cushion moss and fine inner bark fibers for the soft interior bowl, with weed stems, catkins, leaves, cedar bark, wood shavings, strips of plastic and—with heavy-handed irony impossible not to record—a few shreds of shed snakeskin woven into the outer nest.

· · ·

Out back, a garden planted with perfect intentions in May is
in a kind of weedy glory in July, fruitful beyond what I deserve,
given my lack of work behind a hoe. Tomatoes, bell peppers,
banana peppers, snap beans, onions, baby carrots go into the big
pot with cubed venison stew meat, which I'll cook slowly in the
relative cool of night. I'm happy to feast out of that one pot for
a week—hot or cold, lunch and supper—ladling my wild Blue
Ridge gazpacho-gumbo out in generous portions and covering
each bowl with a heap of shaved Romano fragrant as skunk.
Gourds grow into strange, sun-warmed shapes, vines climbing
the porch trellises with coiled tendrils strong as fishing line.
Oily basil plants glisten between heavily laden cages of tomatoes
the way my Calabrian grandmother said to plant them. If you
are living well, sun-warmed tomatoes will fall softly into your
palm when you reach to pick them. When I'm feeling domestic,
I pound the basil into pesto with a wooden pestle that sends
the pine nuts flying. Patch tracks them over his shoulder like a
center fielder but loses interest after a sniff or two.

The farm is fruitful on its own. The showy blooms of April
and May metamorphose into a soft mast crop that feeds and fat-
tens all of us who live here. The woodlots and pastures bear fruit
well. I'd like to gather it all in sacks and baskets some year—
every berry, nut, acorn, seedpod and seed—have it weighed
in town, so that my landlord can claim his rightful share of
the GNP. That's the way to value land, the way to take its true
measure—not its ornamental status when it's "developed" and
"improved," but what the genius of the place naturally grows
on its own. Give birds and small mammals what they need and
the rest of us will live pretty well.

I count myself a critter in good standing and elbow in selec-
tively to get my share as a grazing opportunist. There is cress to

harvest from the strong spring as early as April. I eagerly pick hatfuls of mulberries in June, hats that are often empty by the time I get home. I haven't tried the mean-spirited little berries of multiflora, the off-pink offerings of autumn olive or the shapely fruit of the haw hung out in long-stemmed bunches. Like food that never seems to get out of the refrigerator, even the birds and deer don't seem particularly eager for that fare, except perhaps the haw, which I think the deer do like. Autumn olive, an inoffensive Russian planting, is much overrated by wildlife managers, who have planted the exotic liberally on public lands. The tiny black cherries out of reach everywhere don't do me much good, but along with fox, frost and sand grape they feed the birds well. I make a pungent tea from the spicebush in reach and grind its red berries to the powdery spice for which it was named.

I understand that the theory of spontaneous generation has its detractors, but berry picking in July seems to create sparrows. In any event, when I wade into the blackberry and dewberry patches, cereal bowl in hand, sparrows are a consequence of my near-noon breakfast. They poke up the overripe fruits pretty well, but leave enough for me to eat my fill for three weeks. Untended peach trees produce their share of bird-watching fare. I eat what's obvious as I cruise around in summer; a connoisseur of edible wild plants could not make a better harvest.

There is more to the farm, of course, than its edibles. There is something haunting in the heart of summer days that is hard to see, the essence of the season I wait for every year and miss. The art of summer is spare within the obvious lushness of the season, the woodlots of July full but so quiet they seem empty for much of the day. Anytime you part a curtain of vegetation to enter some rocky or woody nook, you get the distinct feeling that something has just left—a rough green snake silently

threading itself out of view from branch tip to branch tip, deer
rustling away, a gray squirrel ducking into its rude nest of leaves
and sticks or—most often—a space in the air where a bird seems
to have been.

Very often the thin, distinct call of a wood pewee will lead me
on into the cabin hollow, promising me a glimpse of summer
itself if I brave the high heat and prickly weediness of late July.
Eventually, the astute, diminutive fence-sitter darts off, slipping
behind the veil of things, leaving me to walk the fence line
toward the barn gate in that gauzy heat, wondering what I came
out for. But if I press on along the way the pewee suggested,
wading through a weedy sea of milkweed, goldenrod, mullein,
horsemint, ironweed and poke—to mention only what rises up
to my shins and knees—I'll find the odd, instructive wealth of
summer hidden in the open everywhere.

In summer, the air is punctuated with calls instead of songs—
the Morse code of indigo buntings, piping of a meadowlark,
squall of a mockingbird, deep bass fluting of mourning doves.
On a slow walk through the simmering heat, one detail leads
to another—stocky kingbirds on the telephone wire, juvenile
flickers flushing into a sycamore, turkey poults startling themselves away behind the barn, a female bluebird in a poplar, a
thrasher in the haw, orioles in the multiflora, sparrows everywhere. Birds hold the farm together in the heat.

Birdlife peaks in mid-July, in diversity and numbers, when
the behavior of birds is pared down to its essence. Only the well-
named mockingbirds insist on exuberance, although even they
cannot maintain in July the absurd vocal energy with which
they filled the air in June. They are insanely noisy neighbors.
In the high heat of summer, even common residents take on an
aura of rarity—cardinals, titmice, chickadees seem wild with

a seasonal skittishness that hones the eye to reappreciate the significance of their presence. The bright spring red of the cardinals has gone flat as the dusty green of the oaks. The titmice look strong hammering branches like woodpeckers, and the chickadees, stuck with a cloying name in English, look as tough as anything in the woods.

The flight as well as the forms of birds is refined in summer. Economy of motion is the rule—the way mockingbirds flutter to the ground in tight spirals and doves sail stiffly into the tops of pines. The thrasher at the barn spring moves loudly from heavy cover to heavy cover, while a Baltimore oriole, an infinitely quiet bird, browses slowly and mostly hidden. As the insect-buzzing heat builds, everything stays inside of the idea of itself, risking nothing. The fast, level flight of indigo buntings is as serviceable as the darting movement of sparrows. Some days turkey vultures move only when the wind moves them, an inexpensive way to live aloft. Kestrels burn fuel lavishly, like peregrines, knowing that food waits helpless at the end of their stoop. The forces of nature select, as Darwin argued, but do not dictate one way to be a bird. The earth and air are more generous than that.

I'm surprised that Boeing or some task force from the military doesn't set up shop here to study how flying should be done. The F18s that course the low-altitude military air route overhead look clunky by comparison despite the ear-shattering noise they make, although—to be fair—a Carolina chickadee can't boogie down to the Chesapeake Bay in fifteen minutes or supply much close-air support in combat. Still, the idea of flight came from nature and is found in its most beautiful forms there. Toward the end of his life, even Charles Lindbergh preferred the flight of birds to that of aircraft.

Sparrows always repay study—field sparrows, chipping sparrows, song sparrows. Their chips and pings seem barely more than insect sounds, but they live well and come to seem quite hardy if you watch the confidence of their daily lives, their stocky flight and unhurried wariness. When Patch is with me on a walk, his charges don't worry them at all. They rise easily above all his wasted motion. Their principal fear is hawks, not the big buteos, I think, which are slow to get off, but the sleek sharp-shins, which I have seen on more than one occasion with a plump songbird in tow. My hunting seems quite genteel in comparison to that rude harvest of a meal.

If I glean my journals for a yearful of birds here, a heartening litany emerges—red-winged blackbirds, wood ducks, black ducks, ruby-throated hummingbirds, great blue herons, cedar waxwings, ruffed grouse, Canada geese, red-tailed hawks, green herons, cardinals, common redpolls, American goldfinches, house finches, purple finches, turkey vultures, yellow-billed cuckoos, common flickers, bobwhite quail, eastern pewees, black vultures, common crows, yellow-rumped warblers, yellow-throated warblers, pine warblers, pileated woodpeckers, gray catbirds, least flycatchers, rusty blackbirds, American kestrels, northern orioles, tree swallows, dark-eyed juncos, belted kingfishers, red-bellied woodpeckers, wild turkeys, song sparrows, mockingbirds, black and white warblers, brown-headed cowbirds, common screech owls, ospreys, black capped chickadees, tufted titmice, Carolina chickadees, indigo buntings, rose-breasted grosbeaks, American woodcocks, downy woodpeckers, hairy woodpeckers, rufous-sided towhees, scarlet tanagers, blue-gray gnatcatchers, ruby-crowned kinglets, golden-crowned kinglets, northern waterthrushes, eastern bluebirds, white-breasted nuthatches, chipping sparrows, field sparrows, rough-winged swallows, barred owls, starlings, eastern meadowlarks, Carolina wrens, brown thrashers, solitary sandpipers, winter wrens, American robins, eastern kingbirds, golden-winged warblers, warbling vireos, solitary vireos, mourning doves, white-throated sparrows, white-crowned sparrows.

That's alphabetical, in Latin, and all the more pleasing in English for its apparent randomness, which is much like the apparent randomness of birds themselves. I have not yet gotten to the bottom of a year's birds here and have probably missed more than a few residents. Who knows what fabulous migrants have touched down to glean seeds and probe for insects without my knowing about their passing presence? A good birder could easily check off some of the common vocalizations that still puzzle me and add a half dozen new species to my farm list in a single walk. But I'm in no rush to check things off. Birds exemplify the notion that life is to be learned from. What matters to me is the process of identifying, in random order, the life around me—the jazz of trial and error that coaxes my curiosity along. In the end, it is perception itself that interests me, the infinitely variable art of seeing, the way our senses turn our heads—and hearts—about. Life itself is quite flirtatious. The warm looks and cold looks we give and get. After all, that's what triggers sexual interest and, sometimes, love and keeps all species specifying.

A self-taught observer of nature, I'm still prone to what scholars call "howlers"—ripping good mistakes that make the experts laugh in confirmation of their expertise—but except for Patch there are no avian experts here. I once pursued an interesting bird up through the barn woods, thinking I may be on to something new, only to find a robin waiting for me in the beech grove. Not knowing what I was looking at, I soaked

in every nuance of its choppy flight and noted every delicacy
where it fed, noticed more about the bird than I would have had
my mind clicked "robin" at the first sight of it. I laughed deeply
when it revealed itself, bowed to it from the waist for the lesson—assuming my *roshi* had appeared in this guise—and eventually framed that scribbled page of field notes for my desk.

I've done worse. I once stopped in the middle of a grove of
old growth down in the Great Smoky Mountains, where they
are fond of pointing out that there are more tree species than in
all of Europe, to identify a gnarly old midstory tree I was sure
was a rarity. After fifteen minutes of close study with a botanical
guide—dutifully inspecting leaf scars and end buds with a hand
lens—I keyed out a dogwood. This was winter, and that strange
tree looked more mythological than anything I have ever seen in
nature. There, too, was a teacher in the woods, my *roshi* again. I
wish I had a black and white photo of it framed on the wall.

So, for reasons of my own and in defiance of the experts,
I consider the robin and the dogwood rare species, which of
course they are on any other planet but our own. And when
I look out my study window to see the perfectly recognizable
dogwood there, fanned out in April with the white flowers the
Chamber of Commerce likes to publicize to tourists, I remember that other dogwood deep in a true forest—a strangely
beautiful rather than pretty tree, grown wildly beyond what
a botanist would call its diagnostic traits, its bark strange as
dinosaur skin—and marvel at the range of expression of which
even the most common tree is capable.

Not knowing is a virtue if it invites a closer look.

Get up on walnut hill in the high heat of three P.M. and you
get the idea that the essence of summer is the heat itself and the
discipline it imposes. *You want sun,* the gods seem to say, *here is*

the sun. Time stalls in the flat light like a turkey vulture teetering in a weak thermal. The moments and minutes don't seem to be going anywhere. Life looks as disorganized as the riot of weed life in the pasture. The gray horizon into which the Blue Ridge Mountains have disintegrated is as uninviting as it is all year. Not hard to imagine how thin the rivers are, how dusty the trails and dense the bushwhacks.

There is literally nothing to do at the heart of a summer afternoon—no hunting or fishing or woodcutting, no writing beyond, perhaps, a few spare lines of verse. "Where is the summer," T. S. Eliot asked near the beginning of his greatest poem, "the unimaginable/ Zero summer?" That's the question. Time to wait out time passing, to try to exercise that frank habit of being that animals instinctively bring to the task of their well-weathered lives. A pileated woodpecker cries once from deep within the river woods. Crows drag their shadows along the ground. Scavenger weather—the kind of day you see a coyote loping along. Summer hides everything and nothing behind the white noise of insect buzz and jay squawk, fawn bleat and hawk cry. Summer suggests meeting stillness with stillness, asks us to be.

There is scant sign of anything on the hot way back home— fox scat, a turkey tail feather, a box turtle shell gnawed around the edges with the tooth marks of mice and voles. I believe I glass one of the vesper sparrows that have been eluding me, but can't be sure. Life stirs a little in and around the shady woodlots. Fawns that were speckled like brook trout in June are now streaked with parr marks like rainbow trout. With sturdier legs, they are more inclined to flee than hide, although they still zigzag like rabbits rather than bolt like yearlings. Sleek does browse with unconcern.

The humblest things stir in midsummer, probably because
nothing else wants the stage. Box turtles dig nests out of the
sandy soil with their powerful rear legs. Painted turtles bask
warily at the barn spring. Summer is weed time, and the pastures
are thick with the toughest forms of life, native and exotic, each
ground-hugging weed evolved to bear strange fruits and odd-
shaped seeds. The big mullein stalks sprout and flower, poke
thickens and sets racemes of small green berries. A half dozen
species of swallowtail butterflies hover around bull thistles. The
ubiquitous sumac is hazy with rusty clusters of seedpods.

When I can walk up on coiled copperheads across ground
hard enough for them to feel the footfall of field mice, I know I
am walking well. As I was told by a good deer hunter, the trick
is to try not to let your feet touch the ground, or at least to walk
as if you could do that. Keep the bulk of your weight in the air,
up in your shoulders, arms and chest and in your gaze, as it were.
Walking stick firmly in hand, I take some pride in watching
these fine pasture hunters uncoiling under my shadow in slow
surprise, although I back off quickly when a cranky snake coils
and cocks its head in my direction.

Counting coup on copperheads is as good as outseeing a wild
turkey at close range. Something to do in the afternoon anyway.
Since I don't throw the wheeling shadow of a hawk's broad wing,
most of the snakes are disheartened rather than alarmed at my
appearance. The big red-tailed hawks, however, *are* alarmed on
those rare occasions when I can walk up undetected on the snags
from which they hunt the busy grasses of walnut hill. They
fly off silently, vulnerable and exposed, unhappy as the foxes
I sometimes jump, that something other than prey has gotten
inside the zone of their hunting.

If summer has an essence, I haven't found it. The closest thing

I've got to offer are the yellow-billed cuckoos I have seen once each summer three years in a row, each time during the last week of July and each time in the cabin hollow coming home from a hot, dry trek across the farm. They seem to materialize right out of the heart of summer.

The first time I saw them, I'd never seen cuckoos before, but I knew what they were even without the binoculars. Large, slender, graceful birds with a distinctive curved bill, they register clearly in the mind through the naked eye. If you had spent any time at all thumbing through a field guide, you would guess them right off. I always catch the pair in midcanopy working their way down the poplars and walnuts of the cabin hollow. With the binoculars I could see the yellow in their mandible and the artful way that yellow is picked up in the thin ring that circles their large, dark eye. Delicate of movement, their leaning posture on a branch is what I mostly remember, as if the whole bird were built to serve the curvature of its beak.

Seeing the yellow-billed cuckoos in the same place at nearly the same time for three years running may say as much about my movements as theirs. Of course, I keep an eye and ear out for them now, but it's odd I've never seen them earlier or later in the season. Like most birds, they are citizens of the world, with a winter range that extends to Argentina and a willingness to nest from southern Canada to the Caribbean. They must not nest here on the farm, or I would see them at other times, but there is something here that suits them at the height of summer—a meal or two to glean—and their passing presence tells me that the season has peaked, that its hot work is nearly done.

So let's say that for this place, a pair of silent yellow-bills in the cabin hollow is either the essence of summer or summer's way of revealing that it has no essence, that the pursuit of essences is a human need that has nothing to do with the life of things. The pewee clinging daintily to barbed wire was not calling me along the fence line. Nature does not lead us anywhere. You are a part of life or not. Go looking for summer, and you will come home full and empty-handed.

In early August, the Perseids shower the big pasture hill, each thin streak evidence of the rocky matter of the solar system eroding, grain by grain, as surely as the surrounding mountains and the limestone caverns underfoot. The mountains become smaller, the caverns larger, and dust from a comet's tail is threshed against the earth's atmosphere, revealing seeds of light. Each thin signature of a meteor marks a graceful change of state, the falling fire we briefly see as if it were meant for our viewing. Among others, the Chinese, Greeks, and Lakota took note of this annual portent. All sensible tribes take the night sky seriously. Over hours, this sparking of cosmic dust betrays a wildly regular irregularity, a deep jazz rhythm the calculus of which escapes me just as much as does the logic of distracting night breezes that stir the broad vanes of poplar leaves.

Patch flushes birds in the dark as the Perseids flush overhead—sparrows, warblers, and wrens that have star charts in their brains more precise than my knowledge of the night sky. Like meteors the birds announce themselves by disappearing, and Patch contents himself with harassing them away, not good practice for a dog I'll want to point staunchly in October, holding steady while trembling with desire in the scent plume of a ruffed grouse. But he has been busting every passing passerine since spring, out of the lack of anything better to do, intently exercising the half-domesticated birds that nest around the cabin and happily rousting any wild feathered critter we come across on walks. A more rigorous bird hunter would not allow his dog to lapse in discipline in this way, but summer is for laxness. We practice that.

We read no darker message in the appearance of the Perseids than that summer is beginning to end, another change of state worth watching keenly. In fact, my sense of a new year beginning stirs most in mid-August, after weeks of missing the midday life of the farm because of the way dog-day heat discourages walking. Most of what I learn about the farm in the dead of summer has to be gleaned just after dawn and just before sunset, or well after dark when the universe shines beyond a lattice of bat flight accompanied by the whinnying of screech owls. On the worst days, when the shaded front-porch thermometer breaks through a hundred degrees, the big pasture hill, the back woodlots, the old clear-cut and the river woods might as well be in another country.

But summer bends in August, even if it does not break. A cool morning or a cool evening materializes out of an invisible front of hazeless air sandwiched between two humid highs. When a few leaves of the Virginia creeper that drapes the split-rail fence turn red or, here and there, walnut leaflets wane pale yellow, early migrant birds appear in casual, hungry bursts. A flock of blackbirds will shift around the back pasture en masse, or a small clan of towhees—a bird we haven't seen or heard around the cabin since May—will swing back into closer orbit. The presence of these early travelers seems to encourage more earnest feeding by local troops. The premature swatches of autumnal color and the hunger of resident and passing birds are tangible signs of what, to hunters, is the most important change in the year, the long season of provisioning ahead.

Occasionally, an evening walk in mid-August is drawn on

by the call of one or two quail that have strayed from a rare, wild covey. If there is enough of a ground breeze, I'll walk with Patch at heel in a semicircle to get as far downwind of them as possible. I'll watch for the moment when he snaps his head around toward *something,* cocks an eye at me to see if I'm in the game and quivers with a concentrated desire he hasn't felt since last February. *Birds, Patch, birds.* This is not to tell him what he damn well knows but to tell him that I know, too. Then he'll turn his entire body toward them, rearranging his hindquarters behind his beautiful nose, not on point at this distance but pointing and ready to go. I'll cut him loose with his favorite words, *Hunt 'em up,* and months of indiscipline will shiver into the half-wild, intent attention known as *birdiness,* the ecstatic endgame focus of a working dog who knows his business.

He'll cut half circles around the cover where his nose has fixed the now-silent birds, feinting from all sides at once, as if to give his quarry the impression that he is one of a half dozen dogs and there is no way out. During the long off-season he will happily wag his tail like a TV dog and root around for woodchucks or get up on his hind legs and paw tree trunks after squirrels. Rabbits send him into a ground-hugging frenzy that is embarrassing to watch. But with the scent of true game in his nose, he stiffens in the neck and shoulders and works his dainty muzzle through every invisible curl of quail-laced air as his tail beats furiously with the energy he eventually coils, with exquisite restraint, into a rock-solid point.

Or not.

If he holds and waits for me to walk up on his right side to get in position for the pointed bird, I'll know the summer's fun has done no harm. If he flushes the bird on his own and then stands over the empty cover mortified, looking carefully away from the escaping bird as if he hadn't noticed it, I'll know he needs refresher work—in acting as well as hunting. But if he busts the bird and charges happily after it like a puppy pursuing cows, then I'll know I let us fall too far from grace and that we have some serious retraining to do. In any event, these stray birds that materialize in dewberry thickets or out of clusters of small cedars take the measure of us and, from mid-August to the opening of grouse season in late October, we try to improve ourselves as best we can.

Summer slips downstream easy enough, going as it came, with birds. Large flocks of black vultures kettle together. The endless haze of summer organizes itself into fronts that bring cool air and welcome days of rain. After each front, I'll hear birds I don't recognize and see familiar species flocking up and feeding en masse, bursting here and there as if something were in the wind. That baking summer heat may well return in full force, but after each wave of weather, you can feel the birdlife shifting around, feeling the flow of the season with unerring accuracy. Every departing bird takes a part of the summer with it. Every arriving bird brings fall as surely as the early-turning leaves of sourwood and fire cherry. This year a gray-cheeked thrush stopped to glean the branches of the Spanish oak while I was tending the wood racks near the end of August. At first I'd thought it was a veery, and then a hermit thrush. But the active bird dawdled in the oak long enough for me to get the binoculars and the bird book so that I could confirm an Arctic visitor as rare and welcome here as the solitary sandpiper that passed through in April. Makes sense, its presence seemed to suggest, to be working on the woodpile on an August evening.

Time flows generously on summer evenings like a river rippling slowly through a long, deep pool where water dwells

before moving on. I'll watch deer graze into the failing light, a
CD of Thelonious Monk playing in the cabin, which resonates
like a gigantic speaker when the amplifier is turned up. I imagine the great jazz pianist wandering around the chromatic scale
hunched over his keyboard like a bear, mumbling softly to himself as he looks for something he seems to have lost between the
keys. And that is, perhaps, what all this walking and watching
is about—looking for what Monk famously called "the notes
between the notes, the blue notes." That's where you feel life
keenly, not just in the sharps and flats that add piquancy to
otherwise sentimental melodies but in the impossible blue notes
we sometimes find in art or nature.

When it starts to get dark, other music comes to hand—early
Armstrong, Ellington alone at the piano, the Mingus of *Blues &
Roots*. The beauty of the offbeat and offhand—discrete casual
melodies, distilled out of long, hot summer days—not summer
days here, where life is probably too bucolic for most people,
but summer days in Kansas City and St. Louis and South Side
Chicago, summer days in Brooklyn and Boston, Worcester and
Bangor and Erie. Then, thinking of my Russian friends in Inta,
I'll put on some vintage records of Billie Holiday and listen to
her sing through a wobbly hiss as I walk out to watch Aldebaran
being occulted by the moon.

Then the harsh bass of a Norfolk & Southern freight answers
the soul-piercing progressions of Miles Davis's "Blue on Green"
which drift to me through the cabin's open windows and doors.
We rusticate urbanely here. The most citified, brainy jazz sounds
fine and natural on the open air, filling the fields with an art
that complements the nature of this place. "Blue on Green" fits
perfectly. Surely one of the saddest and most joyful pieces of
music ever fashioned, its bluesiness as much small town as big

city. John Coltrane, who heard more than a few freight trains wail while growing up in rural North Carolina, handles the lonesome diesel with ease, making it seem as if a saxophone and a train whistle spoke the same bluesy language. After Miles eases back into the relentless drift of his meditations, pensive and circumspect as always—sharp and quick and kestrel-like in his playing, which is somehow casual and deeply engaged at the same time—I wouldn't be surprised to hear a screech owl, much more mellow-sounding than its name, whinny into the session on the downbeat like a pro.

The end of summer summering. Everything improvises.

*T*he rivers ran hard this September, gathering a good year of rain from the mountains. I fished Poor Farm day after day, as if that twisting stretch of water were going to tell me something. But the river ran as it always does, chattering off the rocks and slipping silently through deep places, a distant thing even when I was knee-deep in it. I admired its aloofness the way I admired the aloofness of deer and birds and trees. I enjoyed listening to its clear, indecipherable language the way one enjoys the bright flow of talk in a foreign place. In the end, I heard from the river exactly what I wanted to hear: river river river river river.

I stayed away from the spawning beds where the brook trout milled and fished the murmuring heads of pools. I could see large brown trout holding in amber ribbons of currents. Although I expected to see them, had come there to find their dark forms poised upriver, I was surprised that they were there in the same way that I am surprised when a deer steps into view or when a grouse flushes from good cover when I am hunting.

Despite their visibility, the brown trout were tough, miles away from me in spirit. Summer had honed their wariness to a fine art. Distilled by the pressures of survival, they were perfectly serene, each surrounded by a field of wariness which put them, in effect, in another world. The cooler flows of early autumn nudged them back onto midstream lies, but they did not come to the fly recklessly as they had in spring. In the absence of a hatch, they took what food came their way, their green forms shifting slightly as they responded to small insects drifting in the flow. Occasionally one would rise sedately, taking something in the surface film I could not see. The wrinkled riseform that bloomed where the fish fed was quickly washed away.

I fished well, stealthily shuffling into place and making long, unobtrusive casts. I presented small, spare flies at the end of long, delicate tippets, making every concession I could to these discriminating fish and to the river and the season. But in autumn wild nature is not so easily touched. Working my way upstream through a rain of leaves, I caught nothing but refusals.

In autumn, in late afternoon, the essence of a river flows exposed to view in an amber light which suggests that something is about to be revealed. Perhaps the idea of revelation derived from such slanting forest light, but I think that sunlight filtered through a hardwood canopy is itself the revelation, as is the river and the fish and the yellow leaves turning in the current, flashing like fish, and the newly arrived ruby-crowned kinglets flitting about in the grapevines along the riverbank. The light reveals that the river is a river and that everything else is what it is.

$\mathcal{L}$ate Wood

I do not see what the Puritans did at this season.

—HENRY DAVID THOREAU

$\mathbf{L}$ate summer thunders against the mountains as if wearing down the leading edge of autumn. For three years, the dark clouds of August were a dry tease. This year the soaking rains will not stop. We'll take the rain and a bumper crop of peppery yellow chanterelles to sauté with stir-fried venison loin steaks. And the springs overflowing into the pastures and the rivers bank-full, too fast to fish. And the migrant flocks of warblers pinned down for a longer stay than usual in the cabin hollow and the gas-line cover and back in the overgrown clear-cut. And the lonely silhouette of ducks overhead against a gray sky rowing hard ahead of the curtains of rain that, for ten days straight, have swept in from the east.

Ninety-nine percent of the time, our weather comes from the west. Once a year, usually around the change of season in spring or fall, a front will come the wrong way—from the Atlantic.

Patch will nose the wild air and look at me with big questions on his face. Perhaps he's scenting the dolphins and whales I love to see when I hole up to work in a beachfront house on the Outer Banks in November and again in March. Or imagining the gulls and terns and cormorants he is suddenly getting a whiff of. Birds that are news to him. He would hunt them all on principle down to the last plover skittering away with the perfect unconcern of shorebirds. I'd like to see him try to lock up on point in the face of a flock of sandpipers. That would make him long for the straightforward secrecy of grouse.

I suppose it's not possible, but up on the big pasture hill I'm sure that I myself can smell the ocean, a faint tang in the air that makes me jealous I cannot be there all the time, watching that version of the year turn through the seasons, those birds coming and going in front of other weather. Perhaps someday we'll give up the mountains for the coast, lose the moody horizon of cloud-shrouded bedrock for the rolling blue reach of ocean.

Summer ends, unofficially, when it's cool enough to start cutting wood again. It's when the crows flock up and get vocal and the jays start massing in the oaks and the poke swells and the goldenrod flowers and every day the unfamiliar calls of migrating warblers distract me every minute. Some mornings it's cool enough for oatmeal and some evenings you feel like hot coffee on the porch for the first time since spring. Monarch butterflies appear, too bright to seem autumnal against the ruddy colors of the turning trees. Carolina wrens come back in voice. Screech owls whinny in the coolness of shortened evenings. The coats of deer turn gray and the big bucks, about to edge into full wariness, look like the heart of winter already coalesced and waiting.

If pastures are for walking, an invitation to take the measure

of things stride by stride, woodlots are for stump-sitting and
watching. Call this hunting, if you like. A grove of standing trees
suggests that something is about to happen—that a turkey will
flush, a sharp-shinned hawk make a deadly move, a string of
does rise into view. A sluggish rat snake or a spry gray squirrel
might draw the eye into the overarching hardwood canopy or
hairy woodpeckers enliven the midstory as crows croak through
at eye level. But mostly woodlots are for gathering light and
filtering it, each a woody prism that fans the otherwise hidden
qualities of daylight into view. Something happens to sunlight
under beech and oak and hickory leaves. Pastures absorb light,
drawing it into the ground, reflecting what can't be stored into a
hazy buzz of insects and nodding seed heads. The farm's invaluable assembly of hickories, walnuts and oaks—to name only the
major players—stir what is, after all, starlight into rich tones of
earthbound air worth watching for its own sake. But watching
daylight won't get wood cut.

Half of the wood I need has been weathering on the racks
outside my bedroom window under the double-trunked
Spanish oak since last winter. In my ideal life, the rest would
have been cut, split and stacked before those *dorotheas* hatched
on the Jefferson in early June. All summer I could take side-
long glances at the six face cords of neatly fitted quarters of
oak, hickory and locust—with the fragrant, shattered limbs of
cherry and walnut mixed in—admiring my own foresight and
diligence. If anyone noticed my collection of deciduousness, I
would demur in a manly way that, yes, ma'am, I had been cutting a little wood earlier in the year.

In my real life, the mayfly hatches of early spring have me
rising to the task of trout fishing with the diligence that my
imagination applies to the woodpile. In a good year, the task

is only two-thirds done by the time an unexpected cool front carries off the summer haze and you suddenly notice the yellow walnuts going bare and the dogwoods reddened and hear the agitated sound of leaves rustling in a nearly constant wind that will not stop until next May when everything is growing again. That wind and that rustling is the sound of the year slipping downstream. That other sound is me cutting wood.

My notebooks as well as the back of my mind are marked with a succession of dead trees to cut and, better, windfalls already laid out for bucking. Any walk during the year is liable to turn into a timber cruise. Although I love living trees, and well understand the necessity to leave rotting logs and graying snags in every woodlot, I cast a lean and hungry look on any dead oak, hickory or locust that looks ready to fall. If it's a straight-trunked beauty, thick in the bole and thirty or forty feet to the first limb, seasoned dead on the stump for a year and free of heart rot, then I mark it as mine, a tangible reward for my afternoon aimlessness. Seasoned split for another year, and used sparingly, there's two or three weeks of cabin-warmth in such a tree. We live a little rougher than most people, whose houses have fewer critters wandering through and no noticeable prevailing wind, but cabin-warmth is one of our most important units of measure.

I've already taken that black oak out of the barn woods, but there is a gnarly old cherry blown over and a ruler-straight ash. I've yet to reap the chestnut oak, scarlet oak and two small locusts I discovered walking the north woodlots. A cluster of dead pale hickories are leaning together along the north fence line. There is a locust down near the deer track I need to get out before bow season, and a twisted walnut—dead for years—right below the cabin that can wait for last. I can get that out without disturbing anyone's hunting. That's enough wood to overlap into next fall. In the best of lives, your woodpile is a full two years ahead of going in the stove.

I'll work short mornings and cut from about nine to dusk for a few days in mid-September to make sure I'm out of the woodlots at least a week or two before bow season opens. I'm well aware that nothing disturbs the woods like the ungodly noise and polluting smoke wreathed around me when I set to gathering firewood with a will.

Working at the steady, unhurried pace I like, I can have a big tree down safely and bucked and sectioned and the first load home and off-loaded by lunchtime. That's a lot of work for one sentence. I'm proud of the way I've learned to read the net bias in an oak or cherry that has grown out every which way. And prouder when I can set my wedge cut so that the tree falls into a narrow opening ninety degrees off that bias, undermined to go the way I wanted. Part of the ethics of woodcutting is not harming living trees, especially the thin-skinned saplings waiting in the wings. I know the trouble in having a tree back up on me if I get my calculations wrong and, yes, I've got a second saw in case I need to cut the first one out, which happened once. But there's real danger in letting a tree hang unpredictably on a miscalculated back cut, and I haven't made the mistake again. You don't want a trunk under the stress of its own weight snapping off the wrong way unexpectedly.

Felling trees is no big deal to a professional, who can turn a tree in any direction with a back cut so flat you have to look close to see the tilt. Judging from the big white oak stumps the loggers left, they pride themselves on that and sign the art of their work with those deft cuts. All those high-backed cuts you see around here, those are mine. Sometimes I saw them off, partly out of embarrassment but also to make a footstool for guitar playing, book stands, and chock blocks for the truck.

The key to any job is how close I can get the truck to the downed tree. I've muscled wood out of steep-sided sinkholes, staggered up the rocky incline of the river woods and toted loads out of that narrow bottom of the barn woods. Needless to say, a big windthrow at the edge of a pasture is a gift of the gods. The bite of winter is cold enough here that my scalp itches when an easy tree comes down. I'll find it on a bird walk or on my way to tend a deer blind. This year a northern red oak blew over in the double-helix, where I can back the truck in pretty close. Its green wood won't be ready to burn properly for at least a year, but I can fill a twelve-foot rack with what is on the ground and have the country satisfaction of watching it weathering anytime I wander out into the yard.

Limbing is a pleasant warm-up for the day's work. The stocky saw feels light in the morning on the strength of a late breakfast and the bracing air. It doesn't take long to undo the tree, trimming the branches off close, eyeing one or two for walking sticks. A few busted stobs prop the trunk up nicely for cutting so I won't have to roll it with the peavey to get the saw all the way through. I pile the thin slash to come back for as kindling and cut the thicker limbs into four- or five-foot lengths. But the real gain begins when I set the bar across the main trunk and let the weight of the roaring saw carry me through years of growth. That's when I feel guilty. That's when the worth of this tree as a tree and my needs clash without resolution.

It took me years to learn how to properly bench-sharpen a saw chain, and once I satisfied myself that I could do it if I had to, I went back to having my set of chains professionally sharpened. In winter and fall, there are always one or two to pick up and one or two to drop off. For five bucks I've got a chain that will cut properly, spewing out big chips of red oak heartwood or golden yellow locust or pure morsels of hickory or white oak. Just sawdust, I guess, but when it's pouring onto my right boot in a neat pile, I can smell the resinous life of the tree I'm working on and see the unavoidable waste of my cutting.

Even though the bulk of the heartwood has been dead for years, a dead tree is, in some way I can't get at, not quite dead. The same way when you start to skin a deer some cold winter morning with your breath dancing in front of you in strange gray plumes the deer seems to be alive, or at least to still be a deer the way an oak is still an oak until you start those cuts through the trunk that disassemble seventy or eighty years of sunlight, water and air stored as wood, bark and leaf. By the time the tree trunk lies in pieces or the carcass hangs bare, red muscles cased in a thin veil of membrane, the tree is no longer a tree, the deer no longer a deer. There's wood to haul and stack or meat to butcher and wrap for the deep freeze.

Tossed in helter-skelter, the upper half of that oak fills the short bed of my truck. I've taken the big toolbox off to make space, and that's a decent load when you don't have far to go and have all day. Having all day—to do anything—that's another key, another standard unit of measure hereabouts, although having all day to do something important—cut wood, hunt, write, read, think, talk—makes what I call industriousness look like loafing. But I stand by the theory and practice of having all day.

It's important to off-load the truck at home before I take a break. As truly hardworking people know every day, you have to match the momentum of your energy to the nature of the task at hand. If I wait to unload that wood, it will only get heavier—as if it lightened up a bit when I tossed it in with the morning's bravado and will return to its real weight when my brain becomes aware of my body's fatigue. You do something often enough and you learn the trick of it.

I toss the fresh sections out on the mounting pile of wood to split, perhaps the most pleasant task to always have at hand. Splitting wood is as satisfying as hitting a baseball with a wooden bat, and a task I save for cool evenings when the sound of green oak or locust popping open resonates like a natural part of dusk, the rhythmic work of some industrious creature undoing the husk of things. The woodpile fills the little yard out back, so it serves a double purpose. The less grass to cut, the better.

Although I'm home with this first load around lunchtime, I'd rather eat in the woods when I'm woodcutting. Canvas work pants covered in sawdust and reeking of gas and oil, I look and smell like something that should be eating in the woods. I put a thick turkey and lettuce sandwich, a hunk of sharp cheddar and a tart Granny Smith in a small cooler. Refill the water jug and grab any tools or supplies I forgot when I went out the first time. There is always something—the bar chain oil, one of the big steel wedges or—God love it—the short-handled peavey that lets me roll big logs when I'm working alone.

Although the chain saw doesn't exactly harken back to ancient times, the axes, mauls and sledges I've collected for this work, including some sweet antiques I've brought back into service, embody a good deal of human history in their simple but brilliant shapes—cutting edges and steel fists on the end of wooden levers that make me stronger than I am and more useful than I would otherwise be. Part of an earlier digital revolution when the unequal density of iron and wood, an old binary relation, enabled man to change, for better or worse, the way things were. I'm not saying I'd last long on a logging crew—half a day, maybe—but working with such tools now and then keeps me more honest than I'd otherwise be, a little more deserving of spending a day with a fly rod or a longbow in my hand, more deserving of being a writer, perhaps, which I think of not as intellectual work but as a final refinement of manual labor. I don't want the hand tools dulling themselves on the truck bed or taking a piece out of the spare tire so they ride up front with me in Patch's nook. They clang softly together as the truck bounces back up the farm road, steely whisperings in Old Norse or Old English, or some old Iron Age tune learned at the forge.

Back at the double-helix, what's left of the oak looks like work. It's the second half of the workday that shows what you have got. I tend the saw and buck another section or two before sitting down on one of them to eat. Just to get some momentum back in the job site. The food disappears quickly and the water tastes bright and flavorful. Hard work uncovers the goodness in simple things. The day is getting a little warmer than I thought, but this wood will pay off in a year or so. For dinner this week I'm eating my usual venison chili with stew meat from a deer I killed last fall. So a two-year span of time here will be lap-jointed from that chilly morning hunt to the chilly evening I put a weathered quarter of this oak in the stove. The rich, red strength a deer gathered from browsing a hundred things on this farm a year ago helps me buck a fallen oak that will keep me warm a year from now as I spend myself writing sentences about deer and oaks. Seems fair in the end, right and good.

Life burns hard and bright in fall. Spicebush berries shine the same otherworldly red as the leaves of fire cherry. Graying deer feed as intently as cattle. Flocks of young turkeys wander around like deer. Warblers swarm through the thinning canopies on the same wind that warns them to move on. Feels good to be out working in that edgy bluster, with flocks of birds bursting in and out of the cherries and clinging to the grapevines hung high in the sunny side of big trees. Feels good to share the needs of animals and the joyful tensions of life—the need to feed and to be wary, the need to travel and stay close, the need to work at life for life's sake until life becomes a serious form of play. On the edge of autumn, the year is neatly gathered, come to all sorts of fruition within which there are the seeds of another year.

The work goes slower in the afternoon, but the beauty of being an amateur is that you can take time with things. When I get halfway down the trunk, the girth of the oak is so large I have to split the sections before I carry them to the truck. So the hand tools come to hand. The green, unchecked wood is hard to read, very often blank. I've learned that the trunk sections split easier from the top down, straight against the way the tree grew, and so I set them right side up. I use the biggest chunk I've got cut for a chopping block so the force of the maul isn't lost in the soft earth that feels so good underfoot. Those blank pieces take some arduous trial and error—painful whiffs when the force of the blow ends up back in my arms and shoulders and spine rather than in the wood. Even a freshly filed maul will bounce off green oak as if the tree had a hard-rubber core, leaving me vibrating like a witless cartoon character. But when the bit hits near enough to a hidden weakness, a lightning-shaped crack will open and the maul will stay put. The give is silent but you can see it and, better, feel it, the force of the blow shivered into the wood where it belongs. I'll dial the piece around to suit me, set my legs and square my shoulders as carefully as if there were men on base, and pop the section open, immensely pleased when it flops heavily in half on the first blow. Double to left, two men in. It's autumn, after all.

What I like most about cutting wood is the sharp scent of the resins that waft up from those freshly split halves. I keep meaning to look up the chemicals involved, but I never get to it. Split wood is sensuous enough without any research, not as sweet as perfume in a woman's hair, but still a wild draw that fills the nasal passages and lungs with rich scents. I didn't know until I got into this woodcutting phase of my life that cherry trees smelled like cherries on the inside. Black locust is the most pungent wood I know, astringent but appealing. Red oak is sharp and sweet though not as sweet as cherry, black oak is a little flatter, white oak dry and subtle, musty. The sweet brown heartwood of walnut is oily and a little bitter, but not as bitter as the husk of the nut. Hickory has a clear, clean, airy odor, faintly aromatic.

The afternoon moves on, the hours fit perfectly to the work I have to do. I split the sections smaller as I go, preferring more trips to the truck than shouldering the heavy sections that only get bigger as I work down the trunk. I'm careful up to a point but don't mind if the truck bed takes a few more dings as the chunks bounce in and settle down. I take mechanical care of my vehicles, but every truck I've owned has evolved from being my "good truck" to my "wood truck." In good times, I'll keep the old one as a genuine wood truck—sans tags and insurance—a status symbol in certain circles. The best of these was a bulldog 1980 Ford F-150 shortbed with the old straight-six engine and three-speed manual transmission. A true working vehicle, it was deliberately short on looks and looked fine for that—all squared off front and back like Fords were before pickups got fashionable and they started rounding off the bodies to give them a sleek, suburban look. That truck could haul. One of the unintended consequences of the New World Order is that used pickups are worth too much money for most of us who need them to keep one as a pet. But even four-figure check in hand, it was a sad day when my old blue truck drove away with its new owner. Now my 1988 F-150, never much of a date-mobile to begin with, is starting to look like the '80 but without the heart for it. Still it looks good piled up with wood.

Knotty sections require a wedge, or wedges, and some pounding with the sledge. I'll use the five-pound hammer to set that beautiful Oregon wedge with the thin, flared edge a third of the way into a big piece. I take the time to set it in good because I don't want that wedge flying out on me when I bring the sledgehammer down on it full force. When I get going right, there's nothing like the ring of steel on steel and, though my upper arms burn and my shoulders groan, a little wedge driving is good for the soul. Must sound like somebody is laying track in the woods. *Lining track,* as they used to say. The blues in it ring loud and clear. All these old forms of work have a sound to them, a beat that is deeply appealing when you can afford to take it slow. And time is what I do have to spend when I spend a day in the woods.

The worst sections take two wedges and a little thought about where the second one will do the trick. No one is there to notice, but it is an embarrassment to the universe to pound away until both wedges have disappeared, swallowed whole by a large chunk of springy green oak. At that point, two of your tools have gone over to the other side, leaving you with quite a poser. Running the chain saw into metal wedges isn't a good idea, and ripping a log will ruin the chain's cutting edges. You could wait a decade or two until the piece dries open and then come back for the wedges. Or you could get a gigantic wood stove, shove the piece in whole and fish the wedges out red-hot. Or you could remember to bring along a crowbar for backup. Attacking a round of half-split oak that won't let go of itself with a crowbar is not the most intelligent or elegant thing I do. When it has to be done, it's just as well there is no one there to admire the work.

At the end of the job I cut what dendrochronologists call a "cookie," a two- to three-inch slab. That way I can study the life of the tree at my leisure. I mark the cookie for compass direction, so I can study its growth in terms of aspect and relate the contours of its natural history to the map I've sketched of this woodlot. Everything in nature leaves a trace of itself—shed antlers, turkey tail feathers, fox skull and turtle shell. But nothing constitutes as well composed a journal as the rings of growth with which a tree signs off on every year.

I note every tree I cut in my journal with the offhand reverence reserved for registering trout and deer and grouse. The rings of this beauty count out to seventy years, some spent growing broadly in sun and rain, some spent biding time during tough conditions. Within the circularity of the trunk, you can see the bias of this niche between the sinkhole and the pasture, the way growth reached east and south and west in waves of wood stirred into being by sunlight. The contour lines within the oak reflect all sorts of other contours, the lay of the land and the life of everything around it competing for—or sharing—light and air and rain. Those rings—parts of ellipses wildly wedded to parts of circles—are, in fact, an oaken signature of the solar system. I imagine a scientist could calculate the tilt of the earth, its wobbling rotation and elliptical orbit, from this section of oak. Perhaps there is evidence in it of eight other planets, traces of comets and meteor showers, tug of the Virgo Cluster. For all I know, this slab of wood embodies the essence of a spiral galaxy or the key to the logic of the Local Group. In any case, seventy well-drawn years—early wood and late wood—are wound tight in it. It will ride up front on the seat with me.

The root wad is surprisingly small, the tap root puny for such a tree. The soil on this site looks more like crushed limestone than earth—very little organic matter, very little give. The upturned roots seem undeveloped, defeated by the stony soil in which an acorn took root. That would have been around 1930, which, as near as anyone remembers, is about the time the original version of my cabin was built. A southeast wind toppled this oak over between three others of similar size, along with a hickory, a large hackberry and a dogwood. If they can stay ahead of the multiflora, spicebush and sassafras will benefit from the release in the short run until the hardwood seedlings scattered all about outgrow them.

I gather the tools, being careful to poke around the sawdust and leaf litter for the wedges. I can't find another Oregon wedge anywhere, and the one I have is among my most valued possessions. You can see the trace where the tree was, but my regret at not leaving a log to rot into a riot of fungi and beetles is assuaged by the image of a chest-high wood rack twelve feet long filled with oak weathering from red to white to gray, with wood left over to get another rack started. Wood for the winter of 2003. Money in the bank.

I walk around one knotty section on each trip to gather things, a two-foot-long, sixteen-inch-thick Zen puzzle in oak I pretend not to notice. Until fairly recently, I would have banged away at it in some misguided attempt to "finish the job." I would have succeeded eventually in busting it apart and be left at home with four twisted pieces that would not settle anywhere on the wood rack. Now I save myself the trouble. This is partly fatigue but also a little wisdom. The four-knotted beauty is the heart of tree, woody nexus of decades of growth. It is to be left, its knottiness, its resistance to my needs and purposes a modest lesson I've learned to respect.

The truck groans up the north pasture. I drive it to the top just to have a look around. The mountains have that fresh green woolly look they haven't had since spring, though the green is darker now and broken up with early autumn colors, brush-work tipped in everyday. The farm is ahead of the mountains for color. The reward today is the well-named fire cherry at the north corner, which today is half bright green and half bright red, as if a child had colored it for fun. Across from it, a sassafras has turned amber next to a ruddy dogwood.

Coming down the farm road, I cross paths with a string of does coming from the barn woods into the sumac hollow. They trot on without undue alarm, the big does looking over their shoulders. The dusk is full of warblers, but I am too tired to get out the binoculars. As I come down the back pasture, the jays are going crazy in the Spanish oaks and a nearly full moon is rising yellow into a blue-gray sky that already has stars in it. This is one of those evenings when the moon rises just in time to replace the sun, the afterglow of which has moved halfway back toward the sandstone ridge behind which it sets in winter.

It feels good to off-load the rest of the oak in the dusky half dark with the moon throwing shadows, dark on dark. The chunks thunk on the growing pile. I try to heave them where they will stay, but some bounce off, taking big divots out of the yard. It will be cool enough to light a fire tonight, get the woodstove going for the first time since mid-May. While I'm

still standing on the truck, a long half vee of Canada geese come
straight on flying west to east, headed for a big spring pond
across the river to spend the night. For some reason, they pivot
north just overhead, the long line of twenty or so birds breaking
up a bit on the turn and then reforming. They are low enough
for me to hear the rustling of their wings and see them straining
forward. Their mellow but plaintive honking is like no other
sound in the world.

I like the heft of woodcutting tools and the way manual labor
makes you feel strong and grainy and tired with nothing left
over. The labor of woodcutting hardens my hands and arms,
stiffening me a bit for the guitar but making me fit enough to
hold the longbow at full draw without the slightest tremble.
Such work helps burn off whatever extra weight I may be carrying, trim me down to hunt properly. If you hunt, shooting well
is your primary responsibility, and a good deal of shooting well is
ordinary health and fitness. The bow and the rifle ought to feel as
if they are not there, except for the shelf and string or the sights
and trigger. That way the let-off or the trigger-pull is a thought,
not an effort. The effort is in the life and the year that brings
you to a steady shot about which you have no second thoughts.
Hard enough to have that year, live that life. The least you can
do is be fit enough to shoot well.

Best to try to be as fit as your game, a kind of fitness that
comes from walking and work and living half outdoors every
day, always headed for one hand tool or another, if only a walking stick. Work shapes the body properly for play—every hammer stroke helps my fly cast, every swing of an ax strengthens
my paddle stroke. The more wood I load and unload, the longer
I can hold that full draw. The heft of a wheelbarrow in July will
help you on a deer-drag in November when the hoe in your

hand becomes a rifle. If you spend enough time watching animals, you get the idea of how to be. And when my hands get stiff
and my fingers heavy on the fretboard and strings, an hour tying
flies or, better, typing words slowly will bring my roughened
fingertips back to the beautiful demands of Sor and Aguado
and Giuliani. And when I work through the simple studies and
lessons I can play, slowly fingering successions of notes as old
as the oldest trees here, it's hard not to notice the faint rings,
early wood and late wood, in the polished spruce soundboard
or the way the notes of the guitar have the resonance of sounds
in an autumn woodlot.

There are finer ways to enjoy woodlots than by cutting wood.
You don't have to cut trees down, saw them up and bust them
open to smell the rich scent of a year coming to fruition. It's
the maturing life of things that draws us on in autumn. By
the time the last thick-walled cells of late wood are wrapping
themselves into place, marking another year, the sheer energy
of the farm and the enormous range of its life hits me with the
poignant clarity of a deeper mystery I have no need to get to
the bottom of.

There is a fine week between the end of woodcutting and
the opening of the bow-hunting season for deer, a mellow few
days in late September and early October when there is nothing
to be done except eye the edge of autumn. Walking changes.
At some point, I'm not bird-watching or cruising timber; I'm
scouting deer, looking for sign, thinking through how I want
to use the blinds I built in August. I move around as if I am
hunting, slowly and into the wind, vaning like Patch when we
are out for birds. When I get to any vista or curious fold of the
farm, I sit down on the ground or on a stump and watch for an

hour to see how the deer are moving. Being still and attentive. That's all hunting is.

With autumn coming on and a high wind rustling through the grain of things, watching is itself awe-inspiring. There is hunting to be done in the coming months, but in late September, it's the long end of the year I'm scouting, signs of time turning along each sweeping edge of pasture and woods, days and weeks disappearing beyond each rise, leaving the fruit of the year and new hours in its wake. It's the year itself I'm scouting in the barn woods, the double-helix, the north woodlots, the old pine planting, the river woods. Set out some afternoon to watch how time moves and you'll get to see everything else.

Between hawk cry and leaf rattle, time is so visible in autumn, so strong in every hour but beautifully fleeting, you'd think you could corner the essence of the passing minutes, hold the glowing electrons of temporality in your bare palms, cling to a moment and grasp it as firmly as a newly arrived winter wren clinging to a weed stem, finally get a close look at what life is, taste the oily seed of it.

Autumn draws you on, but leaves you where you started out—waiting at the cul-de-sac, for example, watching does slowly walk out of the pines late in the afternoon, crossing within bow-shot of one of my blinds. The wariness of the deer, the way the wind leans into the woods, the constant play of birdlife in the air suggests that there is something in the scene just beyond what you can see. Not intimations of immortality, as Wordsworth and the Romantics wished, but just the opposite. We don't save our souls by living forever in some other world; we save our souls by living well once in this one. As Wallace Stevens suggests, death is the mother of beauty, not of immortality.

The gleaming edge of things reveals itself at every turn in autumn, like sunlight soaking into the broad wing of a hawk or gleaming off the newly polished antlers of a running deer. *Sunlight. Hawk wing. Deer antler.* That's what's sane and saving in the world. *Sunlight, hawk wing, deer antler*—those are not signs of some other world; they are proof of the beauty and truth in this one and proof also that beauty and truth are not solely a human affair. Rivers and forests and mountains, winter wren and red-tailed hawk and white-tailed deer—they are not signs of something, they are the thing itself. They lead us on toward themselves, toward their ways of feeling and using the hours. You miss the prize if you want more than that.

That's to scout more than deer, I guess. Wind-stirred thoughts run on in early autumn, tumbling along like chattering leaves.

If summer is an affair of birds, autumn is when the tree life of this place steps forward to demand attention. The trees here are strong company throughout the year. I don't know how else to put that thought. I spend far more time contemplating trees than cutting them down. Trees prompt walking. And when you walk in a familiar place, you walk tree to tree without thinking about it, as if locusts, poplars, walnuts and oaks were a guide to a subconscious sense of landscape, their rootedness as appealing to the heart as their graceful, aspiring forms are to the mind. Trees represent one of evolution's profound practices, a way to use starlight to manufacture a form of earthy life that builds on itself year to year, growing itself on a column of wood that will stand effortlessly for centuries.

Trees don't just grow, they create new habitat around them with the way they distribute sun and shadow. The great American elm halfway up the front pasture draws a world of life around itself. Small copses of walnuts, locusts, cedars and sumac conspire to expand into woodlots. The woodlots aspire to be woods and, unless that awful bulldozer goes to work enlarging the pasture, they reseed and reclaim the farm year by year. The woods, of course, would be forests. The most admirable embodiment of the life of this planet is what is left of its forests, those great gatherings of trees that take on a deep life of their own and reveal to us the true depth of ecological complexity of which the earth's vegetation is capable. Even here on Highland Farm you can see the idea of a forest trying to reassert itself seed by seed, sapling by sapling.

In early autumn, I take the same long walk I take every season. Truth to tell, I take it every week because, as I say, trees lead you on. The Spanish oaks still lead up the hill to the world overseen by the barn gate walnut. Gangs of jays pipe and whistle in those trees, which are full of clusters of small acorns half hidden under leaves turning a glossy shade of orange. Gray squirrels cut acorns among the jays and get up in the big red and black oaks so that nuts smacking constantly on leaves sound like spats of rain. Every gust and long pull of wind winnows hard mast to the ground—beechnuts, hickory nuts and walnuts, as well as five or six varieties of acorns. Years when the walnuts bear heavily you can hardly walk in places.

The black locust and the redbuds and the coffee trees hang long seedpods that rattle for the birds to pick them open. Spicebush and dogwood set gleaming red berries. Sometimes you will see a dogwood so full of cedar waxwings you would think the waxwings were the fruit of the tree. The farm's soft mast has been ready for weeks—papaw, persimmon, wild apple, black cherry, the early grapes and dozens of things I don't know. I'll nibble on papaw during walks. You think, at the first bite, that you won't stop eating papaws, but then that sweetness cloys

about the time your tongue gets tired of gleaning custard from
around the giant, off-putting seeds which don't leave the pulp
much room.

Woodchucks are the real devotees of these neotropical fruits.
The normally circumspect chucks are distracted by them like
nothing else. I once saw a wildly dancing tree back near the
old house site at the locust spring. Even with the binoculars, I
couldn't make out what was going on. When I got closer, what
I thought for a while was a bear cub turned out to be the fattest
woodchuck I have ever seen. It had lashed itself out on a thin,
fruit-laden branch of a papaw tree with its hind legs and, while
the branch careened like a big-game saltwater rod with a marlin
on, it grabbed for the fruit with its front paws. The chuck got
its meals but pulled an awful lot of Gs doing it. The books will
tell you that *Asimina triloba* is a moisture-loving tree, but here
you will see seedlings sprouting up all over the bone-dry pasture
where woodchucks have made their well-fertilized plantings not
far from their burrow holes.

Above the barn, hickories, walnuts and poplar frame a woodlot that fruits in persimmon, apple, cherry and papaw. I watch
the farm's half dozen persimmon trees judiciously as a raccoon.
But it's hard to time the harvest of these tasty if unattractive
fruits, and more often than not the raccoons have gleaned the
trees before I get to them. The oak-hickory of the barn woods
flows around that Fraser magnolia in the little hollow that culminates in the grove of beech. The oak of the oak-hickory is
mostly black and red and northern red oak, including the *falcata*
I have come to know well because I live next to one. An ecolo-
gist could illuminate these relationships; I tend to just enjoy
them. Of course, there are white oaks—the platonic form of
the oak. These oversee the best hunting places—turkey, deer,

jays, nuthatches and every other living thing seem to materialize
under them in autumn. The hickories are hard to distinguish
by leaf and bark but are easy to tell apart by their fruit—the big
mockernuts that burst into bright orange by the middle of bow
season, the smaller bitternut hickories and the less numerous
pignuts that put considerable shelter and food into the farm.
There is also a grove of pale hickories, most of them dead or
dying, along the farm road fence line.

Most of the woodlots play variations off a walnut-oak-
hickory bass line that give each place its distinctive character
and wildlife. The poplar hollow might just as easily be called the
sumac hollow or the box elder hollow although its finest trees
are some chinquapin oak at the foot of it where I bow hunt deer
early in the season. The usual suspects can be found yellowing
and reddening in the understory—spicebush, sassafras, redbud,
dogwood, hackberry, buckthorn, red maples. The smooth black
haw is as elegant as the cedars are scroungy. Sycamores hold
wet places or, grimly, places that used to be wet. Look close
and you'll see a hardwood seedling waiting for release on every
square foot of shaded ground. Stately sugar maples have taken
hold here and there, bleeding sap slowly from woodpecker
holes. Of course, there is a black locust for every black walnut,
as if they were an echoing theme, counterpoint in hardwood.

I've learned the trees here slowly, like the birds and stars,
learning flowers and fruit in spring and fall. If I glean another
list from my journals and maps, the tree life here ramifies like
the birdlife, although my knowledge of trees, especially the softwoods, is not up to the mark—ash-leaf maple, sugar maple,
tree-of-heaven, papaw, black birch, ironwood, bitternut hickory, pignut hickory, mockernut hickory, pale hickory, American
hackberry, eastern redbud, flowering dogwood, round-leaf dog-

wood, common persimmon, American beech, white ash, honey locust, coffee tree, black walnut, eastern red cedar, mountain laurel, common spicebush, yellow poplar, Fraser magnolia, red mulberry, American hop hornbeam, princess tree, white pine, scrub pine, sycamore, sweet cherry, fire cherry, black cherry, white oak, swamp oak, southern red oak, blackjack oak, chinquapin oak, chestnut oak, black oak, northern red oak, post oak, smooth sumac, eastern hemlock, American elm, smooth black haw.

Tree names are among our oldest words—*oak, hickory, maple, beech*—and over time the elegant botanical Latin names for them become as easy to remember as the surnames of friends—*quercus, carya, acer, fagus*. Those are undoubtedly *Fagus grandifolia*—smooth-barked beech trees—whose barks are marred with Orlando's bad versifying in Shakespeare's *As You Like It*. But the practice dies hard, and if you look close, you'll find a beech tree on Highland Farm with a courtship carved into it. It's not unimportant that *beech* and *book* are cognate.

Few forms of life with which we share the same scale have such presence. In evolutionary terms they represent an extraordinary achievement, a strategy for living so successful, so imaginative, they form an important part of the character of our planet. Solid as bedrock in trunk and root, lithe as the wind in their yielding crowns, trees set all sorts of examples. I take them seriously for their own sake. From their rootedness to their columnar strength to the varied aspirations of their crowns, their beauty and utility is unparalleled and perfectly fused. That trees store time, record it carefully as scribes, marks them as strong beings. Those growth rings take you back to the Devonian, when the idea of wood arose. It's rare to find time, so abstract when you try to stare it down, reified with such clarity in something as common and tangible as wood. I assume the appearance of woody-stemmed vegetation that gathered years past to support new growth was one of the great evolutionary steps forward of life on earth. Trees are the planet itself coming to full fruit.

At home there is all that wood to split, all those hours well spent in woodlots come to hand again as new work. It's time to fill the kindling box for the year's first fire. It's time, too, to sight the rifles in and begin to remind yourself of the seriousness of hunting. If you are a hunter, there is no hiding your intentions. To have glimpses of the transcendental significance of nature is not to claim to live transcendentally. The *thock* of the maul, the harsh *crack* of a rifle, that's me being in the world as an intrusion, as, in part, a destroyer of the life of things. That's worth facing in fall, I think. If you love animals, hunting is a hard harvest. But it's there to be done as the year begins to end. Those who don't hunt, don't feel this final pull of the woods on the heart and mind.

New flocks of Canada geese cruise overhead, shifting from the Maury to South River in the evening. Geese augur well, wild life overhead, great honking animation of the chill bluster of the season. As darkness falls, the wind takes rein and shakes those orange-blazed leaves of the Spanish oaks and shakes the early stars I can see beyond the half-bare branches.

In the early morning, when I let Patch out, Orion shines brightly overhead, beckoning us to hunt again.

*B*y the time high autumn comes in on the windy days of late October, the twisted barn walnut will be shorn of leaves. Only the highest fringe of wine-red Virginia creeper will still be bright with color in the walnut's empty crown. But the shapely Spanish oak across the cattle guard from the walnut will be turning through indescribable shades of crimson, yellow and orange rust, unusual showiness for this stolid species. High autumn is a time for showiness, a brilliant response to the brilliant cry of spring when the rewards of late October must have been nesting themselves in the promise of early April.

You hunt against and through these changes, changing, too, hurrying slowly in autumn as the year slowly hurries. You feel the passage of time keenly, like the mixed flocks of migrating birds that burst about, a bit bewildered by the gusty wind and the constant rain of leaves, spurred in several directions at once—as I am—by that familiar, unsettling feel of the beginning of the end of the year. You start to feel, even before it gets cold, that it's time to start a fire.

All those beautiful, wind-driven changes work on a hunter's heart, which hardens itself for the task ahead even as it responds to the eloquent cry of things against the passage of time. But time is flowing for the hunter, too, and the serious business of provisioning yourself and your loved ones with wild food for the coming year is, finally, a way to participate in the beauty of year's end.

One night in late September or early October, you light a fire in the woodstove to ward off a chill that feels like it has some staying power. And then you keep that fire lit, the steel stove pulsing warmth, until some evening in April when, bent to the open door, you realize spring has brought back warmth you haven't felt since Indian summer.

Expecting to Be Surprised

It should be noticed that only by hunting
can man be in the country. . . .

—José Ortega y Gasset

During the first year of their lives, bird dogs learn to their enormous disappointment that men hunt in seasons. Not seasons as dogs sense them in their fur and through their noses, but arbitrary seasons unfathomable to the canine mind. A good dog comes to accept this outwardly—he or she eventually understands that there will be no hunting in April or August—but not inwardly. Scrape a chair back at midnight on some mellow June evening and the bird dog sleeping under your desk will leap to its feet eagerly, sure that the hunt is on. Not hard to guess what it was dreaming. Patch—who is now six—still does this nearly every night, bouncing and dancing in the hallway where my bird-hunting vest is hung, trying to urge me on to a new idea, a radical practice, the Tao of dogs.

You have to laugh. And you have to agree. Why not? Work is hard and, in the end, dull. Why not go out the door on a balmy June night and hunt birds in the insect-buzzing starlight, count coup on Carolina wrens and chickadees with Vega and Altair winking overhead? Get the neighbors up and start a bonfire down by the river to celebrate the new order of things, the world according to dogs. I have no doubt that would be fine. No matter how much they come to love you in that unstinting way dogs love, bird dogs must wonder to their dying day what poverty of spirit, what failure of imagination could have hold of their gun-toting partners during the months when there is no hunting.

We have a long season on ruffed grouse in Virginia, from the last Saturday in October through the second Saturday in February. That's long enough to be not so much a season as a standing opportunity to hunt a great game bird across a good chunk of the year. Partly because of that, grouse hunting has always felt like a complement to trout fishing, a way to get into the landscape and learn things. It gets us out with a fabulous goal in mind, takes us far afield and leaves us rich even when we come home with an empty bag. When we succeed, well, then we feel pretty good.

October to February is a fine wedge of time. We can, and do, hunt the tail end of autumn color in the Blue Ridge on blessedly balmy days when the birds are easy, if a little hard for Patch to scent on warm air redolent with persimmon and apple, cinnamon fern and dying bracken. We hunt November, when the days and the birds tighten up and the mountains look as grizzled as the coats of white-tailed deer and the air is laced with wood smoke from the chimneys of the humble mountain homes I envy, sprawling cabins built on wild parcels of land tucked into National Forest land. We'll hunt middays in December, going out when it's overcast and not too blustery, poking around the

late-season cover we know, trying to figure out what grouse eat
in winter. In January, if we have a big snow, I'll fill the truck
with wood for traction and drive as far into the mountains as we
can get. I'll strap on a pair of bearpaws, which for some reason
fills Patch with extra glee, and we'll walk a forest road, happy
just to be out breaking trail but hoping to cross paths with a
winter bird that will draw us up some unspeakably beautiful
snow-filled hollow. We rarely catch up with those grouse, but
we get to where we are going, tangled up with the winter life
of things.

I get no higher marks as a grouse hunter than I do as a trout
fisherman or as a devotee of white-tailed deer. That is not false
modesty. In my experience, grouse are scarce in the Blue Ridge.
You've got to work hard to find them—*why they call it hunting,*
as the lame joke goes. We hunt the best cover we can find on
public land and move on when good grouse cover grows up
into something else. Grouse, like deer, lead you into the thick
of things. Eventually, I suppose, if you keep hunting you see
everything a grouse sees, not just the solemn oaks and hickories, the shining maples, beech and birch, but tiny frost grapes
hung on withered vines, empty beechnut husks on branch tips,
minuscule spring seeps welling up in thickets of club moss,
mossy drumming logs and sandy dust baths.

We start the season where we ended it last year, poking
around some old apple orchards, hoping to get lucky on an easy
bird or two. Grouse are bunched up early in the season, young
of the year on the prowl and the feed together. If no one has been
through yet with his dogs, we might get first takings on these
gregarious birds. There aren't that many bird hunters working
in the mountains. Year to year, I recognize some battered trucks
with homemade dog boxes and, here and there, a new SUV

with some sort of catchy vanity tag. When I cross paths with someone knee-deep in pointers or setters, we'll exchange a little information but not share any family secrets. The more it seems like a place has petered out, the more freely the talk flows, like conversation at a funeral. A bird hunter doesn't mind admitting he had a good day "hereabouts" five or six years ago. But if he discovered something last week, that's likely to stay classified for a while.

Backcountry etiquette demands admiring the other fellow's dogs, which is rarely hard to do. Dogs are the heart and soul of bird hunting, the life of the search, and it is always a pleasure to see them or hear them working a watershed. You can tell what the other hunter is doing by listening to his dogs. Bird hunting is all dogs. The man with the gun trails along just to bring a bird to earth occasionally so that the dogs can snuffle the game only they can fully appreciate. Bird dogs don't yelp and bay like coon hounds, and they don't have the feverish passion of bear dogs. You just hear the steady clinking of their bells as they jog a search pattern, then that beautiful clanky staccato when they make game. Finally, you hear that tense silence when the dog locks up on point—promising as any rest in an orchestral score. Although *birdy* or *birdiness* don't appear in my desktop *Webster's*, a good dog getting birdy is something to see and birdiness in one's hunting companion is what a human grouse hunter lives for.

I had come across the terms many times in dog books and in hunting stories but didn't really know what they meant until my own dog showed me one promising April evening on Highland Farm. Patch burst into the world in mid-September. I took him home at seven weeks and, after housebreaking and some basic obedience training, started fun-and-fool bird-training that winter. I don't believe in overtraining young dogs. Love of being out is the most important thing. I took him to the mountains, just to let him breathe the big, wild air in the places we would hunt next year. Those were good trips, just going out to let a new dog scent the woods, hunting vest full of treats instead of shot shells. Like all bird dogs, Patch loved the windiness of the world and wanted to chase down every living thing for the sheer joy of chasing. *Ready or not, here I come.* A high wind drove him crazy with enticing information from far and wide, judging from the stoned glow in his eyes and the way his wet nostrils enjoyed the air. We'd sit on a rock outcrop and take it all in. He'd look at me like he couldn't believe the world was as fine as it was—big woods and blue folds of mountains in every direction. *What planet did you say this was? Yee-haw.*

Needless to say, I learned to keep him on a check cord and, before I did, spent some long and lonely hours blowing the whistle to which I thought he had been trained. Without informing me, he instituted mountain rules as soon as we got to the big woods. I learned the brassy taste of that peculiar worrying you do when you begin to think your dog is lost. He thought, and still thinks, that the wider world was just an extension of Highland Farm, which I suppose it is, and that he could always find his way home, which I doubt. He had a few backcountry adventures as a pup, but would always appear back at the truck at dusk or dark, looking ragged and unapologetic.

Despite his natural rambunctiousness and his pointer's tendency to run wide, Patch taught me things from the beginning. From his youngest days he walked in that figure-eight, hunt-search loop characteristic of dogs bred to hunt. Even when he was stalking field mice and rousting whitethroats, he was casually all business. A foolish pup locking up on grasshoppers is a hunter and deserves praise. Never mind how many hoppers it takes to make a meal. And never mind the pup's habit of stumbling into fresh, quivering-green cow pies half as high as himself ten minutes after a bath. I'd walk along the pastures at home and he'd range and circle back, range and circle back. As he got older and started feeling his oats, the circling back got to be a problem—an overnight problem once or twice—and we had some long and hard disagreements about the radius of that circle. Two years of disagreements. But Patch knew what hunting was from the start.

We were working our way up the front pasture one warm evening in April at the end of one of those days when you could watch the farm green up minute by minute. I was walking off a long day at the desk feeling dull-witted and unobservant. Patch was doing his thing. He had grown quickly, as dogs do, and favored his English setter mother for looks—a little shaggy-eared and solemn in the face, with a flowing coat and feathered tail that shed light when he ran. Daylight could barely keep up with him when he ran full out in his early years, all pointer for speed and stamina. Then he'd morph back into a setter when he found something to dignify with a point.

Those points were pretty catholic for a while. I tried to interest him in training dummies doused with what a catalogue said was grouse scent. I'd hide them at the base of bushes along our route and bring him along downwind of them. But he never showed the slightest interest. I came to appreciate that he was smarter in this matter than I was, and I was sorry to have invested as heavily as I had in bottles of artificial grouse scent. Hard to give that stuff away. A pup that foolishly chases crows flapping low across a pasture until they lift off, laughing, into the sky will make a better bird hunter than one that locks up on a hunk of smelly canvas stuck under a bush. Patch's hunting instincts survived my pedagogy.

I remember watching him change into a full-bore hunting dog that evening, hung up on a patch of multiflora and dewberry growing around the base of a haw fanned out halfway up the pasture. His body language was unlike anything I'd ever seen before. I could tell when he was on rabbits or woodchucks, snout on the ground, body squirreling around in an undignified way. Foolishness. And when he made deer, he simply took off and tried to get out of whistle range as fast as possible. This was different. His energy seemed collected in his shoulders. He worked his nose around the air downwind of the cover like he was parsing something very particular. He was more agitated than I'd ever seen him, but under control; aggressive, but delicate on his feet. His impressive speed on the run had been gathered into a deft quickness. His tail beat with a strange stiffness. I didn't know it at the time, but he was birdy, working, making game.

He finally locked right up on the cover—pointing with his nose, right paw up, tail still, creamy April light holding in his feathery coat. He waited and then looked at me over his shoulder as he never had before. All business, he suddenly seemed older. I was slow on the uptake, so he released himself, nosed in a little tighter, quivering all through, and locked up again. He was desperate to have me do something. When I finally leaned in over his point, a quail nearly flew up my nose.

Bird, boss, bird.

I took the quail in as it whistled off and suddenly understood that we were bird hunting. We have no resident quail here, but three or four times a year you'll hear that unmistakable bobwhite call from wild birds set down to glean seeds or fruit. Now when I hear that rising tease of a call, we're out the door. I started to praise and congratulate my brand-new certified bird dog, but he ignored me. Normally a glutton for any kind of attention, he wasn't ready for high fives. He moved along the cover, locked up again and I knew he had another bird.

This is what we do, boss. This is how we hunt.

I encouraged his staunchness with, *Easy, easy, good dog, bird, bird, good dog, easy,* just to get some language going for future hunts. Then I kicked the bird up and made a shotgun sound and pretended to lament the miss, an act he'd see for real many times in the future. He knew he had shown me something important and that I had understood. He danced around our collaboration—*birds, birds, wild birds*—what could be better than that?

Suddenly we were bird hunters. I cut Patch loose with, *Hunt 'em up*—his favorite sentence—and he charged off after the quail, shedding April evening light on the way. He pinned one down in the fence line cover at the foot of the pasture and held it until I kicked it up and—*pow!*—missed again. *Damn!* Then we pushed it through the Logans' woods until we lost it over the river. Of course, Patch wanted to keep going—a good sign. I let him burn off his newfound intensity along the riverbank until dark. The next week I drove to Harrisonburg to buy pen-raised quail to stash around the farm for training, and in the next few weeks he showed me bird-finding moves that opened my eyes.

Patch had no trouble switching from quail to grouse when the time came. He understood, as I did, that, for us, *bird* meant *grouse* in the same way that in the mountains *fish* meant *trout.* The mysterious beauty and subtle ways of *Salvelinus fontinalis* drew me into the mountains years ago, when I wanted a wild landscape to call home and tumbling mountain streams seemed the best way in. The flush and drum of *Bonasa umbellus* drew me the rest of the way into another country of hardwood hollows and long, hogback ridges where bobcat and bear and rangy backcountry bucks lived wild lives in secret places. If brook trout seemed like the finest idea a rocky headwater stream could have—a stunning collaboration of bedrock and cold spring water—ruffed grouse seemed to embody better than anything else the spirit of the woods. They lead the rest of the way into country I like to get lost in, not lost like I can't find my truck at the end of a long day, but lost like Patch used to get himself lost when he was a puppy.

So in October we tumble out of the truck on a frosty morning. Patch dances, clanking away, as I shove water, sandwiches, shells and some dog treats into the bird vest. I've got my brier-busting Filsons on and a wool sweater that doesn't feel warm enough at first. Grab the whistle, grab the gun and the hunting pouch and set out through this old apple orchard to see what we can find.

This year no easy bird greets us by flushing through the twisted trees. I like those forgiving crossing shots when you can see what the grouse has in mind. Swing through the well-spaced trunks until you find an opening waiting for the low-flying bird. It's more likely a grouse would bust out of the bracken and veer off high like a duck startled off a pond, leaving me to twist around and shoot at the sky. But if I'm going to fantasize, I'm going to make the shots easy.

Apple trees pruned by wind and ice take on a hauntingly wild look, and their mottled fruit tastes tart and dry, as if nature were reclaiming the idea of an apple by taking some of the well-bred juiciness and prettiness out of them. The two I pick will add a tang to lunch. The orchard peters out at the head of a hollow through which a strong stream flows. The stream comes out of a rocky cul-de-sac in the side of a mountain north of the orchard, cold water from inside the mountain. Leaf-choked now, half its pools hiding like birds under cover, the stream doesn't so much flow as wait, cool water in rocky bowls, a tiny trout or two in each, dace flashing around together mirroring the flock-flight of blackbirds. Quiet and still, the idea of a mountain stream is there, and in the spring its rushing water will speak volumes and the trout that have come through winter will wax fat on juicy mayflies. When I fish that same stream, lower down, in April, I'll hear the *thucka thucka thucka* of grouse drumming up on the slope where we are headed and remember today when we crossed the stream to hunt the ridge above.

Pleasant as it would be to walk down along the stream, we have to get up on that slope in order to quarter through a mountainside of evergreens and laurel where the birds might be. The breeze we need doesn't hold and except for getting birdy on old scent in the orchard, Patch's coursing around looks pretty aimless. But he is doing what he can with what he has to work with. I whistle him over and we slog uphill to an old logging road that follows the contour we want about a third of the way up that mountainside. I'm hoping that the birds, if they are around, are below us so that we can flush them downslope into the hollow that broadens out around that stream. Otherwise we will have to climb the mountain and quarter back high, which means, among other things, that one of my legs will be shorter than the other at the end of the day.

A quarter mile along that road, Patch gets down to business in some indifferent-looking cover I wouldn't pay much attention to if I were on my own. He's all over the place and scenting low, not finding a living center for his work but nosing through the possibilities in an orderly way. Good bird dogs are thorough, and he knows far more than I do about what's been going on here. I stay behind him to his right, where he has learned to expect me, shotgun up in front of my chest, safety off. Early in the day, the gun feels light and I'm as quick and as good a shot as I will be all day. He worries that cover to pieces for some reason I can't see, and then loops upslope, where he loses interest in his own moves.

The day warms as we hunt along. An October day in the backcountry is like a flaming match—cold, hot, cold. At some point I shed my wool sweater, take a draught of water and chomp around a wormhole in one of those wild apples. We keep to the logging road as the easiest way through the most possibilities. No sense heading into the tough stuff until we see or hear or smell a bird. When Patch whiffs sign, he'll check the woods out on either side. During the course of the season, he'll send a few easy birds to me that way, getting nearly out of earshot and then turning back with a bird between us. I'm not sure how he figured out that move. He'll push a grouse across a logging road and leave me with no excuses for missing. When I bring the bird down in the grass, he gives me the most approving look he has got. When no bird appears, he has an elaborate way of noticing its absence.

Patch follows the wind combing through the terrain, but it gusts and shifts and then dies, leaving us in eddies where we can't do much. I follow Patch's shifting interests, readying myself when he gets intense around blowdowns and other natural openings where poplar and red maple seedlings are growing in thickly amid grape and greenbrier and other tangled growth best referred to as *whatnot*. Grouse get in stuff that's way beyond my words for things. Any plant or vine or shrub with seed or fruit will bring them for a taste. Birds are nature's most eclectic epicures. On public land, where there has been a lot of disturbance and what passes for "grouse management," there will always be coralberry growing wild and autumn olive plantings, but I'm convinced that the natural openings in mature forests do more for grouse than gimmicks involving bulldozers and backhoes. Take an early-morning walk in the Great Smoky Mountains and you will find grouse flushing with pleasing frequency in woods that haven't heard a chain saw in eighty years. That's old-style grouse management—the undisturbed life of the woods. Grouse will take these artificial edges now if that's all you give them, but I am convinced they are deep forest creatures, more kin to black bear than quail. And when management areas are no longer managed—the con game having moved on—they become an impossible mess of exotics grown wild—too thick for even a dog to get through.

After a while, it's clear that although he is working hard, Patch is getting nothing serious out of those pines. A warm breeze from the east that feels like it has some staying power turns our heads. Much as I love being out in the Blue Ridge for its own sake, I hate for a day of grouse hunting to degenerate into a heavily armed walk. Patch comes to heel on the road, and we confer at the head of a boggy opening that leads down toward a hollow we haven't hunted. That will put us back into the wind. Modest as these old mountains are, and as often as we've been here, we can always find a new place to explore. Sometimes, the earth seems turned differently to the sun and you find another way into a landscape full of modest surprises that were waiting there all along.

We ease around a spring hidden in sphagnum moss and ferns with those little ground pines and club mosses that have a Jurassic look to them spreading all around. There's witch hazel and yellow birch, haw and buckthorn, spicebush, little cedars and spindly white pines bordered by ranks of ratty post oaks that are small but probably ancient. It looks right for game, the wind is in our faces and it's a downhill gig. Patch looks over his shoulder at me like this could be the place.

It's a mess getting through there—sometimes what looks open isn't open at all and sometimes biodiversity can be a real pain in the ass. A knee-high tangle keeps me hobbled. Briers grab at the gun and pull at my arms and shoulders. The boggy ground gives way at every step and I feel guilty at every tear in the moss mat. I can feel my wool socks sopping water. My vest hangs up on every other bush. I have to spin and twist from the hip, like a slow-moving running back. Hard to stay steady for a bird. Hard to give a damn about the birds. Patch threads through the post oaks, hitting dead ends of his own. But he is not giving me his *what's the point of this?* look, so we might be on the track of something. You earn your chances bird hunting and you get into the country in ways that are less than lyric. Busting cover is part of the price of admission, if not the most elegant part of the game.

In a couple of hundred yards the spring seep finds itself a rocky streambed and a bench of land thick with cover under a broken forest opening that looks as birdy as a Robert Abbett painting. Patch cuts himself loose and I whistle him right back in no uncertain terms. I like the reluctance in his obedience, but I need to catch my breath. I want him working close and slow—none of that bird-busting puppy behavior that he slips back into sometimes. I'm looking for a point and a hold, not the joy of the chase. If I could, I'd show him an Abbett painting of a setter working just in front of a companion who is ready for the bird hidden in the composition.

Despite the value of prior experience, I probably hunt better in new places where I move along without any preconceived notions about how the day should go. Hunting grouse, you are expecting to be surprised. That's a fine way to spend a day, and a hard thing to do for six or eight or ten hours. On a good day you flush two or three birds in the places I hunt—that's ten or twelve *seconds,* figuring three or four seconds between the *Wha?* of a grouse getting up and the *Shit!* of its being gone. That's ten or twelve seconds out of twenty-eight thousand eight hundred seconds in eight hours of hunting and, of course, the kicker is you don't know when the feathers are going to fly. If you really want to flush a grouse, put your gun down and start to take a pee.

Old haunts are marked with previous years' surprises, which will never repeat, no matter how many times you play the tape over in your mind. You can't hunt well with a narrative already laid out, any more than you can write well with too many preconceptions about how a stretch of writing should go. You never know what is waiting for you in the language that will come to mind on a given morning. You have to hunt grouse word by word, as it were. There is no story, just the woods, Patch worrying the cover with fantastic energy until he freezes on point. *Bird!* In hunting, every moment counts and you need to be ready for whatever flushes from the new day unfolding in front of you and the dog.

Patch gets into a tunnel of greenbrier right away and, watching him work, I have no doubt we've hunted to where we need to be this morning. *Birds, Patch, birds, easy, easy.* He's on good scent, but the bird is not there. I let him do his intelligence-gathering, his hunting bell clinking purposefully. When there is a bird at stake, Patch will tear himself up in the thick stuff, beat the tip of his tail bloody with a kind of canine excitement that goes from being an elegant extension of my hunting to an awesome display of his own raw hunting powers. He never goes off on his own anymore, but when I see him really getting into it, with his instincts firing pure desire, it's clear he could hunt better without me.

But Patch works at my pace—his highest compliment to me—and now that he's on birds I can stay in the open, keeping my feet free to position for a shot. He works through a few ghost birds, crosses the small stream which I can hear trickling softly whenever he stops to consider his next move. The day has warmed up and the heavily scented air is all autumn, the brushwork of the gods in the woods is, as always, quite well done. Would art have come up with nature without the example of it? The forms? The colors? The deft pathos with which life dies down to its root at the end of the year? Not thoughts I have while waiting tensely for a bird to flush, but thoughts I have now writing this, remembering working autumn cover.

Patch does move up on a grouse, which flushes before his flowing point freezes into the stance a painter would capture. Life is not quite like art. But his body language has given me all the warning I need, and I'm set to cover the tough angles into the timber on our right and still be able to swing back toward that beautiful opening in the autumn woods on the left. The bird goes high and left but doesn't get far, its suddenly crumpled flight one of the starkest images of the year, an image of a hard harvest in the yellow woods. I'm excited with adrenaline and relieved to have dropped a bird we came this far to find, but before I even start to bring the gun down I see that Patch did indeed flow into that classic point. And he's not waiting for me to paint his portrait. The second grouse flies low into the timber and, shooting beyond my skills for once, I use the tightly choked second barrel to stop it at the edge of the woods into which it tried to escape.

A poor man's double, I guess, and the only time I've done that. Patch went for the second bird first and waited for me, looking down at it with some sense of the occasion. A true forest creature, ruffed grouse, feathered with the browns of acorns and the red of spicebush and dogwood berries, tail feathers banded black and white like the fins of brook trout. The bird was tumbled over on its back, one wing outstretched oddly, caught reaching in death for one last gout of air. When I picked it up, I could see bloodstains on the sugar maple leaves where it had come to rest. I let Patch get his whiffs and then folded the bird's wings, felt the airy heft of it absent the miracle of its life. I was sobered by my success but unrepentant. I was out in the backcountry with Patch on an October day that flamed in root and branch with the beautiful mortality of things. We were hunting, and hunting comes to this.

Life comes to this, since we depend in one way or another on the lives of other creatures to maintain the vanity of our own existence. That, I think, is the ground on which all life can be said to be sacred, using this word in a purely secular way. Things are sacred because they are. Hunting, so prosaic in its scene and accoutrements, will take you to the bright heart of life and death and measure you against what you think you know about that. It will reveal to you feelings unnamable as the colors of autumn leaves, baffling as the scent of split wood or the tang of wild apples. There are moments, hunting, when you have that uncanny feeling that you are about to remember something very important, like a faded dream is reforming in your mind. That dream or memory doesn't quite coalesce, and you are left only with the rustling autumn day around you. Of course, that is the memory, that is the dream, those rustling autumn hours in the mountains and the feathery colors of a bloodstained grouse, so familiar and so strange in hand, warm bounty of the season that is disappearing around us as we hunt.

I set Patch, no natural-born retriever, to find the first bird in the grassy opening where he gave me that easy shot. He snuffles and circles his way around to it. I sit down on a rock to enjoy what we have accomplished. To suddenly have two plump birds to clean and tuck in the vest is as bountiful a moment as I have ever had afield. I feed Patch a giblet out of hand, but save the rest, since he doesn't like to eat in the middle of a working day. I'm so well off—the season suddenly complete in a way—I feel like sitting on a rock and getting started writing a novel or some other impractical task. It's noon and we're done. We'll hunt on, free now to hunt the day itself, but I am not eager for another bird. We are hunting well. That is already in the bag. We have more than what we came out for, more than we deserve today, but birds perhaps we earned on other days when we kept faith with the idea of hunting but returned home empty-handed.

This rivulet we have followed leads not to the watershed's main stream but to a small creek I've hunted down in the past. This two-bird detour connects a small swath of the landscape I didn't know with the part I know well. So my backcountry holdings have been enlarged by thirty acres in addition to the two birds. The creek takes us back up to a faint extension of the logging road we started out on maybe a mile farther on from where we left it. We hunt all the way back up. I'm at half throttle, but Patch is in his midday groove, worrying the laurel slicks. Once on the overgrown road, the path of least resistance takes us on

toward the rim of the bowl-shaped watershed we are working. Although unfamiliar terrain is a help in keeping an open
mind, I like hunting in watersheds I know nearly as well as the
humble woodlots of Highland Farm, ancient hollows deep in
the mountains that seem like home, that are home at certain
times of the year, some wild extension of the idea of home, like
those tart, dry apples from an orchard abandoned long ago.
Maybe Patch had the right idea when he was a puppy careening
into the world as if it were all home. Today, we've hunted five
hours into the mountains, following our inclinations and the
scent of wild birds brought to Patch's nose on a random breeze.
We hunted in a new place where we had never been before and
then worked our way back to familiar ground until we found
ourselves lounging on a rock outcrop where we've lingered dozens of times before and seen something different each time.

Good hunts come to vistas. I like getting up on the high
ground and being able to see the shape of the land around me,
especially the distinctive outcrops of granite and greenstone
that underwrite the highest peaks. The Blue Ridge substitutes
toughness for grandeur, a quality of age in mountains. These
worn, old mountains may not look like much from a distance.
But you get up in their hollows and you learn to appreciate the
unassuming but rugged landscape into which they have weathered. On the ridgelines, where ancient rock juts rudely toward
the sky, you feel you have gotten up on the working edge of time
itself. At home, where ticking clocks presume to measure what is
immeasurable, we sometimes forget how wild time is. Hunting
in the backcountry, you feel the hours keenly and see them as
fine and strange as the spiry yellow witch hazel blooms that we
have encountered at every turn today, or as full of promise as
mountain ash in fruit that hangs heavy in the wind up here.

There is no finer visual contrast than the beauty of fall—the color of a year of forest life molting eagerly before your eyes—set against a skyline of two-billion-year-old rock whose purpose is to resist change grudgingly and gracefully. Somewhere between the fluttering fall of this year's leaves and the stolid life of granite from Precambrian times, when Earth was strange as Mars, we find a scale of time that suits our own needs and purposes. We hunt in and around the life of things, and despite the birds we've killed today, we are part of the life of things. Perhaps the still-warm birds in my game bag are proof of that. From the point of view of the woods, the birds we killed are gone and we are a strong intrusion. From the point of the granite from which we watch the sky for ravens, we are not even present. Watch granite from the granite's point of view and you will feel yourself disappear.

The ravens we often find here do not disappoint. They are up, a gang of them, playing in the cool daylight, cronking their guttural cry. Ravens use the air as no other bird does. Strong fliers, their great talent is the stall, the way their broad wings and tails enable them to hang in the air battling each other for fun, counting coup with wing strokes and feinted beak jabs until one bird gives up, folds itself and tumbles straight down to another invisible plateau, from which it makes a stand in the air.

Go back far enough in history and you will understand that to see character—and virtue—in animals is not necessarily to personify. It is to remember that in wise cultures animals guided human nature and informed what, ideally, human beings might be. We do not project virtue into animals. Long ago they projected their virtues into us. Despite the claims of culture, perhaps the best of our character is in what we have in common with animals. And, insofar as we have spirits, that, too, comes from our kinship with the things of this earth.

It's not true, what José Ortega y Gasset asserts, that *only* by hunting can you get to know country, *be in* country. Poets and artists and pure-hearted lovers of nature, who are often aghast at the idea of hunting, know the country as well as Patch and I do—better, perhaps. But this is how we do it, how we have found what I hope is an honest place in a landscape we love, and where, I hope again, we leave more than we take.

When Patch gets restless, we push on. Deer hunting is my gig. Grouse hunting is his show. Back in the woods, it's all about following Patch as he tries to worry birds out of the land. I follow, tired and feeling every step now.

There is a roughness to hunting that suits us, man and dog— what the wild carvings of a fiddle are to the orderly strains of a violin, a strain of music closer to the beckoning in the percussion of a grouse drumming in the woods. We hunt maybe as a way of going over to the other side of things for a while, dancing by old fires, each of us a little more wolfish than we would otherwise be. In the end, I can't speak for Patch, but hunting seems to question and answer something in me I would rather not deny and forces me to fess up to my inherent selfishness as well as my mortality. If you love the tragic gaiety in nature, to borrow a phrase from Yeats, there is nothing sad in that. It's rather invigorating to take life for what life is, as a hunter hunting, if you will. Heaven is indeed underfoot, as Thoreau suggested, crunchy and loud in the fall, the air full of earthy perfumes and shards of hazeless light that look like shining windows in the woods. I can't imagine not hunting birds with Patch in October, following grouse wherever the grouse lead.

While you hunt, home and away trade places, and you learn things you would otherwise never know. There is a dark side to that, the violence of gunfire and the birds we kill and take away, the beautiful birds especially, not to mention our own hours, which are gone forever. That aftertaste is pretty sharp after a day in the woods. But those hours would have flushed wild anyway. And neither birds nor bird dogs nor human bird hunters live forever. That's part of the fine, wild edge of things, too, and not a lugubrious thought. Afield, we see them go—birds and hours careening through the bare hickories and the leaf-rattling oaks headed for the safety of the soft-boughed pines.

I call this time of year what my Russian friends call it—*gold autumn,* a phrase they uttered with subdued passion, especially in the Arctic, where the brief, flaming excess of beauty in the willows, larch and dwarf birch underwrites all sorts of hopes and aspirations, not just in a harsh landscape at the beginning of a long, gray winter but in the minds and hearts of people who have been treated harshly by history.

In the Urals as in the southern Appalachians, nature matters, and hunting draws you into the most heartening season and reminds us that nature at every moment is life and death come 'round. It's not just Patch and I and the birds. It's those leathery brown post oak leaves or the shaggy bark of that mountain laurel that tell you something about the life of things. The point of autumn is not its beauty but its truth—that the woods are always the same and always different. In autumn you think you can see why that is. That's why hunting is so fine. Game seems to lead you on, co-opting you out of your own subjectivity, healing that ancient division between mind and body that is part of the cost of culture. Just as the Romantics promised, you can see the truth in nature—touch it, hear it, smell it, taste it. Grouse and deer and turkey—or anything else you choose to follow—will lead you on in the right direction. That sequence of fruiting and flaming and dying back in the leaf to expose the bud of next year's leaf is all you need to observe. Spring may be spawning season for the very young, but for the rest of us, I think, autumn is the most sensuous time of year—a sadder, wiser, wilder season in which the pleasures of being alive are at their most piquant. There is a rich whiff of life offered in every breath if you slow down to take it in.

It's getting late and we have our birds, but on the long way back Patch and I stop at one last stretch of good cover where we might flush a bird just for the sake of hearing it escape. I hunted alone for several years before I acquired Patch. I'd roam the ridges and put up some birds, mostly at random. That was good hunting in its way, but I never liked staying out until dark when I was alone on the trackless ridges. The familiarity of familiar places disappears at night. I've slept many nights in the backcountry, but I still get an uneasy, shivery feel with darkness coming on—a touch of what Huck Finn, watching the broad river that was his home and not his home, called the "solid lonesomeness" of things. For me it was the sudden feeling that I didn't really belong in the backcountry, that I had either hunted too far or not quite far enough and had been caught out, at sunset, on ground that wasn't mine.

With Patch for company, I don't mind dusk catching us far from the truck as we hunt for one more flush of a wild bird in a wild place, just the sound of wings that proves that we are hunters hunting, that we belong in the woods.

In October, as in April, I cannot be everywhere I want to be. The opening of deer season enlarges the farm along the grain of the lives of deer—their habits, needs and hungers. Every subtle fold of ridge, every sinkhole, every edge where woods or a woodlot give way to pasture becomes a hunting place. Before I ever released an arrow, bow hunting led me deeper into the farm and into many fine hours in the woods.

I could hunt the cabin hollow through which deer sometimes cross in the morning browsing honeysuckle along the path where I watch sparrows in the spring. You can see where they come down near the dying sugar maple and follow the lower pasture edge toward the river woods. I could hunt the edge of the back pasture, staying hidden in the dark oaks waiting for deer to come up from the river through new hollow, nuzzling acorns out of the leaf litter as they come. I could hunt the lower barn woods near those limestone outcrops above the fox den spring or lay up in the head of the barn woods in that shady draw below the beech trees. I could wait at the head of the poplar hollow where does make a long, dangerous cross-ing across the front pasture, or I could sit on the big white oak stump down among the chinquapin oaks. I could hunt just off the fence line at the far edge of the nameless woodlot near where deer come out of Baizley's evergreens, or post up on the edges of the sinkholes in the north woodlots. I could sit on that gnarly section of red oak I left in the double-helix and wait for the north woodlot deer to cross up to the big pasture hill. I could hunt the honey locust spring or anywhere along the near side of the clear-cut edge where deer come out to browse on pasture grasses. I could hunt the big twin white oak or sit quietly in any of the openings in the old clear-cut where deer bed down. I could hunt where the good cover peters out on the crest of the river ridge near where I killed that spike buck in the ironwoods. I could hunt above the river woods on that dog-legged ridge the twists and turns of which the deer follow when they are moving up from the river to the far back side of the farm. I could hunt the dense evergreens along the near side of the river woods or hunt the open river woods themselves or get down low around the strong spring or wait in the cedars across the foot of the front pasture from my cabin.

At certain times during the day, during certain weeks of autumn and fall, deer were likely to cross through any of these places, although they wouldn't be anywhere particular for more than a moment or two. These were good places to hunt because they were good places to be—birdlife, trees, terrain, any weather that blew across them, the way the light shifted though their hours. While you wait for deer, there is nothing else to study. I do not hunt from tree stands, which get the sight and scent of the hunter out of the plane of a deer's awareness and make deer hunting a fairly perfunctory affair. I hunt deer with my feet on the ground, eye to eye. This gives them a good chance of seeing me or scenting me and makes for many disappointments, especially with the bow. Most deer I see, see me. Hunting on the ground, longbow in hand, pits you against a whitetail's senses and requires that you learn how to get inside of their extraordinary wariness. Something happens to you when you hunt like that.

ᴀArcher's Paradox

I stood still and was a tree amid the wood.

—Ezra Pound

When you habitually rise in the dark, the night sky is the dominant feature of your mornings and dawn, when it comes, oddly anticlimactic. The itch to wake in full darkness is, I believe on no evidence, a vestigial strain of wildness in some of us—a wolfishness or bearishness that inclines us to seek out the comforting remoteness of the universe before getting down to the simple business of the day. If that business is to hunt, then the taut silence of the night sky seems to justify that serious venture. But a hunter's hours and a writer's hours are the same, and even if I awake to spend the morning writing, it only takes a moment to step outside to confront the vast closeness overhead, so large a distraction that it is no distraction at all, like one's breathing or heartbeat. By the time I reach my desk, I have forgotten both the lingering night sky and the impending morning. This gesture of acknowledging the universe is neither humble nor grandiose. Just old blood stirring, DNA sparking faintly in the heartwood of its double helix, the twisted strands of which I imagine are muscled like ironwood and fragrant as cedar.

Once the Virginia creeper wreathed through the barn walnut has turned wine-red and nights contract with an autumnal chill, it is time to hunt deer. Mornings hunting and mornings writing alternate in October, as if hunting and writing were two aspects of one practice. This seems most to be the case in bow season, the finest weeks to be afield for white-tailed deer, a quiet time to be in the woods, a time when few people know there is hunting to be done. And although the red elm longbow I carry afield is a deadly weapon, the absence of a firearm gets me closer to the heart of hunting, an art through which hunter and hunted are silently united. Those of us who do hunt in this season simply disappear into tree stands or ground blinds and wait, at dawn and dusk, on an ancient chance.

In early October, the thin crescent left from last month's harvest moon has already set, but the morning star presides high in the west when I step outside on yet another morning that might be the beginning of the year. Despite the autumnal cast of hunting—the way you hunt into shortening days and harder and harder frosts—each hunt feels most like a beginning, an affirmation of another year for which provisions must be laid in. Overhead, Venus is attended by Regulus, heart of the Lion. The Great Bear circles low in the north, preoccupied, as always, with something hidden in the sky there. This presence of wildlife in the heavens is reassuring, as is the ground-hugging river mist suffused with starlight that has crept into the pastures and wreathed the woodlots with brightened darkness.

Deer are, of course, common to see. Does and their young

often bound back into woodlots from the pasture's edge during an evening walk. Any search for birds or stars will inadvertently flush deer. The leading edge of things at dawn and dusk is limned with the gray forms of browsing white-tailed deer. Well-cropped honeysuckle and spicebush show where they have been. In the morning, they will be moving through that river mist to their beds, chased by daylight into dense stands of pines and cedars where they can rest and watch for any approaching danger. When the sun sets, the woodlots exhale deer, as if they materialized out of the graying light that makes them hard for the hunter to see. Even out in the pastures, half hidden in goldenrod, white-tailed deer look as if they are tethered to the woods, close kin to maple and hickory and ash.

Nothing embodies the soul of the eastern woods like white-tailed deer. Their wariness is exemplary. The slightest disturbance will send them back into the shadows, where they silently disappear. In any season on Highland Farm deer are abundant and scarce, there and not-there. Deer seem to be everywhere when you are not hunting, though bucks are as rare as a full moon, and big bucks—the noble, wide-racked deer that change your mind about what kind of animal a deer is—you see maybe once a year, usually near the opening of bow-hunting season. I don't think of myself as a trophy hunter, but I can't deny that the idea of them leads me on. Start hunting deer in October and the bucks will disappear and even the does will become scarce, displaced by the scent and motion of your pursuit. Seeing deer in passing is one thing, but being within bow-shot of one quite another. Hunting restores game to rarity, not absolute scarcity in the case of white-tailed deer, but the rarity of a wary animal whose senses have evolved over hundreds of millions of years to protect it from your intentions.

The wooden longbow that I use fits the closeness of the season. A rifle hunter hunts the deer that are there, deer seen at a distance. Bow hunting requires slipping into the not-there, getting so close to deer that you are where they are, within the space of their awareness without them being aware of you. When you bow hunt, you can often smell the animal you draw on. You can see the rise and fall of its breathing, the grain of its pelage, the glistening catch-light in its eye. This intimacy is, of course, unsettling. When hunter and hunted are so close at the kill, what Emily Dickinson called "death's tremendous nearness" suddenly reifies in the hunter's hands, where part of the hunter thinks it ought not to be.

With a bow fully drawn, you can feel the strain of that nearness arcing across your upper body between the palm of your left hand and the fingertips of your right. Locked up at full draw, you can feel the unsprung power of the bow in your forearms and shoulders. You can feel the strain of your stance distributed through your stomach and leg muscles. You can feel the seriousness of your posture in your oddly cocked right arm and in your face and eyes and through the fingers of your shooting glove. If you have drawn the bow properly, you will feel the tense flex of it everywhere except in the tips of your shooting fingers, which will somehow be relaxed on the server. "The bow encompasses the all," Japanese bowmen have been taught from ancient times. Drawn up on a deer, you can feel the all in the bent wild wood and in the strange impersonal center of the hunting mind which reveals itself just before the kill.

When the moment you have been hunting for finally arrives, the arrow shaft may well chatter on the rest, a stutter of what José Ortega y Gasset called "mystical agitation" and a sign that the hunter is poised at a threshold which is as dangerous to him as to

the deer. Punning on the Greek word *bios,* Heraclitus noted that
a drawn bow was an instrument of both life and death—which
is undoubtedly what the Japanese masters meant by "the all."
Hunting is a paradox, a practice that cuts both ways, gleaming
with two razor-sharp edges like the steel broadhead on the tip
of my cedar arrow. When I am bow hunting, the filed edges of
that broadhead are the first and last things in my field of vision
to catch or hold the light of day when I wait for deer to suddenly
materialize in the not-there where I am hiding.

The not-there is a practical as well as a transcendental place.
For me, it is a circle with a radius of fifteen yards. I have no
business releasing an arrow at a deer farther than fifteen yards
away, and I don't. At that distance, I can put nearly every arrow
I shoot into a space the size of a deer's heart and lungs. This
short-range accuracy is a matter of practice rather than talent.
The fundamentals of using a longbow are no more difficult than
the fundamentals of properly handling an ax. Most wooden
tools are designed to guide potential energy in order to take
advantage of a quirk of gravity, some work you need to get
done along the curvature of space. A longbow, like an ax, is a
kind of lever.

The first year I took up the longbow, I practiced nearly
every evening through the summer under the Spanish oaks,
a quiet routine that didn't interfere with watching the birdlife
of the cabin hollow. Over the course of shooting hundreds of
arrows, I fit myself as best I could to the grace and power of the
bow. I learned by trial and error what kind of thing a bow was
and became stronger and more efficient along the plane of its
demands. I did not know I was doing this, but every practice
imposes a discipline. A bow will change you in the same way
that an ax or a guitar or a keyboard full of letters will change

7}

89

you. We become shaped by the tools we use, weathered to our work.

I honed my mechanics as well as my attitude toward the bow. I learned to load the bow by pushing through the grip with my left hand rather than by pulling on the bowstring with my right. This distributes the strain of the bow into your left forearm, triceps and shoulder and then down through your left quadriceps. You should feel a drawn bow in the toes of your left foot. Even at full draw, the bowstring should feel light between your shooting fingers as if you were about to gently pluck a note from a stringed instrument. The trick is to leave the power of the bow in the bow, cycling silently in the tapered red elm limbs and anchored in the firm grip of your left hand and the oaken brace of your left arm and shoulder. When I took up archery, I felt the benefit of all my woodcutting chores in the way the fifty-five-pound longbow seemed underfit to my own strength, a feeling essential to hunting well.

When you have accommodated yourself to the inherent strength of the bow, you can begin to learn to shoot. I trained myself to extend my left arm fully and lock up my right hand to a fixed draw point at the corner of my mouth and, when drawn up fully, to stare hard into the aim point. That was the hardest thing to learn, that archer's way of looking at a point so intently that every muscle in your body shifts to serve that aim. When you draw properly, you can feel your body and mind come together, and the arrow flies straight to the spot without your having a conscious memory of releasing it. You sense the effortless connection a bow is designed to effect. When you are shooting well, the arrow appears where you envisioned it.

That first summer I shot into box targets propped up in front of the woodpile, developing a shooting ritual which incorporated habits of mind and body essential to instinctive aiming. I grooved my eye and mind to the triangulation necessary to sending an arrow where I wanted. I knew from grouse hunting that I shot a little left, and I built compensation for that into my mechanics. I learned the obvious, that an arrow was flawless and would go where it was aimed. Every shot hit its mark, even those that buried themselves deep in the chunks of oak and locust scattered around the target or that flew into the pasture behind it. The thing was to see where you were shooting, to look calmly and clearly at what you wanted to hit. I thought about that as I used a pair of lineman's pliers to pull the field points and broadheads out of the woodpile and searched for arrows in the pasture after practice. Since the arrow was important, I studied what an arrow was—its length and weight and stiffness—and experimented until I was using cedar shafts perfectly fit to my draw length, properly spined to the weight of the bow and balanced with the broadhead I used for hunting. I adjusted the nock point until a fully drawn arrow was dead-level straight and left the rest with just a whisper of departure.

I tended the bow, keeping it clean and dry, and dressed the bowstring with the same beeswax I used to dub fur onto thread when I tied trout flies. Each practice session I tuned that bowstring toward silence as carefully as I tuned the A-string on my guitar. By twisting or untwisting a braided bowstring, you change its length and therefore the brace height or *fistmele* of the bow when strung—the distance between the bow and the server on which the arrow is nocked. Varying this distance fine-tunes the cast of the arrow, increasing and decreasing contact time with the bowstring. You can do this best by ear. The less residual hum the string makes, the closer you are to the proper *fistmele*—a medieval term for the breadth of a fist—and the most efficient transfer of energy from bow to arrow. A bow that twangs is way off tune, vibrating after the shot with wasted energy that never passed into the arrow. A well-tuned bow thrums softly, not even loudly enough in many instances to spook deer, although they will flinch and then freeze when they hear it, deeply curious sometimes about a sound with which deer were once familiar. If you have tuned the bow properly, the *thrush* of the arrow will be louder than the bass note of the release. No bow is silent, but each has a perfect pitch for hunting. Finding that note takes time.

Finally that first summer, I learned the odd passivity of being a good bowman, the fact that you release an arrow rather than shoot it, a condition of what the Japanese Zen masters call egolessness. Assuming your mind and body are coordinated to the task at hand, the arrow will go exactly where you are looking. A bow is flawless. Every arrow is accurate. A bowman simply accommodates himself to that inherent, mutual perfection. A bow, like an ax, will do its task if you let it. Raise an ax properly and gravity will bring the bit to the center of the wood you want to split. Under the big double-trunked Spanish oak one summer, I shot and thought and read about archery until I shot well, releasing arrows easily on their path.

When I could shoot well standing at a fixed distance straight on at the target, I started moving about at random and learned to see the arrow path from different angles. I studied the psychological difficulty of shooting at very close ranges and the practical problem of arrow drop from farther out. I practiced shooting while sitting and kneeling and stooping until I could shoot well from all the awkward postures a hunter finds himself in when deer approach. Then I moved the targets into the woods and watched my backyard shooting prowess crumble.

I shot between trees, over and under branches and through the cross-hatching of brush. I tried to thread arrows through the goldenrod and ironweed. I used my most brightly fletched arrows so that I could find them afterward. I missed in an instructive variety of ways and learned a lot of things I couldn't do. Through it all, the arrow's path never wavered. Every arrow went where it was aimed.

I slowly trained my eye and mind not to be distracted or deceived by all those false visual cues waiting in the woods—the dappled light and shadow which foreshortens distances, the recession of trees which lengthens them and the cross-hatching of brush and blowdowns which defeats the clarity of distance altogether. Not to mention the heckling of crows, the flutter of jays or the scurrying of squirrels or the way the sound of wind and leaves wears at your concentration.

I got better but not nearly as good as I had been in the yard, and I shortened up my shooting distance considerably until I got my confidence back. The woods, I knew, were full of distractions, and so I practiced in the cabin hollow and the barn woods until I had a very clear idea of what I could do and what I couldn't. Inside of those new limitations, I improved. In bow hunting, the goal is not marksmanship but shooting well. And shooting well, after all, is merely a matter of only taking shots you can make.

After all that practice, the first time I had a clean shot at a deer within range I did not take it. In fact, the first season I took that longbow afield, I learned only that I was not yet a bow hunter. I was an apprentice archer in the woods.

I got close to deer that first season with a bow, closer than I had ever been to bucks as well as does. And that was to do well, very well. Everything about my hunting improved, which is to say my presence in the woods improved. A quiet walker already, I learned to be quieter. A slow walker by nature, I slowed down until each step I took from tree to tree was a journey during which nothing happened within my purview that I did not see or hear or smell. When I started regularly seeing foxes before they saw me, I knew I had changed. I was the fox. And when a coyote passed by me thirty feet away without ever knowing I was there, I knew that on a good day I was one step away from being a wolf.

When I got into my hunting places, I stayed still. Not still the way I was with a rifle in my lap, much more still than that. Literally still, not moving. Still enough so that squirrels would run over my feet and jays and crows fly unaware into the trees under which I waited. Still enough to be within arm's length of kinglets and winter wrens. Woodchucks and skunks would walk by and not know I was there. And, toward the end of that first season with the bow, still enough to find myself face-to-face with a sharp-shinned hawk, the wild musty scent of which I will never forget—a visitation at least, a blessing perhaps, and, I hoped, a sign of kinship. Eye to eye with that hawk, I felt every inch a hunter.

But I took no shots that first season, not because I had no shots to take, but because I did not recognize the opportunity when it appeared.

It was still early in the season, too early, perhaps, a cool morning in mid-October. I watched dawn come on, back in the clear-cut pines near the pasture edge where I often hunted. Strings of does sometimes traveled through there on the way to the river woods. They moved silently over the years of pine needles, but you could hear them come out of the dense cover

of the clear-cut and then see them through the open understory. I stood in front of a shoulder-wide hickory at the fence
line trying to wake myself up into a hunting frame of mind.
Later in the season, the cold does that—attacks your senses so
that you instinctively fight back with the kind of concentration
that keeps your purpose clear. Early in the season, in pleasant
weather, there is no finality in the air.

I was enjoying the rustling life of things, thankful to be out,
when four does came through exactly where I expected them.
This happens so rarely that your expectations can become a
disadvantage. I don't remember hearing them. They came
through that cover somehow without a sound and were suddenly turning through the pines maybe thirty-five feet away
and completely unaware of me. There must have been a slight
breeze in my favor. I remember feeling that I wasn't ready. I had
killed deer with a rifle, but this was different. It was too early in
the day, too early in the season. A good hunter's mind doesn't
suddenly fill with excuses. The light was good and although I
was facing east I was shaded by the pines, my telltale silhouette
absorbed by the hickory.

In my mind now it seems like they were there for half an
hour, but of course they passed by in seconds. The lead deer
offered a good shot at the far end of the distance I had practiced
all summer, turning its gray flank broadside to me. I can still
see the soft place behind its shoulder muscles where I knew its
vitals were. I slowly raised the slender bow, keeping its long
tips inside the width of the hickory, pushed through the handle
firmly, loading the bow into my left arm and shoulder as I had
taught myself, leaning into the strain of it finally with my left
leg. I gently fingered the bowstring on either side of the nocked
arrow, made sure my right elbow came straight back, canted

my head over the arrow and then hung up on half draw.

When second thoughts arise, it's best to stop and think. There is much to be learned at half draw. The shot was there, but I was not confident in it. I didn't know then that, even hunting well, I would rarely get such a good look at a deer with a bow in hand. Maybe it looked too far. I had never wounded and lost a deer with a rifle and was intent on having an equally clear record as a bow hunter. I wanted this first shot at thirty feet or twenty-five. That's not the way it was for those few seconds. I know now that a reasonable shot was there, but I was not ready to take it. I had not finished becoming a bow hunter, and a deer turned broadside to me at thirty-five feet didn't change that.

The second deer quartered away without offering a clear shot, but the third tempted me as had the first. If I had really been a bow hunter then, that was the deer I would have killed.

I drew up on that deer, half hoping, I think now, that I would spook it. The arrow rattled softly on the shelf, tapping out my uncertainty. I tried to settle down, felt for my mechanics but although I could see the shot, I couldn't feel it through the bow or align myself with the resting arrow. I had no idea where that arrow was aiming.

Hunting tests all sorts of things in you. While the third doe turned away, the trailing doe got wind of me, or sensed something it didn't like at the fence line with a brightening pasture behind it, something odd about that hickory. That deer froze, lowered its head, shifting its eyes and ears around the way deer do, staring intently at me until it came to a decision and snorted a warning to the others before stotting off behind their flashing tails.

I knew instantly that I had passed on as good a shot as I was going to get that season, but I wasn't sorry not to have released that arrow. Hunting is not always about taking shots. Learning to handle a bow had not made me a bow hunter. Shooting well in practice does not make you ready for the kill. Bow hunting is not archery; there is something profoundly contradictory between that egolessness necessary to shooting well and the aggressive assertion the hunter must own up to in the end.

A rifle is impersonal, literally and figuratively cold. The barrel of a rifle is a product of a forge, not a forest. You don't nestle your eye down against the bullet. No goose-quill fletching brushes your cheek. A trigger doesn't have the feel of braided cordage tacky with beeswax. There is no recoil in a well-tuned bow, no obvious violence. You can feel your self in the resistance of a drawn bow—the yielding wood takes strength directly from your strength. You activate its power, half create the weapon, encompass the all, the *bios,* life and death. There is something in taking up the bowman's posture that stirs the old hunting blood we all carry traces of. Hard to find that blood in oneself and, finding it, hard to acknowledge it as your own. That takes time and practice, too. Not practice shooting arrows, but practice being a hunter.

Hunting is indeed a way, a demanding practice when you undertake it with full consciousness of what you are doing—taking an active role in the tragic necessity built into nature. I didn't wonder that Native Americans and other great hunting peoples the world over understood hunting to be in part a spiritual endeavor, one in which transgression and affirmation were uneasily mixed, and one for which there were many prayers, half for success in the hunt and half for expiation for having succeeded. When the arrow chatters and refuses to settle down, something in the hunter isn't ready for the kill.

Since I was doing something serious, I didn't mind that it was taking me time to learn what I was doing. It would be very odd indeed to go about killing animals without any second or third thoughts. I evaluated the ethics of my hunting as carefully as I tended the bow, the bowstring, the arrows, my hunting kit and clothes. An active conscience is part of the hunter's life, every game meal an occasion for reflection.

Hunting is indeed a way, a Tao. I could feel that keenly when I was out with the bow. I could feel it in the extraordinary level of awareness bow hunting required, in the way it led to learning how to be there and not be there in the woods, and how it slowly made you become like what you hunted until you drew up and released the arrow that identified you as a hunter hunting. But to go from what the Japanese masters called the *egolessness* of archery to putting an arrow into the vitals of a deer at close range—as gross an expression of ego as I can imagine—that was a metamorphosis about which I had not read a word.

This year I hunted dry hollow hard all through October. What I called the river woods ended at the deep groove of a skidder scar left by a logging operation a half century ago. You could see where the deer jumped it. The thick cover of some planted pines ended there and opened up into a hillside of poplar, mulberry, maple, dogwood, hickory and walnut, along with a few big red and white oaks. At the foot of the hill, the hollow was filled with spicebush, sassafras, papaw—slender young trees attended by brushy autumn olive, dewberry and multiflora and then hung with wild grape that occasionally brought grouse around. I'd flush them coming into the hollow sometimes, when I wasn't even thinking about grouse.

Dry hollow was always a busy place, full of birds, squirrels, foxes, skunks and woodchucks. A flock of turkeys would come through there every week or so. Deer sign was everywhere—

narrow game trails threaded here and there, punctuated with scat. You could see their browse marks in the ragged edges of spicebush leaves. In autumn, big scrapes and gleaming buck rubs appeared out of nowhere.

Deer passed through dry hollow from all directions. In the morning, they might be coming from the river woods up into the deer track and the other small islands of cover in the pasture. The big bucks sometimes did that, hiding in not much more than rabbit cover, from which they could see out in all directions. The bucks also liked to track along a ridge to the east, which led them into the clear-cut or to the Logans' river bottom. They moved slowly on that ridge, wary as hell, and they were fine to see in silhouette working their way along into the wind, looking behind them, turning those big cupped ears around to listen.

Does crossed low through dry hollow either way but mostly from the clear-cut across the spicebush flat, up to that ridge which took them the long way back to the river through good cover. I had a blind in some poplars that oversaw those trails through the spicebush and that was my best bet for getting some venison with the bow this year. Some days those does and the younger bucks came straight up the hill, fanning out around my upper blind on their way to the honeysuckle at the pasture edge. And sometimes deer came straight out of those planted pines, hesitating at that gully. Wizened bucks never ran such an obvious gauntlet. Young of the year, too small to shoot, went down and skittered up the side. You could see their momentary panic in the scuffs their hooves left. Young bucks and mature does jumped it and then hesitated when they landed to reset their intense awareness. To a hunter, that was an interesting moment.

You would think that, with all these theoretical deer passing through, dry hollow was easy to hunt. I'm rather encouraged by the authority of my observations here and wonder that I haven't taken stacks of deer in October, when I am fortunate to get a chance at one. Factor in the wind and the way the slope of the land left you always exposed to view, and taking deer there took time. A steady breeze would help you elsewhere. Just turn into it and wait for a deer careless enough to walk downwind. But dry hollow turned most breezes to a disadvantage, and most days the approaches were ruined after a few hours no matter how well concealed I was and how still I stayed. I've earned a lot of karma hunting well in dry hollow with nothing to show for it beyond the minimum wage of a hunter's hours.

Our prevailing wind from the northwest would go right over the lip of that hill just below the deer track but stir the air underneath in passing enough to get your scent around. Any kind of easterly would turn against that hill and sow your scent lavishly, not just behind you, but out in front where deer picked you up long before you had a chance of hearing or seeing them. A still day was best, at least until the deer got close. Then you needed a sudden pull of air to mask you so the deer would come forward into the short radius of a bow-shot. That's asking a lot of the universe, even with a little hunting karma in the bank.

Of course, dry hollow is not the only place I hunt. In late August and early September, I'll cruise the farm and repair old blinds and maybe build a new one based on notes I scribbled last season. I hunt from the sparest kind of blinds. It's not a good idea to build anything too monumental. Deer know what the woods look like. When you bow hunt, you try to hide yourself in the open. You can't make yourself invisible to deer. You've got to look, at least for one critical moment, like you are something that belongs in the woods.

With a small saw and an antique hatchet with an odd, offset handle, I dress limbs and branches and prop them against closely grouped trees that suggest a three-sided shelter. Sometimes I'll nail a few crosspieces to set the brush against. This should break up my sitting form but allow me to look through it and be low enough so that I can shoot over it. I'll cut a chunk off a log for a seat. Clear the ground a bit but not too much.

All this work puts my scent into the place and I don't spend more than half an hour doing what needs to be done and I don't come back to a blind until I'm going to hunt it. Finally, I'll sit in the blind and look at the shooting lanes and maybe tend a few nearby branches with the saw or prune anything overhead that might catch on the upper limb of a raised longbow or the long reach of a nocked arrow. As I leave the blind, I'll check landmarks—large trees, rock outcrops, the lay of the land—so that I can find it in the dark and look to see where the quietest walking will be.

Then some morning in early October I'll go out in the brilliant darkness of four A.M., Orion directly overhead, cross the farm under the stars, navigating by the trees. When I get up to where the farm road splits at the head of the poplar hollow, I'll stop to see which way the wind is blowing. A southeast breeze will send me to the cedar blind along the clear-cut edge, just up from the enormous double-trunked white oak, a good place early in the season when the honeysuckle is still sweet. I've doctored a blind into a tangled grapevine deep in the clear-cut, which works sometimes when there is no wind, but that's a hard place to hunt because the deer can come right up on you from any direction without a sound. A steady easterly will put me in the high blind on the edge of dry hollow hoping that the big buck that beds down in the deer track comes through that way.

Once a year I see this deer coming or going. A swirling, uncertain wind will send me lower down that hollow to get out of the contrary breezes. I've built a three-sided stick blind overlooking a saddle dense with spicebush that deer browse heavily until it goes yellow after a hard frost. A strong northwesterly will ruin many places and put the deer down anyway, but I might try the upper edge of the nameless woodlot or get below those beech trees in the barn woods.

I could hunt closer to the cabin—above the fox den spring, or along any edge of the back pasture, in the cabin hollow or across the front pasture in the cedars. And I sometimes do that late in the season if I need a deer. But in October I like that long walk under the stars and then standing in the cool dark where the farm road splits and, feeling the wind, thinking about how my blinds will hunt. If I choose right and a slight, steady breeze keeps up in my favor, and if the deer are coming that way and I hunt well, I will have a chance.

You don't pursue white-tailed deer. You wait for them. Waiting for them is an art, a way of being in the woods. There are many more ways to fail than to succeed. Nonhunters do not understand this. Hunting is, like writing, mostly failing. You have to be built for that. The hunter waits through hours like the writer waits through hours, watching not for something clever to say but for a fleeting glimpse of the way language is, life turning with absolute clarity through an edge of the mind like a deer coming through buckthorn and spicebush, slowly wending toward you through the woods. It doesn't happen often. You look in one direction and listen in another and try to triangulate a glimpse of the life of things.

October is a busy month, and time passes easily in a deer blind. If I come in at midday, I tend the ruse a bit, adding a few

branches I've picked up along the way and fixing what the wind
has shuffled. I arrange my gear so I can get to it quietly, prop the
quiver in front of me and shove an arrow in the ground. Then
I nock one and settle down to watch upwind, bow across my
lap, literally camouflaged to the eyeballs and looking, I hope,
like a stump.

At first, my senses will be wide open, like a radio with the
gain turned up too high, the background noise hissing like low
surf. When you take everything in, the deer are screened by the
life of the woods. So you filter out the rustling of squirrels, the
squawking of jays in the oaks, the swooping of woodpeckers
from tree to tree. You listen to the wind filling the slowly thinning canopy. In mid-October that's likely to be a gentle breeze
that combs leaves from the bright crowns of trees one by one.
You learn to listen to each leaf fall ticking slowly down. When
things go quiet, you turn the gain back up until you think you
hear a deer walking. Most of the time that sound will become
a gray squirrel or a fox squirrel or a turkey, but you are hunting
and so you listen to everything and watch everything because
you are a hunter hunting.

In a hunter's mind, there are all sorts of deer. There are deer
that turn out to be something else—those squirrels darting
around or those turkeys shuffling through, or nothing, really,
just an empty wind devil of leaves. The deer woods are full of
antlers and eyes and it's not for nothing that when the weather
turns cool and hunting begins, deer turn the color of tree
trunks.

There are the deer you expect to come into view at any
moment but never see, deer that may well not exist. You'll
never know.

There are the deer you saw the last time you were in that

blind, those vivid deer that live in your memory, animals that came toward you and turned away for some reason, drifting out of range on some path other than the one you wanted them to take—a short string of does wandering away, keyed-up bucks too fidgety to come on a straight line toward your blind.

Then there are the very few deer you draw on. Almost all of these deer spook at the last moment. *Something's moving. Something's wrong.* It's your hands, or the bright fletching, or the way that stump has gathered itself and leaned a little forward. Or they have picked up the triangle of your face, the search image of a predator. *That's wrong.* However well concealed you are, more often than not your deadly intentions will reveal you in the final moment when you try to slowly draw the line between hunter and hunted taut.

That's as it should be. That's the deer's way out and the final test of the hunter. Hunting on the ground, eye to eye with deer, you have to risk losing everything in the end. If the deer freezes, eyes glowing, it's as good as gone. You can see flight in its shoulders and in the tensed muscles of its forelegs. That bow was tuned to be quiet, not silent, and there is enough time between the sound of the release and an arrow traveling ten yards for a whitetail to be gone from where it was. A deer spends most of its life poised to flee. And although I have been sorely tempted, I don't release arrows at running deer—no matter how close the animal is when it bolts. No good hunter does.

But the deer that doesn't freeze up at the last second, that's my deer, the wild brother of my hunting, wild food for the coming winter and for another spring. The deer that leaps high and runs its wound out a short distance into the final silence to which its blood trail will lead me. The deer that takes me to an edge of things, an edge at which respect and awe are the only proper responses. A deer dead on the leaves in October, with the weather still mild and the year still full of life, that's the deer that reminds me of the value of what I value and why I spend so much time in the woods.

That deer lying in the leaves brings all the strange, beautiful hours back to me, every sound and sight, the cold mornings, the long uneventful afternoons, the way the farm looks under the stars, the welcome sight of my humble cabin coming home with the moon rising above the Spanish oaks. When you field-dress a deer killed quietly on the bow, removing the warm life of it with your bare hands, it feels like you are unpacking the woods, that every good thing you love about being out in nature is there to drag home respectfully in the moonlight.

Bow hunting white-tailed deer gets you close to the essence of hunting—the pure, fair, tragic idea of it, the way lives are tensely bordered on other lives in nature. If you don't hunt, you don't know what food is. Only hunters know, some hunters, how high and strange and wild the cost of living is. I'm not some paranoid survivalist preparing for Armageddon or a wide-eyed Romantic who imagines he is becoming an Indian in the woods because he has a bow and arrow in hand. My life is part of the life of things and my own death will be part of the life of things. That's all to the good because that is the way things are. Being is what it is. We all hunt that.

It takes me three weeks, hunting on and off, to get an October deer in dry hollow or to come to accept that I am not getting an early deer that year. An early deer is important partly because of the way the season feels. Killing a deer with the *thrush* of an arrow late on an autumn afternoon in that yellow hickory light with the wind high in the trees seems a fitting thing to do, part of a very powerful practice that prepares you for the end of one year and the beginning of another. Dragging a deer home at twilight, feeling the bountiful weight of it and listening to the leaves chant as you pull it along feels right as rain. To be a hunter that way, with that iodine odor of blood on your hands and forearms and your heart still pounding from the approach of a deer that's been dead for an hour. Many people don't accept this, particularly folks who don't spend much time in the woods, but hunting is not about killing animals. No more than life is about dying.

Hard to get at what I mean. I'm leery of every sentence in this book that tails off into armchair philosophy. And the arguments that try to rationalize hunting are quite dull indeed—and unconvincing. But I'm out a thousand hours every year, and that those hours lead to a blood trail in the bright October leaves and a deer-drag home in cold blustery twilight with the scent of wood smoke from my neighbors' homes wafting on those same breezes that made the hunting hard—all that seems good. Gets me out hunting at a time of year when it maybe seems too fine to be hunting yet. But the year turns with or without us engaging the hours, and those hours stop briefly, like birds, and are quickly gone, taking autumn with them. The hours I spent in dry hollow this year, half hidden in the buckthorn and spicebush, were good hours.

One day I got in the upper blind at midday and half an hour later had four does walking toward me down off that ridge. They came through the open timber nuzzling acorns or nibbling tubers. They stayed in line when they got to the flat, a bad sign. The advantage of the upper blind is that I can see so much. The disadvantage is that the deer have to come up past it for me to have a shot with the bow. This group disappeared into the bright yellow spicebush and must have followed the hollow out toward the clear-cut. I could hear them *shush*ing along, closer and closer until they turned and the sound of their walking faded and was replaced with the skittering around of squirrels in the leaves.

Four hours later, just before it began to get dark, I found myself watching a big buck coming straight at me, walking along a game trail with total unconcern. A deer coming straight at you is not a dream come true, and a deer walking up on the wrong side of your blind is a nightmare. I'm attentive in a blind, and pick up sound and motion well, slowly rotating my stillness around the way hunters do. But deer can appear on top of you out of nowhere, and it seems like the bigger a deer is, the less noise it makes when it's close. It's like that last twenty yards in to you the sound has been turned off. I've listened to a field mouse scurrying under dry leaves make more noise than the two-hundred-pound animal that sauntered toward me that second day out. If you are not turned in a position to come to full draw and happen to have an opening in the brush right where you need it, the deer might as well be a mile away because it will see you as soon as you try to reposition yourself. Every time you think of it, you'll wish you were standing, but chances are if you had been standing the deer would have picked you out. Even fully camouflaged, that human silhouette will betray you.

I recognized that beamy, oval rack as soon as I saw it coming. When the twelve-pointer stopped to browse not ten yards away, I turned off the seat, slid to a kneeling position and drew as best I could, hoping the deer would quarter away and then hesitate. The angry, startled look in that buck's eyes was worth the hunt, and the sound of it crashing away with ruthless abandon was as good a sound as I have heard in the woods.

That's not meat in the freezer, but that's a good hunt—the

does that faded away, the buck that came in close. Hard to know what to say sometimes when well-meaning friends ask, "Did you get a deer?" If you answer truthfully, "Yes and no," they think you are making excuses and laugh rather than listen to what you want to say about getting close to deer. Best just to say no.

A few days later I saw deer from the lower blind, which puts me on the near edge of the spicebush flat. This time three does came the other way, tracking up through the spicebush and then back up that far ridge. They passed about thirty yards out, too far. They never made me, but they didn't like it all the way across, kept looking nervously up toward the blind where I hid myself behind one of the poplars. They were headed toward the ridge anyway and weren't going to come my way. They never bolted or stomped or snorted, but each of them was more than usually wary. The last to pass was wound up tighter than the others and just a hair away from deciding there was danger nearby. It hung its steps in what I take to be a warning stance, holding a foreleg in the air, poised to stomp a warning to the others. Odd, to see yourself in the behavior of animals, the effect of your presence on their senses and instincts. I watched them graze nervously out of view.

Some days deer hunting has nothing to do with deer. One day, crows massed in the way they do—all vocal and agitated, tribal and wild as anything you'll see in nature. They got into the poplars and hickories, which still had leaves, and posted in the bare walnuts like red-tailed hawks. I've always thought their wing-spread silhouette was one of the strongest images in nature—their shape a sign or symbol of what a bird is, a warrior shape, I don't doubt, among Native Americans.

You see things, hunting. One day an unaccountable shuffling in the woods becomes a flock of turkeys flowing around you, their heads rowing along, dark eyes all suspicion. It's a fine thing, to be close to the sharpest eyes in the woods and not be seen. When it happened to me one afternoon in my grapevine blind, I was sure a deer would come through behind the turkeys, confident that the way was safe. But the rewards of hunting are not doled out that easily, and the prize that day was the flock of turkeys passing.

Some days you just watch time, the subtle changes of the season—the walnuts that took so long to leaf out in the spring quickly going bare, the hickories thinning, the oaks holding on in their stubborn, oaken way, their leaves dying across a fabulous palette of russet that entrances me every year and reminds me that I want to look up all the words that painters use for colors. When I do that, the words don't fit what I have seen, and I'm left with *russet* as the only honest word I carry afield for what I see hunting in autumn. As the woods blaze and thin, different trees stand out each day until finally they are all bare and the woods have opened into the mystery of how in winter they seem to conceal the life of things as well as they do in summer when they are dense and green and impenetrable. The farm eludes me even as it opens in autumn.

Beyond time there is light to see, the hours themselves, the undramatic way dawn comes on, replacing every measure of darkness with an equal measure of light, revealing the woods in stark simplicity. Spring daylight is like running water, bright as a flashing mountain trout stream. Daylight in autumn glows like wine until it slowly fades at the end of the day, leaving dregs of darkness against which the brightness of the moon is strange and starlight a reminder that the darkness of the universe is pierced with daylight everywhere.

When a deer steps into view, out of nearby cover or moving in the distance, what I call the strangeness of the hours changes and hunting becomes hunting, a practical task that, until the critical moment has come and gone, isn't much helped by a lyric consciousness of things. But those hours and the weather wear down your consciousness until you are only a hunter hunting. Looking and listening for deer will tune you in like nothing else. Hunting has taught me to look not just at the leaf but at the veins in the leaf, at the way the color change bleeds from the midrib.

Evenings after hunting I transcribe scribbled notes that read like the ur-texts of poems in journals, odd, cryptic phrases composed in the fatigue of concentrating on what isn't there. Some mark the intense presence of untouchable deer:

> *The locust blind at 2. No wind. Does flushed coming in. Should be here earlier. 3 — something coming through the heavy cover. Stops. Snort. Gone. Never saw it. 4:15—two does crossing too far below. Squirrels. Doves coming in to roost. Nothing at dark. Coming out—buck silhouetted on the hill. Moonlight. Strong thing to see.*

Some recount their absence:

> *The cedar blind. Woods half shorn. Yellow hickory leaves strewn about my seat like a circle of light. Blind as a center. Gleaming edge of sharpened broadhead. Cool air and cricket chirp. Leaves and twigs rattling down. Breeze picking up suddenly, as if something had happened elsewhere. Quick cooling as sun slants off. Hot afternoon disappears. No warmth in the ground. Warblers I don't know. Then winter wrens, like last year bow hunting at the head of the barn woods, always, like their name on the first cold evenings of the year. Birds as signs.*

Chipping sound. Starting to get cold now, waiting. Hands.
The doves coming late, it seems, to roost. Hunting hardens.
The moon not up yet. Miss it walking out.

Some barely even mention the woods:

Wednesday, October 27, 1999. Out at 6. Brilliant sky.
Full moonlight. Ursa Major standing on its tail up over the
big pasture hill. Venus bright and large two fists high in the
east. Enough light to walk by, enough light to take notes by.
Unreal circle of moonlight at my stand—as if I am being
spotlighted, hunted. New hickory leaves on my seat. Leaves
falling sound like steps of deer. Dressed for cold. Highway
sound. Doves? Leave roost just as dawn neutralizes moonlight.
That blending. That change of state. Freight train drowns
out chipping of winter wrens. Coal train. Moon brightens in
the sky at sunrise, with sunlight, but still looks to be a source
of light, not just a reflector of it. Colder, as it always is, after
sunrise.

The season changed constantly, the wind ruffling things
and then going silent so that you think something is about
to happen. You can feel your human sense of what counts for
something happening refine itself down to the busy work of
gray squirrels, the teetering of turkey vultures in and out of
view, the glint of warblers sparking through the canopy on their
way to the Caribbean or South America or the leaf-thrashing of
juncos and towhees returned to winter here. I log these comings
and goings in my journals like an innkeeper. What's here now,
what's gone. The trees stay put, but they change as profoundly
as if they, too, were migrating. Studying the essence of trees,
the emergence of their winter character, is one of the hunter's
tasks.

There is nothing as constant as change in the autumn woods. October moves off while I hunt. The mockernut hickories that were blazing orange stand empty and starkly strong in the pastures. A warm breeze aloft has become a chill, ground-level bluster that creates a constant rain of leaves and masks the sounds of approaching deer. Frosty nights kill off what is left of the midstory cover, the dappled yellows of buckthorn and spicebush. By the end of the month I can see into every nook and cranny of dry hollow and the deer can see every move I make.

Two days of rain soaked the woods, ruining the last colors of autumn but making the walking quiet. Moving into my blind one morning, all I can hear is the soft scratching of goose-quill fletching and a muted click of cedar arrow shafts in the deerskin quiver on my back. The woods are bare and chill at first light, but I am weathered now, my attention honed down to the hunter's task. Birds and trees don't matter. I want to take a deer today, begin the great satisfaction of bringing wild food home.

Waiting in the wet, disheveled blind, everything seems clear. The ticking fall of a leaf from the top of a poplar sounds nothing like the fidget of a gray squirrel with which I might have confused it a month ago. Better still, the scurrying of squirrels sounds nothing like deer walking and, when I tilt my head imperceptibly to the hint of new sound in the gray air—a soft shuffling of wet leaves fifty yards away behind a screen of cover—I know a deer is coming toward me, not a turkey or a fox.

The shooting shelf of a wooden bow, on which the arrow rests, is offset from the center of the bow. This complicates the flight of the arrow in a way bowmen have been aware of for thousands of years. Archer's paradox, it's called. Even a perfectly shot arrow will wobble from side to side as it leaves the shelf until it resolves the offset pressure of the string and bow and settles on

its path, stabilized by the centripetal force created by the twisted
fletching which spins it. A few yards out, the paradox is gone and
the arrow flies true. You learn to shoot through the paradox.

It was not yet full daylight when the doe approached, coming at me across the bottom of dry hollow. She trended along
the game trail that passed to the left of my blind, nuzzling the
ground here and there as she approached, browsing something
sweet just under the leaf litter. I was frozen in a half-kneeling
position turned not toward the deer but toward the opening in
the blind that oversaw the trail she was following up toward the
deer track where she was probably planning on bedding down
for the day. When the deer raised her head, as she did before and
after every step, she did not see me. I was there and not-there.

At dawn on cloudless mornings, the risen sun will warm the
air on walnut hill before it touches anything else. That warm
air rises, pulling a slight breeze up through the river woods and
dry hollow from the Logans' bottomland. A hunter hunting on
the west edge of dry hollow waiting on a deer approaching from
the east has a slight but distinct breeze in his face.

I drew up when the deer's eyes and ears passed behind the
last stout walnut along her path and then I froze in place again,
still to the eyeballs. I stayed at full draw, right thumb at the
corner of my mouth, patient behind the bow, joined calmly
to its power, as I had practiced. I remember thinking to keep
breathing slowly but deeply, to stay relaxed inside of the impossible tension as the deer's forequarters and flanks approached
the opening through which I would shoot.

The broadhead off-centered in my field of vision, the point
of my triangulated attention, my left arm locked hard, the fingertips of my shooting hand somehow light on the taut string. I
felt the hunter's awestruck amazement at having slipped into the

circle of a deer's life, proud and ashamed at having succeeded. I could feel all the strange hours behind me.

The last yellow walnut and poplar leaves drifted down from the nearly empty trees, each leaf unaccountably loud as it fell. The muzzle of the deer clarified in every hair and detail. I couldn't believe those profoundly wary eyes couldn't find me. The woods were my ruse now, my place. I think birds flitted at the edge of my vision, juncos, maybe. I could feel day brightening and that uphill breeze began to fail.

As the deer stepped into the opening, I could see her beautiful gray flanks heaving slightly with the shallow breaths she took. The cedar arrow strained to chatter, but didn't, as I waited drawn up on a shot I couldn't miss.

*T*he first deer I killed came to me through a stand of cedars as if it were looking for me.

It was very cold but windless, the air hard and still. At dusk a fine-grained snow slanted across my field of vision, as if a wind aloft I could not feel were driving hard. The snow was frozen into tiny pellets that ticked on the leathery leaves of the blackjack oaks that grow along the near edge of the cedar woods. Several game trails that threaded through the cedars were pinched together by a limestone outcrop which funneled them toward the fence line along the Logans' upper field. Even late in the season, with the deer scattered and skittish from months of hunting, this was a good place to wait for deer.

That first season I was not sure what I was hunting for. I loved the hunt more than the prospect of a kill, and what passed for deer hunting in my practice of it had slowly circled its goal for months. At first all the strange hours were enough, this waiting in the woods alone at dawn and dusk. Since coming to live at Highland Farm, I was drawn to that edge of the woods in all seasons. In one way or another, I had been hunting all along. But that first year of hunting, rifle in hand, I badly wanted venison—a cache of wild food with which to restore my strength and senses after an unsettling bout of ill health. Strange to say, it was this visceral hunger for wild protein—a Stone Age craving—that put me, rifle in hand, at the edge of those cedars below where the limestone outcrop funnels deer toward the Logans' fence line.

I remember feeling that it was odd to hunt so close to home. Behind me, a hundred yards across the foot of the front pasture, I could see the yellow light from the downstairs study spill onto the *porch. A thin wreath of smoke rose from the chimney into an ashen sky. Around me, winter wrens and juncos flitted darkly among the sheltering cedars, feeding on their dusty blue fruit. With those apple-round cedar berries in their beaks, the birds were completing a process the cedars had begun. Sometimes at nightfall, the connections between things emerge briefly, clear and still. Everything is in opposition and mutually supportive: sky, snow, cedars, birds, hunter, deer. Enormous distances collapse along the unseen curvatures of space. Dusty blue fruit in the beak of a junco with pellets of snow recently fallen out of the universe clinging to its neck feathers. Cabin light in the middle distance. The near hush of conifers, which seem to breathe. The cold rattling of oak leaves. The still air. The slanting snow. The ground whitening. A hunter half hidden against a tree trunk. A deer coming silently through that snow, that failing light, its hooves stitching a neat path toward a ragged limestone outcrop.*

I shouldn't use the word so much, but it was strange, the way that deer came through the snow and cedars and the hardening dark of a winter night, bringing the hunt to me making me a hunter hunting.

Blood Trail

There is no animal, pure animal, other than the wild one, and the relationship with him is the hunt.

—José Ortega y Gasset,
Meditations on Hunting

Deer teach you to hunt deer.

In late November, Orion hangs low in the west in the hour before dawn. Some mornings, that can be a cold hour. It's odd to be walking up the truck track in the dark, footsteps crunching so loudly you think you are going to wake the nearby town. Nothing else moves or makes a noise. You just hear the rustle of your heavy clothes and your gear creak, feel the cold stock of the rifle in your ungloved right hand. That's the hunter's first hour, that strange and beautiful time before dawn, walking alone hidden in the open.

Along with the solemn trees, the foxes and birds, the rock outcrops and stars, *Odocoileus virginianus* is the finest thing grown here, a being familiar and mysterious, wary with the stillness of the woods, quick as the rivers from which it drinks, deciduous as the oaks and hickories. Whitetail venison is the finest food I know, as transcendental as red meat gets. Truth to tell, I'm hungry for it all the time. If I want to feast on steaks and roasts and wild stews all winter and spring, and still be munching cold venison sandwiches while I wait for trout to rise on summer evenings, I had best fill the freezer to the brim by the end of our long deer-hunting season. This is to be unabashedly carnivorous, a wolfish fault I acknowledge in myself. But after years of eating venison, a good deal of the deer hunter in me is made of deer. In the long run, hunter and hunted are one.

Highland Farm is large and strange in the predawn dark, as if hiking up the truck track to the barn were a way into the larger world, which, I suppose, it is. In the dark, there is no horizon except those stars overhead. Every nook and cranny of the farm feels like backcountry, wild and far off. The red intention of hunting does that. I don't much think about it when I hunt, but it's an ancient task I take up when I go out the door after deer, an ancient need and an ancient desire being played out one more time. In mid-November I waste a glorious week hunting deer every day, partly to enjoy the keen pleasure of hunting deer in the bare fall woods and partly because I am as inefficient a deer hunter as you will find. For a week I let all other work and responsibilities go and keep a hunter's hours.

That next-to-last week in November I keep faith with every cold morning, reluctantly leaving a warm bed a full hour before sunrise. I start the day on autopilot, groggily running through a humble mission checklist: Let Patch out to pee. Start coffee. Let Patch in. Dress by the woodstove, dancing on the cold floor. Vents spun open to a reassuring crackle, the stove pulses while it warms a pan of leftover cornbread, a thickly buttered hunk of which will do for breakfast.

Once fully dressed and fed just enough to keep my stomach

from grumbling, I throttle down the stove and quickly gather the small assemblage of gear laid out the night before—belt pack, canvas shoulder bag, Enfield. Twenty minutes after opening my eyes, I'm out the back door, conscious mostly that I'm not yet fully conscious.

I follow the dirt track without a light while the muted crunch of my footsteps comes to me from a distance. I pass the head of the barn woods, the double-helix and the impenetrable brier field at the end of which the road splits high and low, dividing itself into two fainter tracks. I may well flush a deer along the way, the source of an invisible snort and clatter. Not a deer you can hunt, that animal you cross paths with in the dark. More like the essence of all deer, confirming their wild presence in the dark.

It's partly the colder weather and the bare woods that makes hunting in November so different from hunting in October. But it's the rifle slung over my shoulder that marks me as a different kind of hunter than I was with a bow in hand. In gun season you don't need a deer to walk up within twenty yards of your own breath plume. You can't take anything for granted, but even a Civil War carbine gives me a far larger stage to work with than that longbow. For better or worse, the deep bass crack of that rifle and the way the thick brass butt plate of the stock slams my shoulder reminds me that I am hunting at a distance that is psychological and philosophical as well as practical.

But the Enfield is not a modern rimfire, and a .58 thin-walled minié ball packed over a 120-grain dollop of Pyrodex is not a modern cartridge. I shoot with the rifle on a range in summer to know what it can do and I have learned not to overreach either its ballistics or the limitations of its open iron sights. I've taught myself to doctor the bases of those minié balls so that they flare out enough to properly engage the rifling that makes the Enfield a rifle. Truth to tell, when the freezer is empty I often hunt with a modern gun, but if the season is going well, I like to have the thick walnut stock of the Enfield in hand.

As a practical matter, the stocky but well-balanced gun comes up clean to my shoulder when I'm dressed heavily for the cold, its heavy barrel light somehow on the horizontal. Its balance point sits right between my hands where it should be. It's a great woods gun, not a gun for distance-shooting in the pastures but a gun with the deadly accuracy you want when you bring it up on a deer moving through oak and hickory and walnut, a deer moving toward you unawares, quartering slightly between a frame of trees. The Enfield doesn't require the Zen-like finesse of bow hunting, but it still demands that you hunt well, that you situate yourself to take a proper killing shot and that you have got the gun steadied against a tree or, if you are sitting, your left elbow propped rock-solid on your knee. In the end, there is no question of fairness in hunting. But you are responsible for being good at what you are doing. The Enfield keeps me honest, suits the short-range rifleman in me. I've put meat on the table for friends and loved ones with that gun. And I've never wounded a deer with it.

As in bow season, the wind determines where I hunt. Even with the reach of a rifle, you need the wind to bring deer to you. A southwest wind will put me in the cul-de-sac at the foot of the ridge on its south side. From there I can watch deer crossing through on their way back from the river to the old clear-cut. A southeast wind suggests the deer track, where I can watch the upper edge of the river woods on both sides for deer coming up to the good cover in the cedar islands behind me or my spot below the spring hole on the far side of the back pasture. A rare northeast wind would dictate the high edge of the cul-de-sac, from which I could watch the woods below me as well as the near side of the back pasture. Such a rarity might also put me at the fox den, as would a strong westerly, to command the heart of the back pasture and its best cover from a vantage that also lets me watch the pines.

Being on stand in full dark is an article of faith for morning hunting. I imagine hunters know more about daybreak than any other class of people, except perhaps sailors. I try to memorize every dawn, which is always the same and always different. There is light, of course, that little mystery that makes all the difference. There is the way terrain and trees appear in the early morning, resolving themselves on stage for another day. There is the disappointing way it gets colder at dawn for an hour or so. You have to hunker down and fidget surreptitiously to keep fingers and toes warm. There is that welcome chatter of birdcalls, much briefer in November than in October, the sparest antiphon. By the time gray squirrels start hitting caches in their businesslike way, sunlight seems ordinary again and the day is there stark and plain and simple. Hunters grow by dawns and sunsets.

The hunting books say this and that, but white-tailed deer might do anything at any time of day, especially in November. Even if no deer move at daybreak, it's best to stay put. When the rut is on, deer are in no hurry to bed down and there are almost always deer working their way up from the thick cover and easy living of the Logans' river bottom. Every animal has a natural history, instincts and advantageous learned behavior that guide it through its days and seasons. But within that roughed-out script, wild animals live as individuals. Every game animal belongs to a party of one—the trout rising, the grouse flushing, the buck raising its antlers in the sun—and seems to embody the curiosity, desire and sheer willfulness of an individual whose life you are privileged to observe. We can never get inside of that individuality or understand to what extent and in what fashion animals live with a sense of themselves. Ironically, it is in paying attention to animals as a hunter, slipping alongside the grain of their lives at odd hours, that you see them for what they are and wish to be more like them. Hunting has taught me why Native Americans have so many stories about men turning into animals.

Once I make my choice of where to watch daybreak, there is nothing to do but wait. I have stayed all day, dark to dark, in the same blind, partly out of curiosity to watch the woods in one place for an entire day and partly to prove I had the hunting discipline to wait on the deer I imagined would be my reward. But if no deer comes to me, I'll usually move at midday and then again in late afternoon.

In the middle of the day I may set up to watch a pasture edge, hoping a deer will come out to feed. The back pasture offers a study in light, pale winter light slanting into the unkempt grasses, long-empty seed heads of goldenrod and horsemint, prickly wild rose and honeysuckle tangled in the small, stout cedars that are slowly reclaiming the best of the rocky ground.

This is the passive hunting of long, uneventful hours, day after day, time slowed to an occasional click of branches or an imperceptible shift of light until the quality of the hunter's patience rises, if it does, to the value of his game. All the hours, and the self-effacement of time spent this way, help justify the kill. Hard to say whether the hours are eventful or uneventful. I'll sit on a small canvas stool tucked into some cedars and watch a long, gray afternoon shed the hours. I've learned to embrace the keen passivity of hunting deer this way, this honest attempt to slip between the instincts of such a wary creature. With a slight swivel of my head, I could watch half of the back pasture on my left, cover the game trails coming out of the thick cover in front of me and the open ground beneath the mature pines on my right.

While I wait, I imagine deer appearing from all directions— stepping into the clarity of the pasture, defining themselves against the framework of pines, threading down that fence line toward me. The silken rustle of turkey vulture wings or the raspy calls of crows distract me from time to time. A few odd sounds raise my suspicion, but often no deer appears during those long afternoons. In late afternoon you can feel how the grain of the year has changed, paring itself down to the essence of its gain.

Where to hunt the end of the day is a hard decision. That last hour of shooting light is nearly as good a time to find a deer crossing into view as was the first hour of the day. So I get back into the woods and hunt nightfall in all the places where I hunt dawn, the good places where I have seen big bucks. I have watched the river woods and the cul-de-sac go dark and have secreted myself in the old clear-cut pines and the beech grove. I might hole up in the deer track, where darkness seems to come up suddenly all around me, flowing out of the locusts and oaks and tangled grapevines. Deer move nearly everywhere at dark.

When daylight begins to fade and the cold starts to tempt me with thoughts of being warm in the cabin, I am likely to have my best chance. I know the test of the hours. That river dark comes up through the pines behind me. I watch the front edge of it for deer moving with the leading edge of dusk. The thick cover goes blank, the hatchwork of saplings losing resolution as the long, pale rays of winter sunlight let go of them.

After the woods go dark, there is still a half hour of light back
in the pastures. I'm well set up to take advantage of anything
moving there or to intercept deer tracking up the fence line. But
that distant winter sun can't keep its grip on the big pasture hill.
My conscious expectations fade with the fading light, but I stay
sharp because great chances come at dusk, right along the edge
of day and night, a primal place where human hunters and their
prey have been meeting for tens of thousands of years.

In that last light I may think I see a head and a small rack
moving out into the pasture from the fence line to my right.
Through the intervening branches and tall weeds it's hard to
tell. As I keep watching, I may think I see the outline of a shoulder and a quiver or two of flank. The deer stares my way, equally
interested and suspicious. I freeze for twenty minutes, trying
to see it without being seen. The shadowy form does likewise,
neither moving nor resolving itself into a deer.

Perhaps the buck is an illusion, a projection of my search
image—shape of the animal I'm looking for—just beyond the
range of what I can see clearly in the failing light. But what
seem to be an antlered head and a neck and shoulders come
dimly in and out of focus right where I'm expecting deer to cross
the pasture toward the cul-de-sac. I'm perfectly positioned if it
doesn't see me and moves on while I still have shooting light.
But whatever is there or not there waits on the darkness. We are
toeing opposite sides of that old edge of day and night.

Then doves come in to roost behind me in the pines, animat-
ing the dark air overhead. Their sleek forms flair in from out of
nowhere, wings whistling as they shed speed in twisting banks
above me and stall onto branches, where they quickly rustle
themselves into place. Some come in low right at me, fluttering
just over my head, proving my stealth. Even in the dim light I

can see their rosy breast coverts, tinged like winter dawn, and feel the way they fan the air with their commotion.

Then shooting light is gone. Dusk has hardened into night. A bright gibbous moon throws shadows across the pasture, dark against dark. The stars appear against a larger, different darkness. I cannot even see the place where I think the deer is waiting against my waiting, can barely see the pasture into which I want it to walk. I move back through the pines, out the metal gate and then trudge up the steep hill, cradling the Enfield like a fullback, not knowing—never knowing—if that buck was real or unreal.

Good days pass like that.

Eventually this hunting is successful. One morning you go out and get your deer.

It's strange when you see deer move at dawn from a hunting blind. You expect to see them—that's why you are out hunting at that cold, lonely hour—but when a short string of young does comes into view, or a mature doe walks along, stately and unconcerned, and then a buck, reckless in the rut, comes nosing along her trail, you are suddenly looking at the end of the hunt before you even settled into waiting on your chances.

The rude fact is that a deer killed in the morning makes a hunter's day.

Everything changes when a deer approaches—say that four-pointer traipsing straight up through the river woods following the scent of a doe in heat that must have come through in the dark and bedded down already in one of the tiny islands of cover that dot walnut hill. Thinking of all the mornings when nothing moved in front of you, you can't believe your luck and your only obstacle now is your own excitement. Stay still and wait and you'll have your deer.

The closer you can let the deer come, the better shot you will have. Good hunters, ethical hunters, wait. That's the test. That's where you prove you are a hunter. You hear someone throwing multiple shots at a deer, you know that's not a hunter but just an asshole in the woods with a rifle he doesn't know how to use. The single shot of a muzzle-loader imposes a useful discipline.

That last thirty seconds of waiting, with a deer moving slowly toward where you want it to be when you take the shot, and the last five seconds of that half minute, are long enough for you to get to know what a second is. Those seconds flap by slowly as the wing beats of crows. Watching the deer come on without moving your eyeballs or even blinking, you can feel the beginning, middle and end of each second through which that fine four-pointer steps. Be thankful the buck isn't carrying a rack heavy enough to confuse your motivation and give you the wonderful, if damning, shakes of buck fever. The deer you put on the wall while it's still in the woods is a deer that will find you out, stare you down, flare its nostrils, snort and bolt before you get your shot. It's a deer you will talk about but not hang on the gambrel waiting on the front porch.

If you get the shot and take it and make it, the whole year suddenly feels like it's over. When you know you have made a killing shot on your November deer, not just the hours hunting, but all the hours outdoors in every season release suddenly as actual hours and quickly coalesce as memories bound tight and permanent as tree rings. *That's done,* you think without thinking, and suddenly the whole year comes to mind as a narrative in past tense.

That was the year I killed the four-pointer moving through the beech trees that cold Saturday morning the week before Thanksgiving. . . .

The wounded deer does not necessarily leap highest, as Emily Dickinson suggested, but there is considerable truth in her wise image, a troubling truth because the success of the hunt is predicated on the infliction of real pain. There is no getting around that, the hardest thing in the narrative of any year here. Hunting sheds a bright light on what we are in the world. At its core, a successful hunt is an affirmation of a tragic relation.

A mortally wounded deer will flair its hind legs in a way uncharacteristic of any natural motion it makes in its life, rather like a horse bucking. That's how you know you have hit it. Then it gathers itself and takes off trying to get to cover it will never reach. Even wounded, it's amazing how quickly a deer disappears; the sound of it running over dry leaves settles quickly into silence, sometimes because the deer has run on out of earshot. Deer are great-hearted animals. They do not lie down to die. They run out their lives full speed.

After the shot, you wait, stock-still, partly not to push the deer, to chase it beyond how it would have naturally spent itself. And you wait partly to respect the end of its life. Let the deer find its way, its Tao, leaping high.

The four-pointer ran true to form for deer I've killed here on the farm. I saw it flair, hit well and hard and then it disappeared somehow in front of my eyes, zigzagging uphill toward the pasture behind me. The zigzagging wasn't natural, either. I knew the deer was mine.

I didn't wait long—ten minutes, maybe. I cleaned and reloaded the Enfield, though I doubted I would need another shot. Then I rose, stretching the tension out of my legs, and slung the rifle over my shoulder, enjoying the serious weight of it hanging behind me. It wasn't much past eight o'clock. The day looked good. There must have been birds about.

I walked downhill straight to the spot where the deer had been when I fired, a spot I had marked carefully in my mind as soon as the animal disappeared, telling myself, *There, right between those two trees, the big chestnut oak and that small red maple.* I found there what I most wanted to find—bright red lung blood on the dry oak and maple leaves—proof of a fatal shot. Looking uphill I could see strong sign every five or six feet. *Blood trail.* That's what hunters call it. The most serious path in the woods.

I might have guessed where the deer ended up in the pasture behind my blind and just wandered up that way, but it's important, as a practical and ethical matter, to find and finger those first traces of blood and to respectfully follow every foot of the blood trail. That's what good hunters do. That's part of hunting well.

That trail took me uphill twenty yards, then out into the pasture for a few yards before it looped back into the woods, where I found the deer dead on the earth and leaves that made its final bed. It died, I'd guess, within a minute after I shot it, about forty yards from where it was when I pulled the trigger. That's a hard minute and that's about as clear as I can be about the matter. The deer's wild life was a gift of the gods, part of some mystery I don't pretend to understand. That last part of that deer's journey, I am responsible for that.

It's hard to see where the fatigue of deer hunting comes from— even a full week of it. There is something exhausting about all that intense watching and waiting. It gets to you. A short deer-drag to the nearest pasture edge I can back the truck into is hardly a hard day's work. But that task and heaving a small deer or hauling a large one up into the truck bed uses up nearly

all of what's left of the psychological energy with which I went
out the door. The last of that energy is burned up getting the
deer on the gambrel waiting just off the front porch. Hunting,
like writing and woodcutting, uses up all of what you bring to
the task.

After a long, irresponsible sleep, I'm pleasantly tired all day
Sunday. Not worn out and muscle sore as I would be after a
week of grouse hunting, but depleted of energy, physical and
mental, idling low. I feel a bit like the narrator of Robert Frost's
"After Apple-Picking"—overly full of an experience I eagerly
sought and which my subconscious does not want to let go.
The modest glow of a successful hunt stays in the back of my
mind as I stoke the woodstove with well-seasoned fuel from the
woodlots where I hunt, fumbling among an indoor cache of
straight-grained quarters of red oak and hickory, woolly splits
of white oak, golden husks of locust and the shattered limbs of
cherry and walnut, dark with fragrant heartwood.

While birds come hard to the front-porch feeder, I wash
salty country ham and peppery eggs down with fresh-ground
Burmese coffee and then chase the coffee with cornbread
plastered with marmalade. Miles Davis and Gil Evans's tangy
Sketches of Spain, simultaneously urbane and pastoral, takes the
rustic edge off life here and reminds me that I want to spend
long days in the Prado, hunt birds outside of Madrid and fish
for trout in the Pyrenees. I want to add Basque to my fledgling
Cherokee and Russian, see the cave paintings of Altamira and
walk the town square of Guernica. I want to visit the towns
in Italy where my ancestors lived and worked—in Sicily and
Calabria, in Tuscany and along the shores of Lake Como—see
what other landscapes and horizon lines have formed my consciousness of things. I want to camp in the Apennines and listen

for wolves there. I need to get back to Russia, to revisit a landscape I keep dreaming about, especially those brooding lower
slopes of Gora Narodnaya, the icy headwaters of the Kos'yu
where I caught those fabulous grayling with my humble trout
fishing skills.

That four-pointer is cooling and setting on the gambrel. A
deer is still a deer after it dies. That's a deer you drag through
the woods, its forelegs hooked over its antlers, slack body trailing, profoundly resistant. That's a deer you pull up into the
truck, being careful with it partly out of respect and partly to
protect the meat from bruises. That's a deer you drive to the
check station in town and a deer you drive back home. And,
next morning, that's a deer hung on the gambrel, stiff with rigor
mortis but still sleek and gray and beautiful in the way of deer.
Not something to sentimentalize over, but surely an animal to
admire. It takes about a day for a deer to stop being a deer.

As the meat cools and sets, a lot cools and sets in the hunter.
The beauty of the deer's pelage—black and white and brown
and gray when you look at it closely and touch the fine-grained
flow of it—contrasts with the deadness in the deer's once-liquid
eyes, the brightness of which will never be restored. Nor do I
want it restored. Possession of game—true, full possession of
game—is a hard, fine thing. I butcher my own deer partly out
of convenience, despite the hours of work, but mostly because
the hunt is not done until you feel the animal you killed and
brought home from the woods cease being an animal. You can't
make those first cuts with your broad skinning blade until the
deer has finished leaving the carcass it leaves behind. Then the
work is easy.

A deer hide will pull away easily from the outer membrane
within which the deer's lean muscles are encased. Once you

get the skinning started, the idea of the animal disappears and the work goes quickly. When the hindquarters are exposed, the weight of the hide starts to pull down on itself with a wet, tearing sound. You grip that clean-smelling hide and pull, making deft, shallow feints with the skinning knife, being careful not to slice into the meat.

I feel young and ancient skinning a deer, proud and humble. I've long had an odd thought that no one who hasn't killed, skinned and butchered at least one animal on his or her own should be allowed to buy meat in a grocery store. You need to experience, at least once, how an animal becomes food and see if you are willing to face and accept the death of an animal for your sustenance. If you can't, then you have no ethical business buying meat someone else has killed. In fact, you don't know what food is—meat, in any case—unless you have taken yourself through the full process of the hunt, including the humble work of skinning and butchering, during which the animal you dragged out of the woods becomes food under the labor of your own hands. That is not a grim task; it is a bright one. But like woodcutting, it has an instructive cost. You have to do it to understand that. The true cost of living is more interesting than you might imagine and has nothing to do with money. Bringing a deer home is both the end of something and the beginning of something.

I'm not sure how I got started on this way into hunting. There is a moment toward the end of my first book, in which I am a trout fisherman, when I find myself watching deer hunters drive up along the Rapidan River to their deer camps like modern-day McCaslins and de Spains headed to Faulkner's Mississippi bottomland wilderness. In those years, I fished in fall and late winter, even though the fishing was poor, because

that was my only way of being in the woods. Those passing
hunters made me self-conscious about being such a dogged
fisherman, made me feel as if, in not taking up the joy and
responsibility of the hunt, I was deeply out of season, that this
was fall and it was time to hunt, not fish. *Go home or hunt,* their
passing seemed to say.

I think back then I looked on hunting with equal measures
of envy and suspicion. If you learn to hunt when you are young,
the sheer instinctive joy of it will carry you over questions that
loom large when you are older and more pensive about such
things. There is nothing obviously acceptable about killing animals, for whatever reason. And the purchase of a hunting license
and some game tags raises more questions than it settles. But
years of trout fishing in the Blue Ridge led to fishing for grayling
and salmon in the headwaters of the Kos'yu, along whose banks
I began to become a bird hunter. And once I walked, shotgun
in hand, into that remarkably soft and quiet taiga forest, trailing
behind Valery's Samoyeds, Touman and Chara, the year divided
permanently behind me into the time to hunt and the time to
fish. I came home from Russia a hunter.

Gold autumn, as my Russian friends call it, gold autumn is
the time to hunt birds. And when gold autumn sheds into fall
and time itself seems to go gray like the coats of deer, then that is
the time to hunt deer and for giving oneself over to the demands
of the blood trail in the woods. It's an old thing. There will be
time to fish in the spring. The end of the year is not the time to
look into rivers for things long gone but to hunt into the woods
for a new year ahead, to let your own fate and the fate of wild
animals come together during those long, strange hours only
hunters know, to seek yourself in the wild other and to face like
a man the antagonistic kinship we are fated, for reasons I don't

pretend to understand, to have with nature on this earth.

You can only learn so much from innocence. The blood trail of animals killed ethically leads to knowledge of self and other you will get no other way. Not everyone needs to do this, but I am not surprised that writing led me to hunting and that hunting now informs my writing. Now I hunt in November and on into early winter and know the hours the way a hunter knows them and learn a little more about these things each year. Now I know how a hunter feels at the end of the year—drag a deer out of the woods in November and the woods are still full.

Once you have finished skinning the deer, you have a carcass rather than an animal to deal with. Given that, there is nothing rude or disrespectful when you start taking your prize apart with a bone saw. The head has to come off, and then you halve the carcass down the spine, being careful not to expose any of the good cuts of meat as you go. The ethic of butchering game is to keep waste to a minimum. In the end, wild food is what you hunted for. I section the deer into manageable pieces—forequarters, flanks and ribs, hindquarters—and put the sections in a large marine cooler. I stretch and salt the hide, using a cedar frame. I clean the empty gambrel and rake up the scraps of hide and fat and bone. Then the place where the deer hung in the cold for a few days, luminous with all my hunting, becomes a neutral place again.

I thought, when I started hunting, that those spots where I killed deer would be marked, that I would leave behind some sense of drama in the woods. But that's not really the way it is. I remember where I've taken deer, of course, but to be honest, although every hunt is clear in memory, an ethical kill leaves no emotional trace behind. That's not what the drama of hunting is about.

The viscera I leave behind feed all sorts of scavengers and every blood trail quickly disappears, the leaves washed clean by rain and then scattered by the wind. The woods weather in my absence, healing like a river heals as it flows around the places from which I have taken fish. There is no room in the woods for human guilt. They bear the burden of my hunting without complaint, the winds of every season here blowing across the track of my intrusion with perfect indifference and implacable confidence.

Despite how violent hunting may look to a nonhunter, the drama of hunting is not about the kill. And in the end, I want to assert, hunting is not a form of violence. It is what it began as—a necessity of culture, an intimate and important part of the human assertion of wanting *to be,* which is not a right but a brute fact. Hunting is as José Ortega y Gasset understood it to be, an existential act and an acceptance of responsibility for the intrusion of human being on the world. That is why you cannot take someone hunting in the same way that you can take that person fishing. There is something grotesque and improper, I think, about simply watching someone else kill an animal. That is why hunting videos are obscene. Only the hunter, who is taking responsibility for what he or she is doing, is in fact hunting. Any companion you bring along is outside of the hunt. Only the hunter can examine his or her conscience. Some of the most respectful hunters I know—men who have hunted this farm every year for decades—never articulate these concerns. They simply hunt well. Outside of the hunt, the killing of animals is *not* justified. That is why there is so much ritual associated with hunting among hunting peoples, so many prayers and songs.

It may seem strange to the uninitiated, but the fatal antagonism between hunter and hunted is a way of showing respect for nature. You do not ennoble animals by putting them in a petting zoo or by sentimentalizing them, patronizing them out of what they, left to their own wild lives, would be. Sentimentality strips animals of their fine, wild otherness in the way that zoos and animal parks do. The true hunter pursues his prey as a subject, not an object. There is no more honest relation between man and animal.

To see white-tailed deer, even the deer you are raising a rifle on, as individuals is to see them clearly. Finally, it is the individuality of animals the hunter pursues—their beauty and stoicism and the profoundly moving accident of their lives, which resonates with the hunter's sense of the fortunate accident of his own life. The cliché is that men hunt to prove their manhood. I hunt to prove my humanity, to implicate myself in the way of things, to take responsibility for who and what I am throughout the year.

The hunter respects the ancient sense of difference and distance between men and animals even as he feels most keenly the tug of an even more ancient kinship—the wolfishness and bearishness and hawkishness in himself. There is a primal sanity and a primal honesty in hunting—in the secret, half-hidden waiting at odd hours in odd places, in the decision to shoot, in the kill and the blood trail and in the undeniable heart-whoop of savage pleasure at being a successful hunter.

Time is a two-edged sword. If the hunter were one of the immortals, this hunting would be perverse, some kind of ugly, cosmic sport. But the human hunter is hunted, too, if only by time, those quickly passing hours and days that fall shows to us. Hunting is a great school for mortals and at the deepest, subconscious level hunting teaches us to confront and accept the temporary nature of all life. Hunting teaches what art teaches and what religions ought to teach, that "death is the mother of beauty," as Wallace Stevens puts it in "Sunday Morning," that we value life because of death, our death and the death of all things—that we are participants in life, not owners of it, that we are passing through life and that life is passing through us. That is, I think, a joyful thought and the source of all our keen powers.

The final bond between hunter and hunted is the bond of the I-Thou, to return to Martin Buber's profound distinction. The true blood trail leads to a fellow subject, not an object. At no point in the hunt is the animal a thing, an It. That's what all the hunting hours teach. The hunter's knowledge of the woods is a way of earning acceptance, fair subjecthood, in the woods, by the woods, of the woods. The hunter's solitariness is, finally, the solitariness of the game he pursues, a kinship beyond words and beyond rational explanation, like many of life's finer emotions. Time spent in the woods throughout the year, reading everything as closely as you can, is a way of proving you belong among the equals you find there. The hunter is a subject and the deer is a subject, just as the junco and the golden-crowned kinglets are subjects, and everything that grows or aspires to be by eroding or rotting or running before a breeze like a dead oak leaf turning end to end as if it were going somewhere. Take the long view of the woods and you will see that the nature of things unites us, that we are, at our best, equals with nature in life and death. In the end, it is our own joyful mortality that justifies the kill.

One November the hunter will not be in the woods and neither the deer nor the woods nor the wind will know or mark the difference his absence makes. If you hunt, and if you have taken your modest share of game—not as trophies but as food for your table—then you will understand the beauty in the thought of that unmarked difference in the woods. Folks who are on their way to heaven or some other imagined paradise where the true cost of living does not have to be paid won't understand or accept this. But I am not trying to get to heaven. I am trying to get to earth.

Most years, I hunt hard in late December for one last cache of venison. I hunt right up to the end of the season when the deer have nearly made it through, pursuing them into the contracting daylight hours of late fall and then across the long shadows of the winter solstice. Then I hunt into the slowly lengthening days, with the weather stiffening in the offbeat rhythm of early winter where one year flows coldly into another, tributary to tributary. In the dead of winter, you can see time pool, nearly frozen in the slow flow of hours. And since now I hunt across those hours, that frozen ground, hunting seems to hold the years together.

This last deer must be earned against the grain of much finality. In late December, whitetails are as wary as they will be all year, each solitary buck or string of does tightly woven into the warp and woof of the empty gray woods. I can wait for three or four hours, stock-still and fully camouflaged, at the locust blowdown or the white oak cul-de-sac or behind the poplar blind at the eastern edge of the river woods, and see nothing except the gray squirrels and woodpeckers that might stir themselves at any hour in winter woodlots. From time to time I will see turkey or a fox, but I am not hunting turkey and the fox is hunting on its own behalf, she and I part of a long regress of predation that is always worrying its way through the woods. But for the most part, nothing moves that I can see except oak leaves rustling in the wind or the pines and cedars soughing.

By the onset of winter, their innate wariness and the pressure of a long hunting season has perfected the wildness of deer, the wildness within which nature reasserts itself—that austere, nearly inanimate otherness that hawks and deer and trees and rocks share at the core of their being. You see that clearly and feel it keenly in winter when the pure shape of that otherness bares itself like a worn tooth, a canine in the jaw of things.

This year a cold fall contracted into a cold winter. In mid-December, the jet stream dove south, bringing brittle air that had a whiff of permafrost and pack ice in it. Perhaps Patch was scenting caribou and spruce grouse in his twitchy dreams alongside the woodstove, or chasing Arctic hares through willow thickets along frozen rivers laced with grizzly tracks. Denizens of the northern Great Plains or the Upper Peninsula or the Maine woods wouldn't think much of our winters, but Arctic air is Arctic after all, a taste of an extreme that puts an edge on life, an extreme that is, in fact, one of the great edges of life on earth.

By late December, the rut is long over, the rush of opportunistic hunters in the woods has subsided and a deer's only passion is to survive—the bucks to breed again in a year, the does to birth new young. In a sense, their lives are one long, elegant, watchful wait, although within this waiting I imagine deer feel the complex pleasures of their life afield through all the seasons of their lives. They have time, only time, and no reason to show themselves. From now until next November, when the rut begins again, every step each deer takes is guarded, and although deer are common, in winter they are not commonly seen. Most deer you nearly encounter in winter crash away with timely passion.

No one admires deer more than the hunter at the end of the

year, a feeling that strengthens as winter deepens. To hunt deer during the final weeks of the season is not to pursue their sacred wildness—which would be presumptuous—but to insinuate yourself into the frank otherness of the winter woods, to take your humble place there, to wait between the grayness of a hickory and the grayness of an oak until the wind ruffles a white-tailed deer into view within range of your skill in shooting. A cold moment, to be sure.

But this last deer of the year is always elusive.

In winter, deer don't move at all. Whitetails have evolved a trick of throttling down their basal metabolism when the weather turns frigid, which reduces their need to browse and graze. They become rare, not in numbers but in visibility, a trick of many things in winter. When the farm freezes up, they bed down for the day in the densest stands of conifers, protected by windbreaks of red cedars and white pines young enough to be green to the ground. Of course, the deer are also protected by the superb insulation of their hollow hair and underfur, the same hollowness that floats the trout flies I tie from deer hair. I read that, over time, deer have expanded their range farther and farther north, taking advantage of their tolerance for cold and evolving into larger subspecies with more efficient mass-to-surface-area ratios. Winter may have a mind of its own, but deer are well adapted to it.

I am less well adapted to a week of below-freezing weather, a week of pale days when dawn is a cold affair, a visual change of state that promises nothing except hours of indifferent winter light that will fade into a brutally cold dusk, leaving me a hard walk home to a cold cabin. Warm-bloodedness may be a clever evolutionary trick, but at the heart of winter you can feel the risk of it in freezing feet and hands and in the way your face and lungs burn with cold. Trying to do anything well under such conditions is difficult. Just getting out the door in the morning requires a supreme effort. Once on stand, simply trying to stay still becomes a complex art. On these frigid winter days, there is not much obvious life left in the year and the hunter is a student not so much of the woods but of his own desire to keep hunting.

During the last week of the season, I hunted my best places one last time. At each blind I felt that I was looking for something I had left behind in the year. It's hard not to think of all the deer that pass by your hunting places when you are not there. Unlike earlier in the season, when everything is a reward, I saw less and less each day—as if my hunting senses were wearing out and would not be renewed until next October. The hunter's intentions narrow in the cold. You pick a spot and stay there as long as you can, peering at deer that are not there. You can feel the lateness of the season in the air, see it in the golden-crowned kinglets that flit among the cedars.

On Monday, I watched dawn pale coldly from the poplar blind in the river woods. I got out in the awful cold, hoping that a buck would come up from the river bottom at first light. I settled in my blind in the dark, dressed for a moonwalk. A thick wool balaclava muffled the silence around my ears. Still, I could hear South River rattling in the cold. As the sky paled behind the Blue Ridge to the southeast, the river woods appeared before me as perfectly empty as I had ever seen them. The tips of long rays of cold winter sunlight reached through the bare trees, lit the leaf litter and bits of brushy cover indifferently until that sunlight finally reached me and bathed the blind in that same cold, indifferent light. I fought the cold back with what concentration I could muster, working to stay still and look sharp. Some mornings it happens. There's nothing there until suddenly you catch gray movement at the edge of your vision and a deer comes up the ridge, confident and unconcerned and coming your way.

On Tuesday morning I hunted the cedars above the big spring, waiting in a makeshift blind I hacked out of a large dead cedar that had blown down years ago. Its branches had turned a dull silver, and it looked like someone's Christmas tree left in the woods. Some small plant or tuber grew under the standing cedars that the wild turkeys fancied. They had scratched their way all around the place, churning up the peaty soil as if they were cultivating it. The ground around my post was littered with the berry-laden tips of live cedars cut by gray squirrels and feasted on by the full array of wintering birds that fluttered around me as if I weren't there. It seemed warmer down in those cedars, but I think the sense of a little warmth was visual, a copse of evergreens cozier to the eye than the open hardwood slopes of the river woods. I stayed there until near noon, hoping that a lone buck or a string of does would come the short way up from the river, headed in to the evergreens to bed down for the day.

On Wednesday, I still-hunted through the middle of the day, working my way downhill to the fence line at the foot of the cedars and then along the tilting fence posts and sagging barbed wire toward the big spring where the Logans' ram pump thumped away like a grouse with just one pronounced beat to drum. Down there at the base of the river woods, I was sheltered from the brunt of a northwest wind that must have been driving hard across the big pasture hill. But I had enough of a breeze to work with as I slowly ghosted uphill. I lost myself as best I could, crisscrossing the river woods, trying to be treelike and rocklike, working my way gradually through the deer-gray woods. Those hours slow-stepping over leaves and branches, heart and lungs hanging fire with every step, were exhausting.

To still-hunt deer, you have to try to get inside of deer-time, move slower than their infinitesimally slow midday movements, to have a chance of outseeing their sight or outhearing their hearing. The breeze in your face takes care of your scent and the slope of the hill you ascend tutors slow motion, but this getting inside of deer-time in the dead of winter is a hard business. The pleasure of concentrating eye and mind on the upslope woods eventually dulls to a faint headache that throbs like the Logans' ram pump in the distance. At times I sat down and closed my eyes for a full minute or two, just to rest the idea of seeing, quell that soft pulsing in my head.

Feeling the week was getting away from me, I stayed out all day. The gray hours slipped quickly away. I slowly worked a faint diagonal between the gas-line right-of-way and the fence along the ridgetop where the property ended. As I approached that fence line I could hear the river down below, freshened by the modest snowmelt in those headwaters where I fished for trout in the spring. I thought of the way brook trout immobilize themselves in the cold and the way the watersheds I knew in the mountains would be as still as empty rooms. The farm, too, seemed empty.

Deer were undoubtedly bedded down in thick cover by the river. They had stashed themselves in the dense pines between the gas line and the front pasture and in the old clear-cut and the cedar islands that dotted the back pasture. Unapproachable where they were, I hunted them where they were not, as if my desire for a deer might conjure one out of limestone and oak. Sometimes that pays off. For a change of pace, I'd post myself downwind of the good cover on the far side of the gas line, watching the faint trend of a grassy game trail disappear into a dark tangle. But unless you drive deer with several hunters, which we don't do here, there is no way to make a useful approach to such game. The farm deals an even hand to hunter and hunted. A red-tailed hawk perched on a pasture tree will wait for a rabbit to move. The rabbit will wait for the hawk to fly off. I waited on the deer and they waited on me.

Wednesday night a front moved in and by morning the snow was piling up like winter moving in to stay. The farm whited out around the cabin on Thursday and I was glad to have the day off from hunting. I went out late in the afternoon with the sky clearing from purple to blue but already going dark. Bundled against the tail end of that northwest wind, I cradled the Enfield and walked up to the head of the barn woods through the enlarged feel of a winter landscape. There wasn't time to hunt, so I just cleared the snow from a log below the beech grove and sat down to watch and see if any deer came out of the cover of Baizley's pines, heading across the farm toward the river as they sometimes did at dusk. I imagined deer shuffling slowly through the foot-high snow broadside to me.

Friday, next-to-last day of the season, I hunted against the idea of the season ending without that last deer to fill the freezer. The snow, scuffed with deer trails in every direction, confirmed what I already knew—that deer were everywhere. Nothing reveals the life of the woods like snow—not just the peregrinations of rabbits, squirrels and deer, but the secret life of birds, mice and voles, not to mention those startling places where the wing tips of hawks or owls frame the bloodstained commotion of a kill.

The brightness of the farm only made it seem more empty,

but the day was warming fast, the sun glazing the snow with a sheen of melt. I knew deer would be moving out of the pines adjacent to dry hollow where I had bow hunted in October. There would be forage in dry hollow that hadn't been buried in the snow. Deer would come out of those pines where the kinglets darted about. They would look about warily, but they would come. Maybe just one or two deer. Does. They would clamber down and up the deep vee of the skidder scar and then freeze, gathering themselves, before moving along across that wind-protected slope where they could nuzzle through a light dusting of snow maybe the turkeys had already disturbed. Big weather always favors the hunter after it moves on because it has redefined conditions in the woods so clearly. I knew, that Friday morning, walking up the farm road around nine A.M., that I would get a deer in dry hollow.

I waited for a few hours, enjoying the bright, unsettled feel of the day, watching the juncos and the haggard bluebirds flit about and the squirrels get out in the sunlit canopy and move around according to the jerky rhythms of their lives. Sitting there, I was already looking forward to just being in the woods again without hunting, to skiing around and bird-watching and taking things in with no desire or obligation to bring anything other than a walking stick or a bird's nest home. I was looking forward to putting the guns and gear away and traveling around Highland Farm with a musette bag of notebooks and field guides on my shoulder.

I was glad to see those two big does come across the skidder ditch near noon. I wasn't in a blind. I was on the inside of the barbed-wire fence that separates dry hollow from the deer track. I just sat behind a screen of grapevine and greenbrier, ready to site in on anything that moved across the slope below me. They came out of those dark pines, although I didn't see them come. In fact, I didn't really see them cross the ditch. They were just there, twenty yards below me, on my side of the ditch. As often happens, suddenly the hunt was about to be over, although it took a long fifteen minutes for me to get a clear shot.

When they lowered their heads to feed, I'd ease toward an opening in the vines so that when the deer crossed directly below me, I would have a clear shot between the trees. In the end I was just sitting in the snow, propped up to shoot, sited on the first good opening in front of the lead deer. My only worry was that more deer were coming through the pines and, seeing me move, would snort the hollow empty before I got my shot. But no deer came. I remember a handful of songbirds scattering through between me and the does, a final test of my concentration, an affirmation of sorts, I thought.

Pine warblers, good.

Not sure what such a thought means. Everything in the woods is good—the deer browsing with unconcern, the warblers flashing in the air—bright snow-light playing off their wing bars—and the hunter hunting.

After the deer disappeared, I could see the blood trail in the snow from where I sat. The second doe had bolted back into the pines. The deer I shot ran on in the direction it was headed. I waited a few minutes in the deep silence that follows a rifle shot in the woods. Then I sidestepped my way down the slope.

I found dark blood on the snow and the deer nearby, thirty or forty yards away, up the slope toward the old clear-cut gate. As deer do, it had bled itself out on the run, nearly cresting that last hill before it made a sharp turn and came to rest at the base of a double-trunked gum tree grown up around a small limestone outcrop. The deer was dead when I found it, gone from whatever life is. I felt the awe of that and crouched to look at the prone animal for a moment before I reached out a hand to touch it. There was blood on the deer's legs and belly, but its coat was clear and clean. It was shot through the heart, I later saw, though the pronounced blood trail itself had said as much.

I dragged the deer gently to a flat spot under the pines and field-dressed it, releasing the warmth of its body to the cold air. Field-dressing is a practical task but also a ritual. There is considerable joy—irrepressible joy—at the end of a hunt. Success is sweet, as is the bounty of venison at your feet. But no good hunter unpacks the life of a white-tailed deer without a respectful sense of gratitude and solemnity, an unnamed feeling that goes far back into human prehistory—not a primitive feeling, but a sophisticated one draped in the hanging moss and shifting mist of a subconscious intuition of the sacred nature of life and death.

I carefully slit the hide and felt the warmth of the deer rise around my face and hands. I worked with my knife to free the organs and entrails from the body cavity, impressed, as I always am, by the intimacy of field-dressing. When the bulk of the vitals were free, I reached in under the rib cage and, fingers spread stiffly, pushed my left hand through the deer's diaphragm, the rubbery resistance of which parted against my fingertips. I felt around for the esophagus with my left hand and brought my folding knife carefully to it with my right. Then I brought the vitals back through—a shattered heart, as it turned out, and two blue lungs full of air. When everything was free of the body cavity, I rolled the ungainly sack of still-warm innards out onto the bare pine needles. Then I cut that shattered heart as well as the liver and lungs off and set them aside.

There wasn't but a handful or two of blood left in the body

cavity. I scooped those palmfuls out and cleared the few twigs and leaves that had gotten inside the deer, admiring the delicate tenderloins I knew I would cook with mushrooms and onions for dinner. I tucked the organ meats back inside and closed the empty flanks to keep the meat clean. Then I pulled the deer into the deep shade near the fence line.

When I stood up to gather my gear, my heart was still pounding from the hunt. I was glad to have my deer. Beyond that, I didn't much know what to think. I just felt good, like a hunter after a hunt. "Death," Marcus Aurelius writes, "is Nature's great secret." I can't improve on that.

I cleaned my knife and then my hands and forearms with snow, gathered my few things and shouldered the Enfield, which I had not reloaded because of the strength of the blood trail I saw on the sunlit snow after I fired. I crossed over the fence and headed home to get the truck.

The snowbound northeast pasture was blinding in full sunlight, but the air was stiff with cold and it felt suddenly like one year had ended and another begun while I was working over the deer.

That was the year I filled the freezer on the next-to-last day of the season with the doe that came out into dry hollow near midday after that snowstorm. . . .

Winter birds—sparrows, mostly—scattered from rattling stalks of goldenrod as I trudged up the steep hill.

*S*ome evenings there is nothing to do. The day I took that doe, I milled around outside at dusk, checking the deer when it didn't need to be checked, fidgeting with the woodpile, trying to make it more orderly than it needed to be. Then, still trying to make myself useful, I circled the cabin several times, mentally penning a list of chores that didn't need to be done until March. I think I was just trying to see if I could glean something more from the day, spy the essence of winter slipping into place like a fox come to occupy the cabin hollow for a few months, see some bird I've never seen, catch the cast of long-slanting winter light just right.

I finally ended up splitting wood as darkness fell, enjoying as I always do the rhythm of the work, the pleasant thock of the ax and the way the momentum of each stroke drove my left hand firmly into the crook of the deer-leg handle.

I split straight-grained red oak finer and finer, admiring with absurd pride the way I could halve the successively thinner pieces until they got so thin I knew not to chance a miss and ruin my streak. Then I stacked them in the wheelbarrow, where they would finish weathering, lose the gloss of those pungent resins still faintly bound up in the wood. I could hear Patch charging rabbits in the cabin hollow, flushing them from the hedgerows and then chasing them back underground, their disappearance clearly an affront to his sense of fair play. The wind was our only company. No stars or moon, no geese or even crows moving about. Just day ending in an indistinct rustle, the undefined moodiness of the season suggesting that it was time to call it quits.

Perhaps we are whatever we are doing when sunset catches us, that last outdoor task we try to fit into the day, wishing we had another hour but secretly glad to have to leave off with the task undone.

Working Past Dark

The days are stacked against
what we think we are.

   —JIM HARRISON,
     "The Theory and Practice of Rivers"

Time leaves traces.

In late December I can feel the farm turn away from the sun and burrow into the long nights like a woodchuck. The pastures slumber heavily. In fact, the woodchucks *are* burrowed, seized in a sleep the planet's eccentricity induces, the tilt and wobble that lends the simple beauty of the changing seasons to the middle latitudes. The winter bruise of sky occasionally shreds open, revealing a pale sun that barely arcs above that broken-crown pine I can see from my writing desk. On the solstice, that wan disk disappears behind the gnomon of sandstone across the river to the west, three handbreadths south from where it sets at midsummer. Those handbreadths are perhaps the clearest measure of the year. The deer hung off the front porch, cooling in the dark, is another—wild life brought home from the woods for food.

I slept in, the day after taking that end-of-the-season deer, happily buried until midmorning in the unfinished dreams a week of hunting will give me. Of course, the business of life is always unfinished, and we always dream, our minds and hearts running on the way they do. Most dreams, it seems to me, are neither dark Freudian tangles nor bright Jungian adventures. They are neutral like the woods, opportunities to watch and learn. In dreams, as in the woods, everything is a sign. In dreams I wander my subconscious unarmed, interested in any crow or fox that seems to speak, in any hawk or friend or lover who walks strangely across my path in some place I do not quite recognize.

The only recurring dream I have ever had was a childhood dream about being lost in a forest. I'd be walking happily through some towering dream wood until my sleeping mind accumulated a feeling of being lost or some unsettling sense that I had gone too far. I'd panic and run, losing myself further until I tripped over a twisted blanket of mossy log and then woke up to find myself at home in a room so familiar I can still see the mottle of the ceiling tiles. That forest dream was such a mild nightmare that I looked forward to it, my conscious childhood mind willing to toy with whatever my subconscious was serving up. Some nights I'd try to dream the dream and see if I could get a little farther into the forest before that unaccountable feeling of having gotten too far from home drove me back out of it at a dreaming run that never seemed to get me anywhere. A child of the suburbs, I liked the woods I knew in reality, fragments of forests I saw briefly in summer in the Adirondacks and in New Hampshire and in Maine. The dream ran on for a year or two and then receded until it wasn't a dream but a memory.

Of course, I know now that landscapes naturally gather

themselves into paths. That is the earth's wild concession to the idea of going home. In dreams as in the woods, the way is to follow the grain of terrain downhill, following a ridgeline to a clear crease of stream that cannot help but lead back to the familiar world in the way that one watershed leads on to another. But when I was a child, I did not know the trick of traveling in the backcountry. I did not know there were paths everywhere and thought there was only one kind of home.

One's relationship to nature, if you choose to go that way, is an affair of trust and respect. Trust and respect lead, in turn, to the instructive paradoxes to which time spent in natural places leads us, encounters with what I have been calling the *otherness* of nature, a useful term from somewhere in philosophy. Those paradoxes show us aspects of ourselves—our tameness, our wildness, our at-homeness, our aloneness—about which we would otherwise live in ignorance. I draw no grand conclusions from these encounters and cannot argue for their values in practical terms. I had fewer of them than I hoped when I wrote the first draft of the prologue, years ago now. But, hunting, you never know. It's a way of waiting that promises everything and nothing. Most days you come home empty-handed until, in retrospect—often years later—you see or sense the gain.

There is more to life, of course, than time spent in woods and woodlot and at the pasture's edge. That was the narrow focus of this book which allowed me some purity of purpose in the writing where I sought a kind of local clarity through the austerity of a largely solitary watch. But those preoccupations easily extend to anything else that matters.

Evidence piles up on the news at night that we are a maladaptive species, and that the consequences of treating nature with violent disregard are enormous. That fact may not suit every political ideology, but the facts of life in this homey, wild universe will be the final arbiters of what was wise and what was foolish in our little history. If I imagine any God, I imagine a deity, half man and half woman, laughing through its tears at the gross folly and waste of a world. "God is alone," Thoreau wisely observed. That is all we know about God. The rest is arrogance. As we run out of room on a crowded planet, it is not surprising that we have turned that violent disregard on one another and that the arrogance of true believers of all stripes is busy destroying what common sense and reason, not to mention a sense of joy and fun, might have preserved. But nature needs no human pity. The owl, the hawk, the fox watch with interested disinterest. Even Emerson, a far more optimistic man than I am, suspected some "derision" toward us in the universe.

Humble work waits upstairs in my study. That keeps me focused and, I hope, honest. Of course, that work was, all along, this book itself, or this ongoing *writing*, since it's the process that matters more than the product, the dance of words and things that writers and poets live by and for, a little light shed by some aptness of expression that gets something right. I wasn't being coy when, at the end of the prologue, I admitted to largely failing. That is what writers do, as I understand the craft. There is so much that escapes us for the few things that touch us and that we touch.

Two essays intended for this book remain half written, promising but not yet useful, much like the snowy pile of unsplit locust and oak in the yard. That always happens and those pages will be seed stock for other work. One of those essays is about language itself, a tank-trap of a subject for a writer who works as slowly and self-consciously as I do. Stare straight at the owllike composure of language and you will see the words you share with others and the sentences you have fashioned for yourself waver in and out of focus, familiar and strange at the same time.

When I teach what the schools call creative writing, I tell my students that writers are odd creatures who spend half the day inside of language, roaming around sentences and paragraphs, working like coal miners at a dark seam where the sound and sense of the words through which we think and feel are waiting to be gathered—fuel for the most common thoughts and common emotions that we still have not gotten to the bottom of. I don't assume what the Romantics assumed, but the task of understanding oneself and one's world still depends upon being able to see "the miraculous in the common." And the questions Emerson posed early in his own explorations remain the central questions of any hour: "What is a day? What is a year? What is summer? What is woman? What is a child? What is sleep?" Those questions get you outside of language for the other half of the day.

The pursuit of the meaning of such questions matters as much as the answers. The deepest prejudice of my hunting is that attention to the tangible details of experience—not a forced literary creativity or what used to be called *fancifulness*—will lead us into the life of things where what we can know waits passively for us, ready to enrich our imaginations. As Coleridge noted, the imagination *discovers* or else it founders on surfaces, and no amount of self-conscious creativity will, in the mind of a hawklike reader, make up for that. Metaphors must have ground; words, roots.

I keep a chunk of bedrock on my desk to remind me of that. This five-pound helping of Blue Ridge basement rock is flat on one side and peaked on the other in a ridgeline that mimics the regular irregularities of the mountains from which it came. The rock has weathered into miniature watersheds defined by creases that zigzag from what look like wind gaps in its crest. Those branching creases, in turn, look like streambeds, dendrites of rocky tributaries gathering together on their way downslope to my desk. Light from a window or a lamp throws shadows across the rock, deepening the relief of the illusion that this fragment plucked from the banks of the James River is not only part of the horizon but a perfect image of the horizon—stony mimesis of parent rock, simultaneously fragmentary and whole.

These correspondences between the chunk of granite on my desk and the mountains I can see through the window behind my computer monitor are neither accidental nor fanciful. The features I have described were, after all, weathered by the same forces that weathered the mountains.

The pink and gray rock leads off in many directions, as any found object does. The pink is potash feldspar; the gray—a distinctly bluish gray—is quartz cooked above six hundred degrees Fahrenheit, an event which turned the normally icy-white, translucent mineral opaque. The heat for this metamorphosis was provided by the pressure of twenty-five miles or so of the earth's crust and the heat of the mantle below. At such depth the molten gumbo of minerals cooled slowly into coarse-grained granite that formed part of an extensive batholith, which was eventually overlaid with younger sedimentary rock of watery origin. After being rumpled by the tectonic forces that shuffle the earth's continental plates over Olympian time spans, the horizon that currently draws the eye here emerged as erosion slowly uncovered what is, in effect, a Precambrian image simultaneously coming into view and disappearing. The rock—like Highland Farm, like the earth itself—is my home and not my home. Just as home is fact and metaphor, figure and ground, tenor and vehicle of a need and a wish.

The other unfinished essay is a mountain piece, a kaleidoscope of good things seen on long walks in many places. "Mountains Walking," I call it, after a phrase from *roshi* Dōgen. That essay got so far beyond the Blue Ridge that it didn't fit here anymore, but it was conceived between "Karst" and "Late Wood." All my walks and thoughts start in the Blue Ridge, but that piece grows into a book of its own, the idea of it lap-jointed into this one. That is the kind of connection that holds a writer's mind together, an orderly way to let thoughts run on.

Downstairs, a venison roast simmers in the cast-iron Dutch oven set on the woodstove. I'm a cook, not a chef, and satisfied myself by dousing a beautiful sirloin tip with salt, pepper and garlic and then rolling it in flour. I propped the roast on a thatch of sassafras sticks I gathered for the occasion and set in the Dutch oven; poured in enough water to support a steady simmer; diced celery, onions, carrots, new potatoes and crimini mushrooms around the venison, which rides, high and dry, on the raft of sassafras.

When I lift the heavy lid of the Dutch oven, Patch points the woodsy fumes of the roast, which glistens under a rising cloud of sassafras steam. Because it has so little fat to cook off, the venison has only a faint aroma, a subtle aura that does not overpower the earthy scent of cooked vegetables. Venison from any wild game is like that, lean and healthy as heartwood. After sprinkling in a small handful of juniper berries, I clank the lid to and half a week of wild protein cooks itself. I will work the thin roux into a gravy, borrowing bits of mushroom for the task and, when the moment is right, pop a cast-iron tray of cornbread well laced with cinnamon into the stove. Later, I'll slice that roast on a diagonal, to show the fine moist grain of the meat, add salad, jazz, a stout Merlot and good company and have a meal with considerable soul, a meal the cost of which has been paid for with the effort of living well here.

Back outside, I pick at the edges of chores a nonhunter would have finished in November—rake up snowy piles of brush from the fence line, prune the lower, near-side limbs of the walnuts in front. After visiting the roast, which must not overcook, I turn to the few weekly chores that cannot be ignored—check the fluids in the truck; shuffle porch wood inside, seasoned wood to the porch, unseasoned wood to the big rack under the Spanish oak; split the little kindling I need, with the woodstove having taken on a life of its own, usually red with coals sufficient to ignite even a chunk of locust in a few seconds.

A low, gray front encourages me to move quickly from task to task. While I work, Patch cuts here and there, burning off his unused hunting energy, busting songbirds out of the thickets of wild rose and frost grape that are taking over the fence line. I prune this tangled, thorny cover back when I have to, but I admire its encroaching wildness, the assertiveness of every odd form of life here—the stout thorns and graceful tendrils of being reaching out—just as I admire the opportunism of the wrens and nuthatches that come to the feeder, not to mention Patch's verve, which can no more be contained than that of the wild rose or the frost grape or the careening birds.

I whistle this good companion for a walk, marveling at his undirected joy and envying his high spirits. Unless I bring him to heel, a walk with Patch is like a walk with an electron torn between two nuclei. He'll loop those hunt-and-search figure eights he has limned since he was a pup, slinging himself out ahead of me to some possibility in the pasture I cannot see, and then loop back on free return to orbit and encourage me before slinging off again. *Hunting requires hunting,* he seems to suggest.

Much sentimental ink has been spilled over canines, but it is a privilege that they constrain themselves to live in our world by our sides, roughly by our rules. We tame that canid wildness and then aspire to what is still unruly in it, nostalgic perhaps for our own wild origins, for a life of instinct rather than thought. With their native health, intelligence and enthusiasm, dogs set a good example and, given a chance, improve our rules. Like children, they know life from the inside and waste none of it.

I stop to admire the big walnut at the barn gate, which unlike Patch will stand still—in space if not in time—for any inspection. I've photographed it in every light and season, and used its old, wise form to teach myself to sketch, but I have not begun to understand it. It has taught me, taught me early on, that it is not there to be understood. Like everything in nature, it sheds the wrong questions easily. When no one is looking, I bow to it, humbled but made happy by its being—not the centuries laminated in it, but its perfection in the moment. The massive, twisted walnut, whose thickly furrowed bark is as grave as a dry riverbed, is the teacher here, a *roshi* in all seasons, wildly branched master of the Tao of karst and blue mountains.

Patch clears the barn spring cover of birds and, satisfied with that work done, courses the foot of the big pasture hill, beautiful on the run—sleek and fast, gathering and extending himself in a gallop that sets his coat flowing with light. When he gets looking too independent, I turn him with the whistle to remind him that we are together on this walk. He heads himself instantly, although the wideness of his turn back toward me is his way of saying, *I have a choice here. We hunt together but differently.*

The barn woods glow in late afternoon. Juncos lead me to the grove of beech trees, where I watch pale winter sunlight descant along those perfect boles. Nothing moves except that light and the birds. It's something to see.

"There's a certain Slant of light,/ Winter Afternoons—" Emily Dickinson wrote—for her a metaphysical glow, for me a nearly but not quite unearthly light that simultaneously intimates our kinship with nature and our distance from it—an attractive but oppressive, austere beauty in things that is the clearest measure of the uncanny difference this writing, this hunting, has been pursuing all along. We are hurt but not, to follow Dickinson, visibly scarred with the "internal difference" we feel inside ourselves from these encounters with something in nature we cannot name or quite see—a chilling sense, exciting and dismaying, that we are at home in the world and not at home.

Each day we find ourselves poised between local noon and deep time. We are free to make of that what we will. If anything, home is an affair of the soul, as is—I hope—the kind of hunting I have recounted here, a secular reverence for things as we find them, for the nature of things, including ourselves, fact and mystery. Perhaps we are whatever we are doing when sunset catches us, working, walking, the ends of the earth all around us—on Highland Farm and on this hard-used planet—everything aspiring to be and to show us what it would. Either everything matters or nothing matters. Either we are all always at home or all everywhere homeless.

Halfway up walnut hill, I turn to look back at the cabin. The wood smoke piping out the chimney reminds me that it will soon be time to return to the roast. But I stop for just a moment to admire this good place bathed in the dullest winter light—watch the canopy of the cabin hollow fill with darkness as birds fly quickly to their roosts. *Home.* I turn to whistle Patch back from the horizon, but he is standing right beside me, vaned into a northwest wind, eyes gleaming, right paw up, pointing an approaching snowstorm that even I can smell.

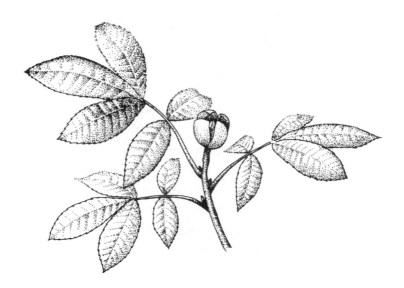